BED ABSOLUTE

A teenage diary of TB in the 1960s

BARBARA SALTER

How unlucky I am that this should happen to me. But not at all. Perhaps, say how lucky I am that I am not broken by what has happened ...

Marcus Aurelius, Stoic philosopher, in 2nd century, during Antonine Plague (a pandemic)

DEDICATION AND ACKNOWLEDGEMENTS

For my daughters, Hester and Sadie, and the many friends who were early readers.

Thank you all for your encouragement and constructive criticism.

Especial gratitude to Sadie Houghton, the first reader of the very rough initial draft as it was being produced.

Without her enthusiasm, on those walks during lockdown in the Winter of 2021, and her frequent questions about how close it was to being published, I might have given up many times.

This book is also in remembrance of my mother, Phyllis.

Without her strength, love and support, and her decision not to treat me like an invalid when I came out of hospital, I could not have gone on to have the life I have had.

Thanks, mum Bx

BARBARA SALTER

CONTENTS

INTRODUCTION

Sorting through a box of old papers during one of those long, empty days in lockdown, I came across diaries I had written as a teenager 1959-1961. Back came the memories of how I was diagnosed with TB, that year in the sanatorium, and the difficult period for my family that followed. I thought about how hard to believe the events recorded in those diaries would be for most 21st century readers. Being cut off from normal life had seemed as endless then as it did in the 2020-21 pandemic. I thought especially of young people, as trapped and bored at home as I had been in hospital. I wished there was a way of letting them know that life does come bouncing back.

The diaries begin just before I was diagnosed in November 1959, when I was 13. I was in the second year at Helsby County Grammar School for Girls, Cheshire, having passed the 11+. I had hated primary school and missed a lot of it through illness. I preferred this quiet school, relieved I was no longer the odd one out because of how much I read and the vocabulary I used.

I lived in Runcorn with my parents and my sister, Sandra, who was in the Lower 6th at the same school. Runcorn was then a quiet market town, surrounded by countryside but dominated by ICI chemical industries. Dad was an insurance agent with the Prudential, collecting payments, selling further policies, and paying claims. His work record was erratic – he gained and lost a variety of jobs during my childhood –

so my mother also worked to ensure we always had a regular if basic income. At that time, she was working as an assistant in a shoe shop although, having run her own business, she was more than capable of being the manager. We lived in a pleasant 1930s' semi-detached house in a residential area, suggesting a standard of living which the family income did not always support.

Sandra had been conceived before my father went with the RAF to India and Burma during World War II. I was born in October 1946, the child of his return. My father was a Roman Catholic (as it was then called) when he met my mother. She was Church of England. This religious divide, and the fact that, because my dad had lost his faith, we were not being brought up Catholic, caused some tension between my mother and her in-laws. Her parents, Nannie and Grandad Wakefield, lived in Runcorn and my father's parents, Nannie and Grandad Salter, lived across the Mersey in Widnes.

All of what follows is true and as recorded at the time but most names have been changed to protect identities. It has been edited and expanded in places to make it less repetitive and more comprehensible. The language is as written then, as is most of the spelling and grammar. At the end is a Postscript which describes how my life turned out as an adult, a separate note on tuberculosis and sanatoria, lists of the films, books, and plays referred to, and a couple of newspaper articles from 1961. Explanatory footnotes give a 21st century adult perspective. What you will read is still vivid to me but I am not sure how reliable a narrator I was.

The beginning of another dismal, lonely + miserable week. I know now I'm here until I leave. I've promised to stick it + so they'll never see at home how much I hate it here. When I get out I may tell them but until then I couldn't ...   Strange as it may seem today, at home we never did discuss what happened to me in Crossley. You, reader, now have the full story. By the end, perhaps you will be able to answer the question that I still cannot: did my parents make the right decision when they agreed to send me to Crossley?

Barbara Salter   July 2021

barbarasalter.writer@gmail.com

BARBARA SALTER

NOVEMBER 1959

MON 9: Back to school. Wish it was still half-term. I hate getting up when it is so cold. The novelty of not being a first year has well and truly worn off! What a welcome back! Everyone in the 2nd year had to have needles stuck in their arms near the wrist to see if they needed a BCG vaccination against T.B. Some of the girls made a fuss, even the ones who are already 13, like me. Janet, in our class, fainted! Didn't bother me really. Me and our gang walked round + round the field at lunch time, even though it was a bit chilly. I am SO glad we are all in the A form together, even though I HATE Latin.

TUES 10: I got a merit mark in French! I don't know what happened. School is very boring. I hate wearing my glasses. Pale blue frames – yuk! I know I look awful in them even though mummy says they suit me. I was only allowed to choose National Health ones.[1] I told Miss Mee in History that my copying up mistakes were because I couldn't see the board properly. She just said "So you have no excuse now."

---

[1] *National Health glasses: Then, as now, children could have free spectacles but there was only a limited range from which to choose without an additional fee so everyone knew if your parents could not afford more than those. Like wearing hand-knitted school cardigans, or not having exactly the right shade of green school uniform because it was from the Co-op, not the official outfitter to the school in Chester, these were indicators of social position and relative wealth, not that I realised that then.*

WED 11: Nothing much happened at school. On the bus home I sat by myself. Went to Girls Friendly Society in evening.[2] Only stayed 'till 8.30. Pretty boring. V.cold in hall and I was tired.

THU 12: P.E. and double maths, not my favourite lessons. I looked forward all day to being by the fire watching T.V. but it was rotten so we turned it off. Mummy and I read. Sandra was doing her homework in her bedroom. She has a LOT now she's in the 6th form. Daddy was out, as usual. I also learned my memory passage for the Sunday School exam.[3] Last year, I enjoyed the Scripture Classes and won the Emery Prize for the highest marks, but it's getting to be a bit much now I have so much homework as well. I like meeting Valerie there.

---

[2] *Girls' Friendly Society: The Girls' Friendly Society (GFS) still exists. It was founded on 1 January 1875. It is a charitable organisation that seeks to empower girls and young women 5 to 25. It was non-sectarian but, in my day, had a strongly religious ethos with an emphasis on family values. The focus then was on wholesome activities for girls.*

[3] *Bethesda Congregational Church, Runcorn: I first joined this church a few years earlier because my cousin Valerie went there and it was the only way I could go on their Summer outing to the seaside. It was a very friendly place and although neither of my parents went – my father was a lapsed Catholic and my mother a non-attending Church of England believer – I became a regular member, going to Sunday School and joining in all the activities (of which there were many for young people). One I particularly liked was the Bible Class, held on a weekday evening, but I also liked the concert rehearsals, the Christmas and Summer Bazaars.*

Although she's a year younger than me and my cousin, she's still my best friend outside school.

FRI 13: I got my essay back in Eng. A - the highest in class! Our class had our mantou tests examined. Mine has gone very red and raised but so were a lot of others in my form. Yipeee! It means we have natural immunity so we won't need the BCG injection![4] I'm glad 'cos it leaves a big round scar on your arm like Sandra has. We were given a letter to take home about it. Mum said when she was my age T.B. was as bad as cancer is now. It was called 'consumption' and a friend of hers died of it at 17. I know the Bronte sisters had it and so did some of my favourite poets. They all died.

SAT 14: Horrible weather but I went anyway because of the Sunday School exam. It wasn't too bad but I think I got a bit mixed up on one section. I couldn't be bothered to go shopping after, it was too wet. Mum and I had our usual Sat night T.V. with a bag of sweets. Dad was out, of course, and Sandra was out with Barry again. Looking serious!

SUN 15: I didn't go to Sunday School 'cos I had another cold. I didn't mind as we'd only be going over the exam. I stayed in bed reading for most of the morning and did homework in the afternoon. I watched T.V. at night with mum. In bed, I finished reading "Under the Greenwood Tree" for school but didn't think much of it. Sandra is doing "Jude the Obscure" for A level Eng Lit. She said it is better. I

---

[4] *See separate Note on Tuberculosis (TB) at the end.*

can borrow it. I like the poetry she's doing, especially John Donne, a "metaphysical" poet.

MON 16: I am off school 'cos of my cold. Temp. 99.8 to 100 all day.[5] I actually do feel rotten. I don't mind being away from school but wish I hadn't missed Art. Glad I'm missing Latin though! Mummy should have been at work but stayed with me. She said they're never busy in a shoe shop on a Monday so it's ok with Mr Fletcher (the new manager).

TUES 17: Off school – again. Temp only a bit above normal for most of the day but I feel awfully ill. I wonder if I'm a hypochondriac like mummy's friend Irene who always has something wrong with her but is never really ill? I'm always being off school. Mummy says it's my age – I'm 'outgrowing my strength'. She was working but came back at lunch time. Mrs G. (the new cleaner) was here for a bit in the morning. She said "What's wrong with you this time?" She's sarcastic in a polite way. I don't like her as much as Bertha. I'm glad she's having a baby but I wish she was still our cleaner.

---

[5] _General health_   _Whether these high temperatures were a sign of the latent TB now becoming active I do not know. I was a sickly child and had missed a lot of my primary schooling. I had endless tests to find out why. In the end, my mother was told I was 'physically fit but constitutionally weak', whatever that was supposed to mean. I was thin and pale. I preferred sitting inside reading to being active outside._

WED 18: My third day off school. I'll be missing loads of work. I hate copying up. I lay on the settee all day. I just feel tired although my temp. is not high anymore. I was fine by myself all day reading but it seemed a long time til 4.30 and Sandra was back from school. Mum said she's had a letter saying I have to have an x-ray 'cos of the positive mantou test. I wonder if I'll see my friends there as they'll need x-rays too.

THU 19: I feel better today but mummy said not to go to school until I've been better for a full day. I got up and got dressed and made a hand puppet. Nannie W came to look after me. She said I should eat more I'm too thin. My arms are 'like knots on cotton' according to her. Also, "you're like a piece of elastic, the taller you get the thinner you get". I wish she wouldn't say such things. I hate being so skinny. I know I'm the thinnest girl in my class. I wish I had started my periods and had got a bust. Some have already.

FRI 20: I didn't think it was worth going to school for one day and, amazingly, Mummy agreed! If I'd gone, I'd have weekend homework and I don't want that. Mum said I should get dressed and walk down town to Nannie Wakefield's for dinner to see if I'm really better. We had my favourite – chips with a fried egg on the top! Grandad winked at me when Nannie went into the kitchen and put salt on his, which he's not allowed because of his blood pressure. After, I went to the library with Nannie and got two new books - from the adult section! It's ok 'cos I read mummy's and daddy's and Sandra's books anyway. Mummy came after work and daddy picked us up about 6.30.

SAT 21: I went to Warrington shopping with Nannie. I got my first pair of HIGH HEELED shoes! They are black leather with a strap and a little heel. Mummy says I can start wearing nylons for the school Christmas party! When I got back, I tried on a pair of Sandra's with her suspender belt. My legs are so thin they wrinkle round my knees and ankles but mum said new nylons will fit me tighter. I don't like the feel of the suspender belt but she says I'll get used to it. I am starting to feel grown up!

SUN 22: I went to Sunday School and saw Valerie. I've passed the Scripture Exam First Class with 78%! Mr Cooper who is the Superintendent of Senior School said in front of everyone "Well done. You are our shining pupil." I'm sure I blushed. In the afternoon, I got ready for school tomorrow. I always feel a bit nervous when I've been away about how my friends will be. I know there'll be a lot to copy up. I hated it when I was off at my junior school and found I'd missed a party or something. Bet my friends have paired up on the school bus without me. Oh dear, I do NOT like sitting next to someone I don't know.

Mon 23: School was school. I like the grammar school and it's in a nice, country setting, but I do wish it wasn't so far away. It's a long day. I have to leave home by 8 for the bus and we don't get back until about 4.30. Mrs Dumbford was ratty 'cos I only got 2 out of 20 for the Latin test. She seems to have forgotten I was away all last week. Liz, the cleverest girl of all, of course got 20! Masses to copy up, especially Biol. AND homework to do. Ugh! I need to be off again to give me time to catch up on being off! I sat by Wendy on the bus. She filled me in on what's been going on at school (which is nothing much really).

TUE 24: 2nd declension in Latin. How I hate Latin. I wish I could drop it but no one can and stay in the A form. French is only a bit better. I was so cold in hockey my fingers went numb. As usual, I was a reserve 'cos no one picks me for their team. I don't care. I know I'm useless at sport. Thank goodness I'm good at English. I've had EXCELLENT four times already this term in my exercise book.

WED 25: Bliss – I didn't have to get up until 8.30. Dad ran us (me + mummy) to the Cottage Hospital[6] for my x-ray. I'm the first in my form to have one. I had to go on the ordinary bus to school after. I didn't get there until break time. Everyone asked me if it hurt! I told them the woman goes behind a big screen, which is a bit frightening but I didn't say it was. I just said it felt cold on my chest. All the girls with negative mantoux are having their BCGs on Friday, poor things.

THU 26: Boy, is Religious Knowledge boring!

---

[6] *Local hospital*: *Like most small towns then, Runcorn had its own Cottage Hospital, with some wards (usually for convalescence or for old people) and where x-rays and blood tests were done and consultants seen.*

Scripture at Sunday School is better. I got into trouble in Latin because I wasn't paying attention. Miss Dumbford made me sit at the front so she could 'keep an eye on' me. The Maths. test was pretty difficult but I finished. Miss Dale was vile in gym but she had to let me sit out because I just couldn't keep up on circuit training.

FRI 27: Not my week. I'm fed-up with school, my family, my life, me. Sandra was in a mood, something to do with Barry, as usual. Mum and Dad are not speaking because of something to do with money he'd promised to give her from his commission. I bet it's gone on whisky as usual. I wish I wore a brassier and had a boyfriend and I wasn't so thin. I was so embarrassed today because the School Nurse weighed and measured everyone. I weigh 5st 8lb and I am 5ft 1in tall. My vital statistics are 28"-24"-30". Mummy took me to see "High Society" with Bing Crosby at the Empress.[7] It was great. Oh to be rich!! And grown up.

---

[7] _Cinema: Throughout that period, when I was at home, I'd often go to the 'pictures' (as we called the cinema or films then) usually just with my mother, and on a Friday night. Our local cinema was the Empress, Runcorn but for a special film we would go to Widnes or Warrington. We usually sat in the stalls but, for a treat, we would go in the balcony. It was normal to have a news feature, perhaps a short cartoon, and a 'B' film before the main film, so it could be a long night. Sometimes, it was hard to see the screen through the haze of cigarette smoke. When younger, I'd also go on a Saturday morning most weeks to the children's pictures._

SAT 28: Today we found out I have T.B.[8] I will soon be going to hospital. Mummy said that although it used to be serious, there are drugs now so I'll be O.K. once I've been treated. I got up late and was still in my dressing gown by the fire when mum and dad came in. I thought mummy was at work. She said she'd been to see Dr Staunton, the GP. I asked her if she was ill. She said, "No, but you are." Daddy started to get very sentimental like he does when he's had too much. He said it was God's punishment because of his drinking and he'd promised God to stop if He'd make me better. Mummy said I'll get better anyway because they can treat T.B. nowadays. We won't know more until we see the Chest Specialist. Everyone fussed around me all day, even Sandra, and Scamp sat on my knee as if she knew too, although she's just a dog. For once, we ALL watched T.V. at night. Boy, I must be REALLY ill for Sandra to miss going out with Barry and dad the pub!

SUN 29: Mummy said I can't go to Sunday School in case I am infectious.[9] She said there must be a carrier at school because there have been so many positive mantoux tests. I hope it's not me. If someone else has T.B. as well, we can be treated

---

[8] *See separate Note on Tuberculosis (TB) and Sanatoria at the end.*

[9] *See separate Note on Tuberculosis (TB) and Sanatoria at the end.*

together. Sunday School sent a big bunch of dahlias and a card. Daddy went to Widnes to tell Nannie + Grandad Salter. Mummy told her parents yesterday. Nannie Wakefield was v upset. Mummy is going to get a Flatley clothes dryer[10]'cos apparently it's bad for my chest to dry clothes round the fire. She's wanted one for ages. I can't see the point if I'm going to hospital soon but I didn't say anything. I didn't do my homework – no point. Maybe it's not so bad being ill after all!

MON 30: The Health Visitor came. She is very nice. Mum asked her if I could be looked after at home but she said it's not allowed for T.B. Nannie + Grandad S came to see me. They brought me some chocolates. Nannie S kept crying and saying there's a lot of it in Ireland 'in poor people' but she never thought she'd live to see one of her own with it.[11] Charming! Mum tried to shut her up but she couldn't. Sandra said she'd seen my friends at

---

[10] _Flatley clothes driers_ were a short-lived fad. The dryer was a metal box with a heating element in it at the bottom and wooden rods at the top over which clothes were hung. The lid was then put on and the clothes dried. It was faster than the alternative – putting clothes on a 'clothes horse' in front of the fire, or on a rack suspended from the ceiling - and there was less condensation but so many caught fire that they were later banned.

[11] _Irish background:_ _Nannie Salter's family (my father's side) had come over from County Mayo, Ireland) at the end of the 19th century to escape extreme poverty. TB (consumption) was then rife in Ireland and was associated with poverty._

school and they were really shocked and sad for me. I just lazed around all day and read and talked to mum (she's on holiday from work). Mummy said Mr Fletcher said the shoe shop can manage without her for a week so she can be off to look after me. Great!

DECEMBER 1959

TUES 1: Nannie W came. She brought me brandy snaps AND chocolate AND a dog ornament AND a book called "Paddy-the-next-best-thing". She kept going on about how pale I was my skin is 'transparent'. Rubbish! She said she knew something was wrong because I'm so skinny and get tired easily and I'm always off school. Well, she never said that before! Mrs G came, although it's not her day, and gave me some sweets. Bet she wishes she hadn't acted as if I was pretending to be ill. I wish I was just pretending. I keep wondering if I'll be really ill and die. I want to ask mummy but what if I am? She is very worried so maybe I will. I am frightened in case she doesn't say it won't happen.

WED 2: I went to Liverpool in daddy's car with mummy and Nannie. Mummy said the doctor said we could as long as we didn't stay long and didn't eat anywhere. I feel like a leper in the Bible. No one I know has been funny with me yet but even Mummy said I must be careful about which glass I use at home. I got a pale blue, quilted cotton dressing gown with deeper blue roses on it and blue brocade slippers with pretend fur trim – very posh! I did feel tired today but I don't feel ill and I have no cough at all so maybe it is a mistake? If I do have T.B. it must be only a bit so I'll soon be better.

THU 3: Lazy day. No P.E., maths., or Latin for me – hurrah! I got up about 11.00 and had a bath and washed my hair. It needs cutting it is so thick and frizzy. I like my new dressing gown and slippers but

I wish my feet weren't so long and thin. I washed and re-arranged my ornaments in the afternoon. Usually I enjoy doing that but today it made me sad because I was saying goodbye to them. I watched T.V. at night with mummy but there wasn't anything much good on. She made us perked coffee for a treat! I am worried about going to see the chest specialist tomorrow in case he says I am going to die. I keep thinking about Jane's friend who dies of consumption in Lowood school. [12]

FRI 4: Mummy and I saw Dr Hughes at the Cottage Hospital. I had another x-ray and he examined my chest for ages. He said I have to go to Crossley Sanatorium. An ambulance will take me on Monday. Mummy asked if it could be delayed until after New Year but he said no. He said I'll be there for about 10 weeks. I'll miss some school next term! I don't mind that but I hate being away for Christmas. Mummy's friend Edith came at night. She had T.B. 15 years ago. She is cured but still has to rest. She made a sanatorium sound like a holiday camp with arts and crafts to do and people coming in to entertain the patients, especially at Christmas. She said she was told "never to sit if you can lie, never to stand if you can sit." I don't like her. I don't want to be an invalid. After she'd gone, mummy told me they'd had to choose between a children's hospital near Liverpool or the one for adults that is only at Frodsham. I'm glad they

---

[12] *Charlotte Bronte's Jane Eyre was a favourite of mine. I kept noticing how many people died of TB in books.*

picked the one close to home. She thinks I'll be better off with adults than with a lot of little children.[13] I don't want to go anywhere. I cried in bed but I didn't let mummy know. It feels real now and I am starting to be frightened.

SAT 5: When I woke up last Saturday, I didn't know. Now, everything is different. All day people kept arriving with presents – chocolates, writing paper, soap, talc. Everyone is very cheerful and says things like "You'll soon be home" and "It'll be like a holiday" and "Aren't you a lucky girl, getting so many presents". Sandra is being very good about the fuss. If she minds, she's not saying. My last Saturday night T.V. with mummy for a few weeks. I'm glad daddy and Sandra were out, as usual. We had pop and crisps as well as our normal weekly bag of sweets! I cannot believe this time next week I'll be by myself in hospital. Mummy says I have to be brave so I tried not to cry but in bed I had to.

---

[13] *Choice of hospitals: I was told, at the time, that the choice was a children's hospital at Liverpool or an adult hospital, nearer home. Because I was 13, I was considered just about old enough to go to an adult hospital but would have been allowed to go to one for children. Because Crossley was nearer – only about 20 minutes from home by car – and because I was thought to be a bit 'precocious' (because of my wide reading, vocabulary and attitude) - they thought I'd be better off with adults than with children who would be a lot younger than I was. As I said in the Introduction, I leave it to the reader to decide by the end if that was the right choice.*

SUN 6: I wrapped up all my Christmas presents for my family and school friends. Mummy said she will find out if they have to be fumigated before they can be given to anyone. Nannie said I have to leave the Paddy book at home in case it gets damaged by being fumigated. I was really upset by that. I am taking the two dolls Nannie knitted ages ago because they can be washed when I come home. A bit babyish but that's how I'm feeling. I am also taking some of the presents I've had. I'll definitely need the writing paper. We were all quite cheerful. I kept pretending I was getting ready to go on holiday. Mummy made my favourite meal, chicken, chips and sweet corn, with her special chocolate cake after. Mummy said I can sleep in her bed with her tonight. That's where I am now, writing this. I am finding it really hard not to cry. I am trying to memorise this room so I can close my eyes and be back here tomorrow night. I just can't imagine what it will be like to be in a hospital bed in a ward with strangers.

MON 7: I woke up very early. I could not go back to sleep. Mummy was already up. I had a really strong dream. There was a big house and snow all around. There was a squirrel and a nurse with a red cloak. The ambulance came at 10.50. Daddy and Sandra had stayed to see me off. The last thing I did was give Scamp a good cuddle. It was awful waiting for the ambulance. When it came, I thought I was going to be sick. I wish we could have gone in Daddy's car. We were here by about quarter past 11. It is like a stately home in its own grounds and there are squirrels, but no snow. Mummy was allowed to stay while I undressed and got into bed. I am in a corner bed with a window behind me in a six-bedded ward on the middle floor. The floor to ceiling windows in the bay – next to my bed – are open, even though it's cold and windy. Mummy left at 12.10. As she shut the ward door, the wind blew over a vase of red tulips in the bay. It shocked me into crying for some reason. We had dinner – yuk, like at school. I have a bedside locker.

TUE 8: Crossley Hospital[14] – or Sanatorium as some people here call it – is quite nice really. Everyone is very friendly. Connie is in the bed opposite. She is quite tall and could be pretty but looks 'hard'. She seems to have something to say on everything – the expert on TB! Next to me is Mrs Benfield (about mum's age and a smoker!). Next to Connie is Jill. She's really glamorous – wears red lipstick to match her hair - and quite jolly. Next to that is Eileen, an old Irish woman who coughs a lot. I was examined by a doctor but he didn't tell me his name. We have to take our temperatures night and morning and put dots on a chart. A nurse is doing mine at the moment. I have to stay in bed ALL THE TIME! I didn't expect to have to do that! It's called Bed Absolute.[15] I am not even ill. I have to use bed

---

[14] *Crossley Hospital/Sanatorium: Looking like a red-brick stately home in its own grounds, it was near Frodsham, Cheshire. For further information, see separate Note on Tuberculosis (TB) and Sanatoria at the end.*

[15] *The Beds regime in place: All patients began on Bed*

pans – ugh!!! Everyone can hear. I even have to wash in bed – NO baths! There's a horrid lidded sputum cup on my bedside locker. I have to spit enough into it for them to check if I'm infectious. I don't cough so how can I do that? Will some people be coughing up blood like in books?

WED 9: Visiting is from 2.00 to 4.45 today. Daddy and mummy came. She could come 'cos it's half day closing. Daddy can make up the lost time tomorrow in his job he said. Mummy said everyone who had a positive mantoux has been x-rayed. No one else has T.B. now. The whole school has to be x-rayed to see if there is a carrier. I feel awful. What if I'm the only one ill with T.B? Will that mean I am the carrier? I feel ashamed even though it's not my fault. It's quite hard work talking for nearly three hours. Other people can hear what we're saying. Mummy says I must do everything I'm told to do if I want to get better. I cried when they went. The nurse told me off because when she

Absolute which meant NO getting out of bed at all, so bed pans, bowls for washing, and bed baths. That soon became being allowed to go to the toilet once (or more) a day in a wheel chair ('chariot'). In theory, a Bed Absolute patient should not get up to go to the window, or water plants, etc., but I did. Bed 1 meant I could walk to the toilet once a day. Bed 2, twice a day. Once a patient was allowed to walk anywhere, the number of times and where became hard for the nurses to monitor so it gave some freedom but not as much as Bed O. Bed O was Bed Ordinary, which meant you could walk to the toilet as often as you liked and have a proper bath. Most patients on Bed O were pretty much up but in nightwear and visited each other's wards, went to the central tea point etc. Even flagrant breaches were usually ignored.

came to give me three more glasses of milk, I'd not drunk the ones she'd left this morning. I have to drink THREE pints a day![16] It is warm and creamy and makes me feel sick. My temp. went up to 100. The nurse said if that happens again, they'll stop my visitors. Surely they can't? I'll die if they do.

THU 10: I was woken up at 5.00 by Nurse Harvey. She took me in a wheelchair to the central part of this floor which everyone calls The Square. It separates us from the men's side. She gave me a "gastric lavage". [17] She tried to make me swallow a horrible rubber tube. I just couldn't. I thought I

---

[16] *Milk: I was underweight for my height and it was important that I gain to show I was getting better. I had to drink three pints of full-cream milk a day, delivered as three half-pint glasses in the morning and another three half-pint glasses in the afternoon. I was in trouble if I did not drink them. The milk was always warm. I hated it.*

[17] *Gastric lavage: Using a gastric lavage to get sufficient sputum was quite a barbaric thing to do to anyone, let alone a 13 year old, taken from her bed early one morning to have it done without warning. A tube, via the mouth or nose, is passed into the stomach. As I kept gagging when they tried putting it down my throat, it was put down through my nose. The aim was to have sufficient samples of phlegm (coughed from the lungs and swallowed) for it to be possible to grow on it TB bacteria and then try out the different drugs to see which killed that bacteria the best to decide on the most effective treatment. We also had regular sputum tests to see if we were positive (could pass it on) or negative. Although I never developed a cough, and never once used my sputum cup, I made sure I never again failed to 'spit' enough for a test.*

would choke. Then another nurse held me while Sister pushed the tube up my nose, down my throat and into my stomach. It was the worst thing that's ever been done to me. I thought I was choking. Then she pumped water in and back it all came. Even though I was crying, she wasn't a bit sympathetic. She said it's my own fault for not using the sputum cup as I'd been told to. My nose has been bleeding on and off all day. A teacher came but I felt too ill to see her. I HATE it here.

FRI 11: I feel much more cheerful today, thank goodness. The teacher[18] is really nice. Her name is Mrs Mawson. She'll give me lessons in bed in Eng, Maths, History and Geog. She will come every day for an hour. It will be like having a visitor! Her daughters are at the grammar school and her sister teaches there so she knew all about me. Her sister is the teacher who took me for swimming last year and told me off for not doing a 'brave jump in' all year. I bet she's sorry now she was cross with me. In the afternoon, the occupational therapist came to see what I'd like to do. I am embroidering a tray

---

[18] _Schooling in hospital:_ _I had a general teacher and, a bit later, a French teacher and there is reference to a male maths teacher. For months, the lessons were in bed, in the ward. Once I was up on 'hours', I was able to go to the school room nearby. I don't think I was a fair judge of how good these teachers were but it does seem to have been a bit ad hoc compared to how Hospital Schools operate today with their Individual Health Plans and liaison with parents and school. However, the lessons kept my learning going and that was enough. Lessons also helped break the daily tedium._

cloth to start with but Miss Growcott said I can do some leather work next week. I think I'll make a purse first.[19] I was really hot and sweaty at night and my temp was up again. Well, they can't blame visitors today!

SAT 12: <u>Visiting</u>. Mummy, daddy, Nannie Wakefield and Nannie Salter came. Nannie W brought me a roast pork balm cake[20] and a custard. Delicious. The meals here are boring and usually cold so I need this food to put on weight.[21] Nannie S and Nannie W talked to each other more than to

---

[19] <u>*Occupational therapy:*</u> *There was a resident Occupational Therapist, Miss Growcott, whose centre was in the basement. She visited the patients in bed but, once on enough hours, her store and office were a popular social meeting place for patients of both sexes. We also had a female <u>Physiotherapist</u> who came to teach us how to breathe correctly. While I remember those visits, the diary does not mention them. People who had had operations required quite a lot of rehabilitation exercise from her.*

[20] <u>*Barm cake:*</u> *a soft, round, flattish bread roll, common in the North West of England*

[21] <u>*Food in hospital:*</u> *The hospital food was typical institutional food – like school dinners – and was brought to us on heated trolleys from a kitchen a long way away so wasn't very hot either. To supplement these meals, all patients kept extra food – as well as chocolates, sweets, cakes, biscuits, fruit – in their bed-side lockers (and sometimes things like chicken and ham, although we had no fridges). In addition, the lucky ones (like me) had families who brought food – full-plated hot meals sometimes – every visiting day. Diary entries list everything I ate in much greater detail than I have included in this edited version. Food was very important!*

me. Daddy went to see a friend called Jack who is in the men's side so mummy and I had a natter. I liked that bit best. Three hours seems a long time but then suddenly it's over and they're gone. I tried not to but I cried when I kissed everyone goodbye. I feel awful now 'cos I know mummy will worry all night. I will try extra hard to be cheerful when they come tomorrow.

SUN 13: Dorothy the old orderly gave me a blanket bath this morning. She put a screen round the bed and undressed me. She kept me covered up but washed each arm and leg in turn. Then she told me to turn over and she did my back including my bum cheeks. Then I lay on my back and she did my front to my waist. She then gave me the flannel and went the other side of the screen. I didn't know why. After a bit, she said "have you finished?" I said "finished what?" She said "down below". I was SO embarrassed. Visiting Mummy, daddy, Sandra and Aunty Laura (Nannie W's sister) came. We had a really good afternoon and I was perfectly cheerful when they left. Aunty L brought me a really funny Get Well card and a basket for my embroidery. Temp ok at night, thank goodness. It's not fair, I can't cheat like the others do, 'cos a nurse takes mine. Is that 'cos I'm new or 'cos I'm being treated like a child?

MON 14: I had three letters today![22] I've had at least one every day and some days two. I like

---

[22] _Letters:_ _Letters were the only way that I could_

replying. It gives me something to do and makes me feel less lonely. Connie, the one with a comment for everything, and the nastier the better I am now realising, said "Enjoy it while you can. People get fed-up when you're in here for years." I said I was only going to be here 10 weeks. She said "Oh really" and sort of smirked. She upset me. So did Mrs Mawson. After the lesson, she chatted about the Christmas parties at school. I managed not to cry then but I did once she left. I could not eat any lunch. Thank goodness I have a bed in a corner so I can face the wall, away from everyone. I don't mind the rest hours – 11.00-12-00, 2.00-3.00 (apart from on visiting days) and 5.00-6.00 – because I put the headphones on to listen to the radio or read.

TUE 15: I got 11 letters today from G.F.S. and four from other people! Miss Growcott left me the leather purse pieces and a metal wheel to make dots which I then pierce with a prodder. I have to use two needles and special thread to sew it together. It's going to take ages. Connie is on Bed Ordinary. That means she should stay in bed but can go to the W.C. as often as she likes and have a proper bath. She is ALWAYS out visiting other wards. I think she's in her early 30s. Her face is thin and pale and she has staring eyes. She has been in hospital for

communicate with anyone outside my ward. The post was very quick in those days. Every week, I would write to and have letters from my family, even though I saw them three times a week. I cannot remember what I found to say to fill so many pages. I also wrote numerous thank you and other letters to many relations and some friends. There were no mobile phones so no calls or messaging or emails of course.

T.B. before, which is probably why she can be nasty at times. I'm sorry for her but it's not my fault. I've not yet worked out what old Eileen is on. Some days she's up and dressed but sometimes she stays in bed. Mrs Benfield (the motherly one) is on 4 hours so she gets dressed for lunch in the canteen and can use the day room downstairs. The others call her Betty but I don't like to, she's mum's age. Sarah (not mentioned before because she's out all day) is also in this ward, up 10 hours. She has all her meals in the canteen. She was an art student. She's tall with long straight shiny black hair and wears a lot of black clothes, like a beatnik. I wish I looked like her – she's super. She's waiting for 12 hours and her "date" to go home.[23] She's 21. She's been here almost TWO years already! Help!!

WED 16: I've now met some of the patients from the 4-bedder. Sally and Judy, and May from the 5-bedder, are all from Liverpool, like Connie. Judy is

---

[23] *Hours regime: 1 Hour meant getting up and dressed after morning rest hour and going down to the canteen for lunch. 2 Hours meant a further hour dressed after lunch, but back for rest hour (2-3) 4 Hours meant being up from late morning until late afternoon. This gave time to go to the Day Room after lunch, or visit the Occupational Therapy room in the basement, or even go out into the grounds. 8 hours meant almost a full day so up by about 10am, with all meals except breakfast in the canteen, and being eligible for home leave. 10 hours meant up after breakfast and free to watch films in the canteen (hall) at night. 12 hours meant up for breakfast for the whole day. This happened close to the 'date of discharge' being given and the end, at last, in sight.*

18 and really pretty. She and catty Connie know each other well. Sally Stevens is a mum with two children. She's very lined and looks older than Mrs Benfield. May, I can't guess. She is on 12 hrs and will be leaving soon. She is hunchbacked and has a withered leg because she had polio as a child. She's had two operations for T.B. already and has been in and out of hospitals most of her life. She ought to be a sad person but she isn't, she's hilarious. She has dyed blond permed hair and wears thick makeup even though she's quite old. She's a right Scouser, always cracking jokes. Some of them are quite rude! She makes us all laugh. <u>Visiting</u>   Had a lovely time, just mummy and daddy. When I started to get upset at the end, mummy said I had to start trying harder to be brave. She said I am making it even worse for her. She goes away and worries about me. I know that but I am the one here.   I promised I will try not to complain or cry anymore. Daddy said, again, that he has promised God he will stop drinking if only his little girl can soon be better.   He says he has. I hope so. They say at Sunday School that "God has his reasons". Perhaps it'll be worth having T.B. if it does mean Dad really will stop forever this time. After visiting, I felt separate from everyone and the feeling stayed with me all night.

THU 17: Super Sarah is organising the Christmas decorations for our ward. She really is an artist! She's drawn and cut out of cardboard a snowy rooftop scene with chimney pots for us to paint. Even me in bed! She is painting Father Christmas herself. Connie is doing the reindeers. We keep singing "Connie the red-nosed reindeer"! No catty comments for once! The others are spending more time in the ward while we are doing this which I like. I'm still shy but I am starting to join in more. I never thought I'd say it while I was here, but I'm actually enjoying this!

FRI 18: Sarah is doing all this art for us even though she's going on leave over Christmas. I wish she wasn't although I know that's selfish. I like Judy because she's young but she's not in our ward. She seems nice and friendly but when she's with Connie, they both ignore me. The oldest one in our ward, Irish Eileen, I don't like at all. She is always using her sputum cup. She asked if my mother had bought me such big slippers "like narrow boats" for me to grow into. Cheek! Mrs Benfield is supposed to be "keeping an eye open" for me mummy said but I don't think she likes me for some reason. She is always going off to the toilet for a smoke! I hate the smell when she comes back, even though I should be used to it from home. We finished the decorations today. They look great! Sarah took some photos. I can have one!

SAT 19: <u>Visiting</u> Mummy had to work as the shop is busy this close to Christmas. Daddy and Sandra came, so did the gang from school – all five of them (Josie, Susan, Jackie, Celia, Linda). We had a real party! We had crisps, jellies, pop, cake. Crossley doesn't mind if you have a lot of visitors at once. It was great! They told me about school and their boyfriends and Christmas parties. I know they are kind to come and I should be glad but it was so hard work pretending and smiling all afternoon. I do want them to come again even though it upsets me. I managed not to cry in front of them. Daddy was with Jack in the men's 6-bedder most of the time. I could smell whisky on him when he came back but maybe it was just a Christmas drink with his friend. I really missed mummy, even though I do understand why she couldn't come. I cried after they'd all gone. Mrs Benfield wasn't very nice. She said I was lucky to have friends who'd bother to come. She went on and on about how her "so called friends" had kept well away in case they got T.B. I'm not like her – I have never been infectious because my sputum test was negative. She then got upset about not being with her children at Christmas – her second in hospital – and I felt really sorry for her and them. I'd rather be the ill one than mummy. We couldn't manage without her for that long 'cos of dad.

SUN 20: <u>Visiting</u> Nannie S came with mummy and daddy. Daddy spent ages with his pal Jack again today and got told off for it by his mother! Nannie S and mummy still don't really get on. Nannie S has no idea what her precious son can be like or what we've been through 'cos of his drinking. Mrs Stevens (Sally), pretty Judy, and good ol' May came into our ward tonight and we were all talking about Christmas. First of all Mrs Stevens and Mrs Benfield started crying about missing their children, then Judy and Connie got upset 'cos they're missing out on parties and fellas. I started feeling really weepy too. Then Eileen said at least we all had something to miss, which is more than she can say. That should have been sad but the way she said it, we all laughed. May then joined in with her Scouse wit and had us all laughing even more. Poor May, she's the worst off of all of us. Jill (the one with the red lipstick) and arty Sarah suggested we sing some carols but Irish Eileen started on pub songs. It got so loud the night Sister came in and sent them all back to bed.

MON 21: Sarah goes on leave for Christmas tomorrow, lucky thing. Anyone over 8 hours can. No one else in our ward or the 4-bedder is but some in the 5-bedder and singles can. Others I've heard about but don't know yet are Helen, Andrea, Angela and Mave and someone they call 'the mad woman' in a single, and an elderly lady they call Miss Smythe. Connie was quite funny but in her usual nasty way about them all, but especially Miss Smythe and Margaret. She said Margaret is "simple" and was in Deva, the mental hospital nearby,[24] until she got T.B. I saw her once when she came into our ward by mistake. She looks like Mr Rochester's mad wife in Jane Eyre. She wears a long white nightie, stained front and back, and has long black hair that needs brushing. Connie said she ought to be sent back and the nurses agree. Miss Smythe, Connie described as "weird" and said she'd be better off in Deva too.

---

[24] _Deva:_ _Deva Hospital was originally an old-style mental asylum, dating back to 1829. For more information, see separate Note on Tuberculosis (TB) and Sanatoria at the end._

TUE 22: Another day of nothing much happening. I could just write "ditto" each day. I didn't sleep very well. Margaret came into our ward twice last night. The second time she sat by the Christmas tree and cried until they took her back. The nurses are fed up with the extra work. Even though they knew about that, we were still woken at 7.00 as usual.[25] Then it's temp. time. Then I'm brought a cup of tea, followed by a bowl of water (to wash) and after that, breakfast. Then nothing, unless it's a school day, so I write letters or do crafts or read. I like it when others are in the ward but, apart from rest hours, those who are up are usually out somewhere. I haven't even started any treatment yet even though its ages since that 'orrible gastric lavage. The rest of the day is morning rest hour, dinner, another rest hour, two hours of nothing, tea time, yet another rest hour (including back and bottom rub to stop bedsores), supper, more time to pass somehow, bed. At first I was embarrassed but now I like having stuff rubbed into my bum, especially when it's Dorothy's turn. She has big hands – and feet that make mine look small! – but she's gentle and kind. She's had T.B. and so an orderly in a sanatorium is

---

[25] _Hospital routine and rules:_ Like all hospitals, there was a daily routine that gave a structure to the day, but, at Crossley, it was fairly lax and staff often turned a blind eye to rule-breaking. Perhaps that was because a lot of the staff had had TB themselves, or because even those who had not could sympathise with patients who spent years in hospital, left, then returned for a further long stay.

the only work she can get. Hope that that's not all I'll be allowed to do when I'm grown up.

WED 23: <u>Visiting</u>   Mummy and daddy came. They had to bring my Christmas presents because Matron said no visiting is allowed on Christmas Day! We were shocked and upset. Matron said there could be NO exceptions as it's not fair on the families to spoil their day! It made me think about what a burden I am. Mummy is here on Wednesdays, her half-day, and rushes up on a Saturday in her lunch hour if she can have a longer one. They both come on Sundays so miss their day of rest. Maybe they will get fed-up coming three times a week if I'm here more than a few weeks. Some people have been here years and only seem to get one visitor a week, if that. I just about managed not to cry when they were leaving. I said "I'll have to be ill again if I get this many presents!" but I'd rather have none and be at home on Friday. When they'd gone, I was upset so I put the headphones on because I didn't want to have to talk to anyone. Then catty Connie had a go at me. She said I was selfish for wanting them to be able to come on Christmas Day. I said Christmas mattered more to me than to her 'cos I am not a grown up. Mrs Benfield then burst into tears and stormed out. Connie said it was my fault. How did I think Betty felt, being away from her children yet again. I felt awful. I can't help being upset. I do know everyone else is too. In the evening, a group of bell-ringers came to give a concert in the hall for everyone on Bed O or above. I was really fed-up, I was the only one who couldn't go. Then Dorothy put me in the wheelchair and pushed me into the corridor and the bell-ringers were there! They did "Rudolph the Red-nosed Reindeer" for me. By then, the other patients were coming back. I know it was kind of them but I felt embarrassed, everyone was looking at me. I heard one woman call me "the little girl". I am NOT little, I am 13.

THU 24: I have felt depressed all day. I hate it here. It is a complete waste of time. I'm not even having any treatment. I might as well be at home. I could rest in bed there. Everyone is fed-up. Connie, at her catty best, and pretty Judy had a row and aren't speaking. Mrs Benfield keeps weeping and going off for a fag. The only one who isn't bothered is Eileen. It's the sixth time she's been in hospital for Christmas!![26] She says it's better than being by herself at home! I tried reading but nothing cheers me up. I wish Judy was in my ward. She really is very pretty. She wears her hair in a French pleat and she's got pierced ears. The only other one near my age is someone called Helen who is in a single. Connie doesn't like her – said she's "posh" – but then Connie is nasty about almost everyone. Jill is a bit "posh" too but she's so kind and funny that Connie is ok with her. Jill is the only one who is nice to me all the time. She's in her 30s, very glamorous, with red hair and red lipstick and a brightly coloured dressing gown she said is a

---

[26] _Long stays_: the older patients, infected before the advent of the drugs I was on, had often been in and out of hospital for years. I remember being afraid I would be too.

kimono. Her husband is good looking. They don't have any children. I wish I had a special friend of my own age. Maybe I would have been better in the children's hospital? I bet mummy thought the adults here would be good company and would be nice to me. How wrong she was.

FRI 25: CHRISTMAS DAY. I was excited to have so many presents (34). Everyone has spent loads on me! I had some duplicates – two identical writing sets and three lots of talc – but I also got books, dog ornaments, chocolates, games, craft kits, jewellery, a really gorgeous yellow satin embroidered bed jacket from Nannie W, and the usual page-a-day diary from Sandra. Jill and Connie ended up sitting on Mrs Benfield's bed, watching me open mine because they didn't have as many. Everyone was nice to each other for once. In morning rest hour, Sister Harvey came round dressed as Santa, pushing a medicine trolley with presents for us – yet more writing paper! The best present of all was that I did see mummy and daddy and Sandra and Scamp after all! Just before lunch, I heard a 'yoohoo' and there they were, outside! They'd come just in case they'd be let in. They weren't. I waved to them from my window. I cried, first of all because I was so happy to see them, but then because I wasn't with them. They had to go after a bit 'cos it's very cold. I had a traditional Christmas lunch, by myself, in bed. Everyone else was allowed to go to the canteen for theirs but not me 'cos I'm on Bed Absolute. If mummy had known that, she'd have been really upset. I was crying when Nurse Evans came in after lunch. She said she was bringing Kathleen in to see me. Kathleen is "very ill" and all by herself so we could be company for each other. I'd never seen her before because she is in a single. She's about 20 I think and is very thin. She has very white skin but red cheeks. When she talks, she gasps for breath. Although she's young, she doesn't have many teeth. I wonder if that's 'cos of T.B.? She's Irish and speaks very softly. I couldn't think of anything to say. After a bit, she said she was tired and asked me to ring for someone to take her back. It took ages for anyone to come. If her visit was meant to cheer me up, it didn't. Boy, was I glad when the others came back! They were a bit merry as they'd all had a drink! I didn't feel like being jolly and Christmassy with Matron when she came round later. It's her fault my family couldn't come in. At night, Dr Houston, the head doctor, came round. It's the first time I've seen him. He is very funny and friendly. The others call him Johnny (but not to his face). After he left, Connie went off to yet another party. Then she and Judy came back for Mrs Benfield and Jill. Even Eileen went! I kept thinking of how ill Kathleen looked. She's young but looks like she could die. Ugh! I HATE it here. Happy Christmas Barbara – I don't think.

SAT 26: <u>Visiting</u>   Mummy and Sandra came. I wore my new bed jacket from Nannie. They had to come on the bus because daddy is ill. I hope he's not started drinking again. He always does. It takes three buses and about an hour and a half, but only twenty minutes by car. We all seemed a bit fed-up but trying not to show it. Sandra liked her purse and mummy said her tray cloth was pretty. I also gave them some of my duplicate presents and a big box of chocolates 'cos I've got so many. Poor mummy and Sandra on such a cold day having to wait for buses. I know it's not my fault but if I wasn't here, dad being "ill" wouldn't matter, just be life as usual. After they'd gone, Connie told me about Kathleen. She's got "galloping consumption".[27] Drugs aren't working and she's too ill for an op. I'm not even on any drugs yet. I might die. No one has been here for less than a few months and some have had T.B. for years. People "get better" then they have a "flare up" or a "set back" and are back in hospital. What a thought. Is anyone ever really cured, even if they don't die? I don't feel ill or look ill like Kathleen or cough like Eileen but will I even be at home by NEXT Christmas? Will I get worse and die? At night, there was another party in the men's six-bedder with booze! I can't believe they get away with it night after night! They all went, apart from Mrs Benfield, who was so miserable I might as well have been here by myself again. Even Eileen went and she's really ill at the moment. I just lay on my side, so I could pretend the ward wasn't there and read and read. I am so unhappy I can't even be bothered to cry anymore. I HATE CROSSLEY.

---

[27] _Galloping consumption:_ _This was the term used by patients and staff at that time to describe a sort of TB that took hold very quickly and against which drugs were ineffective but the patient was too weak for an operation._

SUN 27: Judy and Connie told me all about the party last night. They got drunk! Eileen was so loud singing that the Night Sister came in and broke it up! Judy and Kenny (he's about her age I think) and Connie and Peter (who is older but not as old as she is) went into the lift and necked apparently!! They are both patients in the men's 6-bedder on our floor. The naughty girls have both got high temps. today. Eileen has been spitting in her sputum cup a LOT – ugh! Mrs Benfield told them they were stupid for carrying on like that and they were "cheap". Connie told her she was stupid for smoking. When I'd said to Connie a few days ago Mrs Benfield was silly for smoking, Connie said "Wait until your second Christmas here before you start criticising other people". Anyway, they ALL ended up having a row. It was awful. <u>Visiting</u> Daddy, mummy, Sandra and Nannie W came. I wanted to tell Sandra about the goings on last night and how nasty everyone is to each other but didn't have the chance. I daren't let mummy know about any of it or she'd go mad. It was our turn to have the T.V. on a trolley[28] tonight. I wish we had a T.V. here all the time. It keeps the others in the ward and it stops them having a go at each other. Sally Stevens and Judy came in to watch

---

[28] _Television:_ _The only opportunity I had to watch TV when I was confined to bed was if it was our ward's turn to have the TV trolley brought in. Later, I would sneak into one of the singles as some people had their own TV. Towards the end, I had a TV in my room but I can't remember if it belonged to my family or the hospital._

with us. They brought bottles of Babycham. Jill's handsome husband had left her a bottle of sherry and some peach brandy. Connie's mum had given her a bottle of Cherry B. I tried a bit of everything! I like Babycham best and sherry worst. I got really giggly! When the T.V. finished, they all went off to another party on the men's side but they said I couldn't go with them. I didn't really mind. I'd had my treat - my favourite heart-throb, Flint out of "Wagon Train" on TV.[29] I hope I dream about him!! When I'm an up patient, I'll be able to watch in the Day Room. I might even be invited to their parties by then!

MON 28: Christmas is well and truly over. I made a silver paper picture with a set I got. I've now been in Crossley three weeks. It feels much longer. I'm getting used to things but don't like it here. At least I'm now allowed to be taken in a wheelchair to the toilet when I want to do more than a wee. I was constipated so they said they'd see if that did the trick. It did! Now, I'll go every day, whether I need to or not, just for the "outing"! Wonder if they'll believe me if I say I have diarrhea? I'm still not having any treatment but I was x-rayed today.[30]

---

[29] "_Wagon Train_": _This American TV series, set in the pioneering days of America, was one of my favourites, especially as it starred Robert Horton who sang as well as acted. I had always watched it with my mum._

[30] _X-RAYS: During the course of my stay in Crossley, as well in the weeks before and for years afterwards, I had many, many chest x-rays, from different angles and at different_

That really was an outing! I was taken in the wheelchair down to the basement. I had to wait ages but I didn't mind – I was out of the ward! The x-ray lady was a bit rude about how thin I am. She said she had to change all the dials just for me. She took loads, all at different angles. She hid behind a screen. I had so many I must be radioactive by now like "The Isotope Man" in that book I read just before I came here. Catty Connie and Mrs Benfield had another row tonight. Mrs Benfield said it would serve Connie right if someone told her boyfriend about her "carrying on" with men here. He didn't deserve that when he'd stuck by her all this time. Connie said Mrs Benfield's kids didn't deserve a mum who smoked when she had T.B. and that if she really loved her kids she'd stop. Then Mrs Benfield called Connie a "slut" and Connie said it was a fact that T.B. made you feel "randy". If Mrs Benfield didn't then she felt sorry for her husband 'cos she must be "rigid".[31] He was probably having his end away with someone else all this time. I was shocked. Jill and Eileen said nothing, even when Connie went off for a bath, but the atmosphere now is awful. I HATE it here.

TUE 29: May was in our ward a lot today. She's a bit strange but I like her. She's leaving soon. She says she's glad but not excited. She's spent so much

---

depths. In those days, the dangers of over-exposure were not understood – even shoe shops used them - although I always noted how keen staff were to keep well out of the way.

[31] *I understood a lot of the 'adult' talk but not always fully.*

of her life in hospital she knows she'll be back. She is an amazingly cheerful person. She told us why Eileen has been moved out this morning. She's positive and is spitting blood apparently. I thought that only happened in books in the past. She's been moved from 4 Hours to Bed Absolute. That must be awful, to be back to square one. Connie and Mrs Benfield still aren't speaking. I don't want to fall out with either of them but if I speak to one, the other might stop speaking to me, so I've not talked at all except to staff. I have invented a new game. I call it "Roving Camera". I hold my hand mirror at different angles then pretend to do a T.V. commentary on what I can see. When I'm by myself, I speak out loud, which is best. Sometimes, I do it like it's a stately home or I look at people's plants and flowers and it's a nature documentary. I've also started watching the people in the ward as if they are in a play, although I don't use the mirror or say anything out loud. I'll be glad when our artist Sarah is back from leave.

WED 30: I was quite cheerful yesterday but not today. Eileen was replaced yesterday evening by an even worse old cougher and spitter, Mrs Wilson. She is ancient. Her face is covered with red spiders' webs and she has wispy grey hair and watery eyes behind her glasses. She has the ugliest feet I've ever seen, all yellow and crooked with nails like snails. She shouldn't be out of bed 'cos she's on Bed Absolute but she wanders about the ward. She's got a miserable moaning voice and complains about everything. She has SO many bedpans and gives us a running commentary from behind the screen, with sound effects. Ugh! <u>Visiting</u> Daddy brought mummy but then had to go as he's behind with his collecting because of Christmas. I was so miserable I could not hide it for once and I cried. When I told mummy about how horrible Mrs Wilson is, she told me off for being heartless so I felt even worse. It was the worst visit yet. I can't stand it here anymore.

THU 31: New Year's Eve. I wish I was at home with mummy, watching the T.V. Daddy and Sandra will be out and she'll be by herself, like I am. I don't mind Mrs Wilson being old but she's so depressing. All she talks about is illness, death, her bowels and God. She is VERY religious and a Catholic, like Nannie Salter. My nose bled again today 'cos of that tube. She came across to my bed to press a "holy relic" on it to make it stop. She is like a witch with a spell. I didn't want her to touch me. She went back to bed in a huff. When the others came back, she told them I'd been rude to her. Even though I told her it was from my nose, she said I'd been spitting blood. I hadn't and I got really cross. Since then, I've had first Mrs Benfield and then even kind Jill telling me to "try and be nice to her" etc. They have no right to tell me off. It's alright for them, they can escape Mrs W. I can't. I'm the only one stuck here every day, just her and me. I feel they are ganging up against me, sticking up for Mrs Wilson. Poor Jill, her bed is next to her. Yuk. I bet it's smelly over there. I put the headphones on and didn't look at or speak to anyone all evening. I am going to try to go to sleep early tonight. I want this day to end. I can't bear the thought of being here for who knows how much of the year ahead. I don't believe the 'only 10 weeks' anymore. People are here for years. I also now know not everyone is cured. What an awful New Year's Eve.

JANUARY 1960

1 Fri: Happy New Year! Yesterday I was VERY unhappy but today I don't feel too bad. Last night, when I was trying to go to sleep, Judy came in and gave me my dressing gown and slippers and I went <u>in the wheelchair</u> to a great party in the 4-bedder![32] It was May's farewell party as well as a New Year party. Although I'm on Bed Absolute and Sister Savage saw me in the corridor, when we said Judy was taking me to the toilet, she didn't stop us! Jill and Betty – I actually managed to call Mrs Benfield that for the first time - were there, so was Connie, and Sally Stevens, of course. There was a LOT to drink and mince pies and crisps. We saw in the New Year by kissing everyone! It was nearly 1 in the morning before I was in bed! We all had to try to be quiet and not wake up Mrs W! May went home at 9.30 today. She went in a taxi because she didn't have any family who could come for her. We all

---

[32] <u>Parties and alcohol:</u> *Hard as it may be to believe, there were many parties – often mixed and going on into the early hours – at which there was plenty of alcohol as well as food, and a certain amount of flirting that developed, in some cases, to more serious 'hanky panky' (as I would then have called it). The night staff were thin on the ground, were often ex-TB patients so sympathetic, and only very rarely did they stop a party. More serious liaisons would be held in the lift, parked in the basement (the floor where both the Occupational Therapy centre was and where bodies were taken on their way to the mortuary). Babycham was a very popular drink for 'ladies'.*

waved and cheered as they drove past the front of the hospital. Connie said "Let's say au reviour not goodbye because she'll be back". Trust her to have to say something nasty. I hope it's not true. I got 3 New Year cards, first-time I ever got any! Mummy and Daddy came to see me but they would not let them in. I'm glad they wanted to see me and I wish they had been allowed in but, arr well ne'er mind eh! At least I didn't have to make sure NOT to tell them about the party last night!!

2 Sat: Boy, was I tired in the morning. I don't know why, it was the night before I was up so late. I was called at 7.30 but it was 8 before I started to wash! I have a LOT of thank you letters to write still from Christmas but I don't mind, it gives me something to do. <u>Visiting</u> Mummy, Daddy, Nannie W and Nannie S came to see me. They were late arriving. They had a puncture on the way here. Three in three weeks! Mummy had to leave early 'cos the shop is busy with people bringing back slippers they'd been given for Christmas. I didn't enjoy visiting much apart from the food. Nannie W and Nannie S don't really get on but still talk to each other more than to me. Daddy was gone ages and then was off visiting Jack so I didn't see much of him. I missed Sandra. I have decided I must try to see Mrs Wilson as a nice old lady but oh! how depressing she is.

3 Sun: Had my usual 'bird' bath this morning. Dorothy gave it to me. She is funny. She sings about "What you going to do when the love bug bites" 'cos she's in love with Dr Johnny! The others tease her –she's big and has straight grey hair and isn't pretty but I think she likes it when they do. <u>Visiting</u> Sandra, Barry, mummy and Daddy came to see me this afternoon. Barry had to go at 3.00 to get back in time to milk the cows! I was amazed he'd come at all. It must be getting serious if he's coming to see his girlfriend's little sister! I really like him. He is VERY handsome. I was a very good girl, I never got upset. Boy, was it an effort but they never even saw a glimmer of a tear. Mrs W's main topic today was her bowels of all things! Really!!!! We hear them enough from behind her curtains every time she has a bedpan. We don't need to be told about them as well! Last night Mrs Benfield smuggled me down to be weighed. I was 5st 10lbs! She said that was far too low for my age and height. Well, hey, tell me something I don't know! I wish they'd start weighing me on Sunday mornings with all the others. Perhaps they will once I start on some drugs. STILL nothing.

4 Mon: AT LAST! I had my first treatment today. Every day (except on Sunday, don't know why not then) I have to have an intramuscular injection of streptomycin[33] in my bottom. I have to lie on my side. Sister Savage did the first one. It didn't hurt as much as I thought it would but it feels quite sore now. Dorothy gave that cheek a good massage as she said she could feel a lump.[34] I've not done any

---

[33] <u>Streptomycin</u>: *for more information, see separate Note on Tuberculosis (TB) and Sanatoria at the end.*

[34] *The daily injection was usually a slightly painful jab in a muscle in the buttock but with an inexperienced or careless or*

work at all today. All I've done is read and look at the birds through Grandad's binoculars. (Of course, I also talked.) Mrs W keeps on and on about her bowels etc! Everything we mention in the food or drink line is constipating or bowel shifting or bad for you! Poor Mrs W! We all feel like laughing now, when she starts, so it's no longer just me that can't stand her. We seem very cruel I suppose but she's so depressing. If we didn't laugh we would become very miserable. Her daughter is so nice and sweet but a typical shy spinster. It must be awful to have such a dreadful old mother.

5 Tues: I started my wallet for mum today but I couldn't do much as I hadn't got the prodder. It is very soft tan leather. I'm also embroidering her a dressing table set. Oh I have been bored today. I've now tried all the craft kits I got for Christmas. I want something NEW to do! I usually go in my chariot at 4.45 but today for Nature Reasons I went in the morning. As a result at 4.45 I didn't want to use the toilet but I wanted to get up! So I said I did! While I was up, I watered my hyacinths and changed the flower water. <u>BAD</u> ABSOLUTE!

6 Wed: Dr Houston didn't come round til about 1.45 into our ward and so mum and dad had to wait

---

rushed nurse, it would be extremely painful both at the time and later. The needle seemed to be in a long time. We all had days when a lump formed at the injection site which made sitting painful or it 'hit a nerve' and we had shooting pains down the leg. The bed rubs – massages to stop bedsores primarily – we had when confined to bed were also given sometimes to ease the pain caused by an injection.

outside. Still they stayed till nearly 5 o'clock to make up for it! I wasn't expecting anything. Dr Houston gave Mrs Benfield her 6 hours. He told Connie that she might need an op. on the other side. He told her so bluntly that he made her cry. Poor Connie. She has had TB since (I think) 1954. She has already had one op. The visiting was lovely. It's much easier when it's just them. Luverly food and lots of it! Oh I do love mummy and daddy! I wish it wasn't so long until I see them again.

7 Thu: Got a letter from Sandra and one from cousin Valerie. Replied to both of them. I am worried. We've been best friends for years even though Valerie is a year younger. Now she's in her first year at grammar school, she'll make new friends so will we still be friends when I'm home? I also wrote to my school friends with a joint 'thank you' card for the Christmas presents. I am glad they are my friends but I do worry about whether they will still like me by the time I leave here. Mrs Mawson didn't come today. She gave me work yesterday. I suppose I should be glad to have something to do but it's so BORING. I don't want to fall behind but I can't see how doing these few hours a week will stop that. My strep injection did hurt today. It hurt a lot when it went in then I had an ache in the injection spot and a stiff leg. Shenola did it! She's new. She's sweet but she isn't very good at sticking the needle in fast and deep. Sister Savage supervised but let her do it. She told Shenola she had to be tougher. She has to practise with an orange! Charming! My bum is not like that surely!!

8 Fri: Did some more of mummy's wallet. It's awfully hard to sew through four thicknesses of leather. When my teacher came, I was on my side, facing the wall, under the covers, so she thought I was asleep. I sort of heard something but didn't check. When she'd left, I sat up so everyone thought I'd heard her come in but I hadn't known it was her. Mind you, if I had I might have pretended! Connie thought it was really funny but Mrs Benfield was a bit sniffy about me "wasting the teacher's time".

9 Sat: Finished mummy's wallet but I'm not going to show it to her yet, not until I've done dad's wallet and something for Sandra. Visiting Mrs Benfield's son brought their dog to see her. Awfully cute. We looked at it through the window. It's ok for her 'cos she's up for visiting so she could be outside with her dog. It made me miss Scamp. Mummy went at 2.45 with Daddy which left me with Aunty Laura and Nannie W. Visiting was very nice and I got a bunch of mimosa (off Aunty) and bunch of iris (off Nannie). I said nice things about both lots of flowers as I know there is a bit of sisterly rivalry still. Actually, I like the mimosa best 'cos it curls up when I touch it, but both are really pretty. This evening, Connie and Jill took me in the wheelchair to be weighed secretly. I was 5st.13 ¾ lb! I was really happy I'd gained but catty Connie said people always weigh more at night so probably I haven't.

10 Sun: Got weighed, officially, today![35] I'm 5st 10lbs! YES!! I've gained 2 ½ lbs since the school nurse weighed me! Connie was right, it's not as much as last night, but still I have gained some lbs. Visiting was very nice, just Mummy, Daddy and Sandra. When they'd gone (not before) I cried. I do love them so. I no longer think I'll be home in weeks, as I was told when I was first diagnosed. Getting out in as little as a year is considered "good", according to what people here say. The thought of about 10 more months away from home depresses me terribly. Another thing that's depressing me is the fact that when (if??) I eventually get back to school, I'll be in the 2nd year and my friends will be in the 3rd year. I haven't really been doing much school work here so far. Part of me knows I have to try harder to keep up. The other part thinks it's all a waste of time. What's the point of doing any of it? Can't see the point of working for a future until I know I've got one.

11 Mon: My teacher came in her new green overall and NAME badge. Why? I know who she is and I don't think she teaches anyone else here. She'd told me she was going to come at 9.00 but didn't arrive until nearly 12.00! I felt fed-up, waiting all morning for her. She didn't say why she was late. I didn't dare ask her in case it was 'cos she knew I'd not really been asleep the other day. We just started

[35] Weight gain: _On 17 November 1959, aged 13yrs, I was 5ft 1in and weighed 5st 8lbs. At my first official weigh-in at Crossley on 10 January 1960, I weighed 5st 10lbs. The amount of weight I gained, or lost, each week was a matter of great importance to me (and the doctors) as it was taken to indicate how well (or not) I was progressing. My weigh-ins are noted throughout the diary as of importance to me then._

Africa then it was dinner time and she had to leave. It made me realise that I do like her coming even when what we do is a bit boring. It's better than just lying here in bed by myself all morning. Wrote to home plus four other letters this afternoon. I've started my lavender stationary today. It looks and smell so nice, I feel like writing to myself! Not quite as cheerful as usual today, but in my letters I was! By the time I'd written the last one, I'd almost convinced myself I was ok. <u>Mens Requests</u>[36] Got records off Peter, Uncle Jack, Kenny, the 6-bedder cowboys! Most of the time, there is proper radio through the headphones, but twice a week we have patient requests, done by patients who are up. I don't know the people who send me requests but I do like having them! I know Kenny and Peter are the two Judy and Connie were necking with at Christmas. Judy said they are good looking!! Jack is

[36] *Hospital radio and request shows:* *A radio station was available through the headphones we each had plugged in by our beds. It would have been the Light Programme (like today's Radio 1 or 2). I do not remember if there was more than one but I'd have only have wanted the one with pop music anyway at that age and Radio Luxembourg (then the best pop service) was not available. Through the headphones, we also received the Men's Requests and the Women's Requests, done on different nights each week, with 'up' patients as the DJs. They would read out requests from patients to patients – a source of many a romance – and play records. At first, I looked forward to these sessions but, as time wore on, because of poor reception, scratchy records, and who knows why else, I stopped mentioning them so I either lost interest or they were discontinued?*

dad's friend. I can see the men's 6-bedder, like ours but at the opposite end of this middle floor. We all wave but I don't know who I'm waving to.

12 Tue: Got a letter off THE QUEEN today! I wrote to her and she sent me a letter saying she was sorry to hear that I was in hospital and she hoped I'd soon be well! Wasn't that lovely! I didn't tell anyone I was writing in case they said I shouldn't. I didn't really think she'd reply (well, it was a lady-in-waiting on her behalf as catty Connie pointed out, not the actual Queen herself). If I'd told them and no one had replied, I'd have felt silly. I don't care what Connie says, she's just jealous. Got a lampshade frame off Miss Growcott. It's for a cane covered Mateus Rose bottle that Super Sarah gave me. Dad's doing the electrical part and I'm going to make a blue raffia lamp shade. It will look lovely in my bedroom. Can't wait to be back there again. Mrs Wilson's daughter came to see her at night. She came over and told Mrs Benfield that she'd been given special permission because her mother is very ill 'cos of her heart. The daughter is a very nice person and was sad, so I'm sad for her. But if Mrs W is that ill, she should be moved into another ward, or even another hospital.

13 Wed: Dr Houston didn't come round. Poor Connie, she was waiting for her hour and after what he said last week she especially wanted it. I can't see the point of her getting any hours up if she's going to have an operation but I didn't say anything. Visiting Mummy and Daddy came to see me. I am SO glad half-day closing in Runcorn is on a

Wednesday or I'd only properly see mummy on a Sunday. They brought me a whole pile of magazines. It was a lovely visit.

14 Thu: Nurse Evans did the strep again today. She puts the needle in very slowly. Ugh!!! I think she's even worse than Shenola! Shenola has given me a white flower called, I think, chincheree. She said they grow in her country in Africa. Dr Houston did his round today. Connie didn't get her hour. Poor Connie, she feels very down. He didn't promote anyone else either. I had a nice little talk with him, he is funny. When he said that he wanted to listen to my chest I thought "This is it! Examination before he gives me Bed 1" but no such luck! Would it be really bad for me to be allowed to walk to the toilet once a day? Started the leather purse. I haven't done much of it though. Womens Requests were spoilt tonight because the needle of the gramophone was an old one and it was so crackly it was too bad to listen to. I haven't sent in any requests yet but I am part of the "girls in the 6-bedder" ones Connie sends for us all.

15 Fri: I have been very lazy today. My teacher didn't come again. She's not been since Monday. I think she should at least send a message. I hate waiting and waiting. I end up doing nothing. Margaret (the mentally deficient patient) left for good this morning. I don't know if she went home or back to Deva. I did feel sorry for her but she'll be treated better in Deva. Jill is going to go into Margaret's single when it's been fumigated. I wish she wasn't, she's the nicest, kindest one in my ward.

I shall miss seeing her smiling red lips and bright red hair! Still I suppose I could go and watch TV with her when I am up. Until I'm on Bed Ordinary, I won't see much of her, and it will be ages before I am. I bet Connie will spend even less time than ever in our ward. Although I am always a bit nervous about what she'll say, she is better company than Mrs W. Mrs Benfield and Sarah are out for most of the day too 'cos of the hours they are on so can't count on them for company.

16 Sat: Started to make the lampshade today. I've changed the design. The raffia was driving me daft. Now I'm binding the frame in blue bias binding and I have got pale blue plastic panels to make the shade and braid to trim it with which I glue on. Visiting was very nice. Mummy, Nannie W, Daddy and Sandra came first of all and then mum and Nannie went home and Daddy brought Aunty Gladys but not Valerie, her daughter! She said Valerie is too young to be allowed in. I don't see why she can't come in if my friends can, only a year older. The best bit was when Daddy was taking Mummy and Nannie home because that was just me and Sandra. That is the only time I talk about what it's really like here and how I feel. At night, I kept thinking about Nora Henson who lives near Nannie W. She's a humpback, like May, and is very little even though she's mum's age. Nannie said she rolled off a sofa when she was a baby but mummy told me, years ago, she had T.B. and it stopped her growing properly. I'm still growing. What if I end up like that? She works in a cake shop and runs the Brownies so at least she's not ill. Mummy said before I came here that T.B. is now curable and I believed her. Now I know not everyone is cured, so how do I know if I will be or not? If I get "better" enough to go home, will I be deformed by then?

17 Sun: Yesterday, Nannie brought me two lovely, not yet opened, pink hyacinths in an earthenware pot. I hope they last longer than the other one did. I don't know if I gave it too much water or not enough. Visiting Mummy, Daddy, Grandad W and Grandad S came to see me today. It was not an easy visit. Grandad W is very shy and said hardly anything. Grandad S talked mainly to dad. It was a relief when at about 3.00 Mummy's friend, Mrs Fenton, came with Tracy. Because Tracy is only 6, they had to take it in turns to stay outside with her but then she came in once for about 5 mins! Sister Harvey saw her!! Nothing was said. In the end, I enjoyed visiting even if it wasn't the usual Sunday type visit. After Tracy today, I kept on wondering why Aunty Gladys hadn't brought Valerie with her yesterday. Maybe Valerie didn't want to come? Oh dear, the start of losing friends?

18 Mon: I had a very lazy day today. I only read, I didn't do any 'handicrafts' at all. I didn't write any letters. No Mrs Mawson, again. You'd think I'd be well, doing nothing, but quite the opposite. Tonight I had a temperature of 100.2 but the funny thing is - I don't feel ill! I've had a back ache all day but that's all. I can't understand it. I had to take 2 aspros before I went to sleep. I'm having my temp taken at 6.00. Mens Requests Got records off Peter, Kenny and Uncle Jack. I must start sending requests back. Even if there's nothing on the headphones, I put them on as much as I can to drown out Mrs Wilson. She is really getting me down, bowels and now piles! Ugh! In such detail too!! Thank goodness my temp. was down to 99.6 by this evening.

19 Tues: Today I wrote three letters and got a letter off Daddy. I think he really is trying to be good. Mummy promised she'd tell me if he started drinking again, but will she? He is funny and I like him when he isn't drinking but hate him when he is. I do hope he keeps his promise for once. Went for my second exam today with giggly Dr Vamor. I blew 2,100, last time I blew 1,800.[37] He said "Very good" again when he listened to my chest. So I was very pleased. My temp was 98 today. I still feel like yesterday, fine! My back ache's even gone today. I bet that was caused by being in bed all the time. (Hint hint – time I was on Bed One!!) <u>Womans Requests</u> Got a group record from this ward. They played some really great records. I sent records to all of them but just said 'To the ladies in the middle

---

[37] *'Exams' and blowing tests: As well as regular x-rays, we all had 'exams' which consisted of chest examinations (primarily with a stethoscope but with a bit of knocking and listening) and a test which required us to blow into a contraption that measured our lung capacity. For reasons never explained, from 12 August, under the new hospital regime, such tests were discontinued, but, until then, being able to blow as much or more each time mattered a lot.*

floor 6-bedder from Barbara". I cannot bring myself to send a named one to the awful Mrs W.

20 Wed: Dr Houston came round early today. He gave 8 hours to Mrs Benfield and 1 hour to Connie. The lucky things! I'm awfully glad that Connie got her hour. It's cheered her up a lot. I wonder if it means she does not need the op now? He examined my back (because of the ache) and my chest (while he was at it). As usual, he didn't say anything about how I am. <u>Visiting</u> Mummy came by herself. She said Daddy was working. It takes her an awful long, cold time when she has to come by bus. I was really happy, just us, but then I thought I was going to be sick and had to have one of those nasty tin "receivers" to be sick in. I felt awful – in front of visitors. I was so embarrassed. I feel guilty because I know Mummy went away more worried than usual. Apart from that, I really enjoyed the visiting, like old times, just mum and me, lovely! Daddy came to collect her ten minutes late! I hope he really was working. Mummy says we're lucky he is an insurance agent because he can choose his own hours. She was being nice about him but ?? Hope he doesn't end up getting sacked again.

21 Thu: I now have a proper school timetable. Mrs Mawson comes from 10.00 to 11.00, mainly maths. and English, and a French teacher with a name I can't say, comes from 11.30 to 12.00. She's nice but I don't think my French is good enough for her. I am truly glad that lessons have been sorted out and I will do the work. But I still can't see how it can possibly make up for all the lessons I am missing in

2A. I liked going to school to be with my friends. Sister Savage said there's another young girl in a single, Helen. I know, but I've not met her yet. I think she's about 15 or 16. She's the one catty Connie calls 'posh'.

22 Fri: Hurrah, hurrah my temp was normal today – 98.4. Wacko! No one seems to know why I had a temp. for a few days. I just hope it's not a sign that the strep isn't working. Would anyone tell me? Had a history lesson today off Mrs Mawson. Started on Henry III. Not very interesting really, well, not the way we're doing it. John, one of the '6-bedder cowboys', went for his op today. He has gone to another hospital for it, in Liverpool.[38] He will come back here to recover in a few days. Nurse said he was 'comfortable'. We sent him a card from our ward. I don't know him but Connie and Judy do. Vincent polished our floor this afternoon while I read "Jane Eyre" (again). He has a big machine with circular brushes. It makes quite a soothing wooshing noise. Mrs Benfield said he's from Eastern Europe. Sometimes, the floor is polished by Fred. We prefer him 'cos he chats to us. Dorothy has a crush on him so if she comes in when he's here, we start singing "Sitting in the back seat, kissing an a huggin with Fred"![39] After that I wrote

---

[38] _Broadgreen Hospital, Liverpool: This was where patients from Crossley went for their operations. For more information, see separate Note on Tuberculosis (TB) and Sanatoria at the end._

[39] _"(Seven little girls) Sitting in the back seat (kissin' and_

to my American pen friend, Barby,[40] and told her all about "it". I wonder if she'll still write to me now I've told her I've got TB? I do hope so. I really like her letters about life in South Dakota. She is at the school that some relation of dad's side of the family teaches at. I wonder if I'll ever see her? I'd love to go to America one day! Oh I hate Friday – I'm always depressed on a Friday as well. Why? I should be able to look forward to visiting for the next TWO days but instead I'm worn down because of the TWO days I've just had without visitors.

23 Sat: Visiting day was super! The gang from school came to see me. Sandra came also. I was glad she was here so I can talk to her about what they said next time I see her.   Daddy didn't stay and he came back late so we could all have a good natter! They brought some egg sandwiches and marshmallows and a bottle of cydrax each as well. Delicious! Wish the cider hadn't been non-alcoholic!! They all seem to have boyfriends now, even Susan the shy one. They all seem boy mad. I

ahuggin' with Fred" The Avons, 1959.

[40] *American pen pal: Barby (Barbara) Seefeldt had been my American pen friend for a few years by then. It had started when, in junior school, we were encouraged to have a 'pen pal'. One of Nannie Salter's sisters (who had been sent to America when young) had become a teacher in South Dakota and, through her, Barby and I began to write. Although we lost touch a few years later, in 1987 we met for the first time when I was living and working in America and I visited my relations in South Dakota with my family.*

think that they've gone a bit babyish in a teenage way. I AM glad to see them and I DO feel they still want to be my friends BUT I felt really really fed up when they left. They are living the life I should be. I feel much younger than them in some ways – no boyfriends here! – but also much older because of what living here is like. I cried at night and Mrs Benfield heard me so she sneaked me with her into Jill's single and we watched Flint from Wagon Train on Jill's TV. Great!!!! Now if Robert Horton was available I would definitely want a boyfriend!

24 Sun: <u>Visiting Day</u> again today. Nannie S and Nannie W, Daddy and Mummy came to see me today. Nannie W brought me some lovely tulips and daffodils. Nannie S brought me some more of her damson jam, I just love it! I've got the knack of not biting the stones!! It went quite well today, although I prefer Sunday with just Mummy and Daddy. When it's just Mummy and Daddy or Sandra, the time flies but this afternoon, it felt like a long time. I was still sorry when it was over. Sunday night nearly always seems dull and flat and if you're not careful, depressing. As soon as visiting was over, I started to feel down. So it wouldn't get worse, after we'd eaten, I put on headphones and I made a leather purse for Susan's birthday. I'll give it to Sandra to give to her. I can always make another one for Sandra. It's not her birthday until April.

25 Mon: My French teacher came again today. Boy, can she speak French fluently. Gosh she jabbers away and expects <u>me</u> to answer her! (Some hope!) I struggled with French when I was having proper lessons at school so not much hope for me now. Mrs de H (can't spell her name) said that having individual lessons should actually be better for me. We'll see. Wrote four letters. Not much to say when nothing happens and I've only just seen them all but somehow I can fill a page or two. Then I finished Jane Eyre. It's a really great book. Crossley is definitely better than Lowood! Every book I read seems to have someone in it dying of T.B. Consumption sounds worse. Connie's going to read it now. I'm amazed she'd never read it! I read it first in primary school. I can't decide if that is my favourite book or Wuthering Heights. Miss Growcott has helped me with my lampshade so I'll begin stitching soon. <u>Mens Requests</u> I got records from Kenny, Peter, and the Disc Jockey.

26 Tue: I had a very lazy day today. That is apart from lessons (ugh!). I say, ugh, but I don't really mind, it passes the time. I just wish it was more interesting or Mrs M was livelier. I do miss being in class with my friends. I saw Helen today. She's got long, dark wavy hair and dark eyes. She smiled at me from the door of her single when I went past in the wheelchair. <u>Womans Requests</u> I got a few records. Already, I don't really care who sends me one (on women's night anyway). The requests are a bit boring but I love the records. I sent one to John to welcome him back after his op, and one to all middle floor girls. I'd like to send a Valentine to John really but I daren't ask mum and I daren't ask anyone here to buy me one from the shop so I don't know what to do. If I did send him one it would be a funny one. I am silly, after all he's 17 and I'm "only

13" and I've only ever seen him in the bay window of the men's six-bedder. Still it's nice to think about. It makes me feel more like my friends. Maybe I'm not so different from them after all – if I had the chance to be the same about boys!!

27 Wed: Dr Houston didn't come round today. Mrs Benfield was going to tell him about her pain but she won't tell him next week as she's expecting 10 hours. I don't know what I'd do. If she has a pain that can be made better, she should tell him. If it's to do with her T.B. then she might be having a relapse and be back to square one but he still needs to know. We all want to get better and be cured so we can go home but the aim seems to be mainly just to be allowed to leave. <u>Visiting Day</u> Sandra, Mummy and Daddy came to see me today. Sandra had her hair up and black nylons! She looked great – awfully modern! The time went really quickly. I enjoyed myself so much. Super Sarah went to Warrington and brought us a tin of 'bubbles'. She is very close to going home so can go out during visiting. She goes to shops, cafes, etc. I like her and I'll miss her. She's more sophisticated than the others + never nasty.

28 Thu: Last night all lights fused at about 9.10. Sister said they'd be out all night but they came back on at about 10.5. Oh, well. Not that I was going anywhere! At least it was something different for once. Connie and Judy were getting excited about going over to the men's side in the dark so they were disappointed. Did some more of my lampshade today. I had four exercises and an essay to do in French. I've not even started them yet! I'll never have them done for Monday I'm sure. Why can't I talk myself into liking schoolwork? Ugh. Depressing Friday tomorrow. I do wish I had a friend like Connie has Judy. They aren't in the same ward but are both up enough. I wish Helen was in our ward. She's near my age.

29 Fri: Dr Houston came round after dinner. Mrs Benfield's pain isn't bad, it will soon go, and it's nothing to do with her T.B. She didn't tell me what it was so I'm guessing it's something embarrassing. I didn't get Bed One. I wish I had. To think – I've been here 2 months on Monday and I'm NO further ahead. Oh I do feel depressed today. Somehow I always do on a Friday. I know I should not as tomorrow and Sunday are visiting, but I do. Catty Connie has turned against me. She keeps making "digs" at me or my family. She says things like I'm spoiled and my mum is old fashioned and she doesn't like my dad and I have too many visitors! She's always doing it, it's horrible, I wish she wouldn't. What have I done to make her be like that? I think she's jealous 'cos I do get more visitors than she does AND I'm not as ill as she is. After I'd said what she said was "irrelevant" and "of no consequence to me", she said "Ooh, swallowed a dictionary". When I said I had not insulted her family so what right had she to speak ill of mine, she said "You and that stuck-up Helen should get together. You'd suit." I wish we could! I do feel sorry for Connie but it's not my fault so why take it out on me. Anyway, she should talk – her mum looks a lot older and wears awful cheap clothes and her hair is obviously dyed black!

30 Sat: Today was visiting day. Mummy, Daddy, Sandra and Nannie came. They all stayed all afternoon, mummy too! It was lovely. Mummy went to see Dr Houston this afternoon. He is very pleased with me. He says that I'm improving and my T.B. is very very slight.[41] In fact it's <u>one tiny shadow</u>. It isn't a cavity. It isn't at all serious. If I keep a steady temperature and stick to BED ABSOLUTE I'll "whip" through my hours. I'm not getting Bed One for quite a few more weeks though 'cos of my age – still I don't mind, now. Mummy showed me on a chocolate box picture of the sea how big my 'shadow' is. It is less than the size of my little finger nail. When I was showing Mrs Benfield after, catty Connie came over and said Mummy was telling me lies. She said no one's shadow is that small and I probably have loads of cavities anyway because TB eats holes in your lungs. Why does she always have to say something bad about anything good? I do feel sorry for her. She's been ill a long time and she may still need an op. But it's not my fault! I believe my mum!

[41] _How serious was my TB?_ _The description I was given by my mother made me believe I only had a slight shadow and no cavities. Whether that was true or not, I still have no idea (even though I now have an x-ray plate, taken to secure me an Australian visa in the 1990s). All I know is I have gone on to have a healthy, long life._

31 Sun: Today, visiting came awfully quickly, I was so busy all morning. I think I was still feeling happy because Dr Houston was pleased with me yesterday. I will NOT let catty Connie depress me. Mummy, Daddy, and Aunty Laura came. I enjoyed visiting, the time absolutely flew by. I had a gorgeous tea, salad with lettuce, tomato, egg, chicken, on a plate. I felt <u>very</u> full afterwards. The good feeling stayed with me all evening so, even though no visiting for more than two more days, I'm OK. I asked Mrs Benfield about Helen. She said she's in a single and doesn't mix. She is posh but Mrs Benfield thinks she's shy and trying to be good, not stuck up. She said she thought she might be a friend for me once I am up a bit.

FEBRUARY 1960

1 Mon: My French teacher came again today. Oh dear, I hate reading aloud, my accent is awful. It is so embarrassing having to speak French (badly) in the ward when others can hear. The others who are up go out when I have a teacher but it still means Mrs W is listening in. I don't know if she can speak French – I hope not! In the afternoon, I wrote letters and read. Didn't feel like doing any leather work or embroidery. <u>Mens Requests</u> I got one off Kenny and one off Peter. The most important - one off John! It wasn't to me alone but I was at the beginning of the list. I don't know why, 'cos I've never actually met him, I keep thinking about him. At least he is young enough to be my boyfriend. During requests, I embroidered a black lamb on a hankie and a blue anchor on another. I will give these away but I haven't yet decided who to and whether separately or together.

2 Tues: My French teacher didn't come today because her mother has got flu, but she'll be coming tomorrow (worst luck). She's given me learning homework. I hayt hur! Whenever she doesn't come, or Mrs Mawson, I'm sort of glad but also sad. I wish they'd just come and talk to me. I want to have them here but I do NOT like the work I have to do! I started my pencil case today. I've stitched the zip in. It's in soft red leather, very nice. <u>Womans Requests</u> Played some good records. I got quite a few 'gang' records. We got one "to the man-mad girls in the 6-bedder Middle Floor." from Disgusted. The record – "Men are good for nothing" by Rosemary Clooney. Mrs Benfield said it wasn't funny, she objected to being lumped in with Connie and Judy. Connie said, "Don't worry, no one will think you've been with anyone!" Mrs Benfield took that as an insult and they had yet another spat. I don't know who the request meant 'cos Judy isn't in our ward anyway, I never go anywhere, Mrs W is too old (and ugly – ugh), and Sarah is not common like that at all.

3 Wed: My French teacher came today and gave me piles of Hmk! Horrid old xxxxx. Dr Houston came round. He gave Mrs Benfield 10 hours and leave, but he didn't give Connie her hour. Oh, I did feel sorry for her. I think she's now given up hope completely. She realised she's not going through regularly 'cos of more surgery. Oh I do hope not. I think Mrs Benfield felt bad for her too, even though they don't get on, 'cos she didn't go on about her own promotion and leave. Next time Connie is nasty to me for no reason, I must try not to mind so much and remember she's ill and very unhappy. Visiting Just mummy and daddy came. I really enjoyed it. Daddy went to the toilet twice and once he went to see Jack. Mummy gave him a 'look' when he came back the third time. Apart from that they seem OK with each other. I'm hoping that means he's not drinking. He is also good company at the moment which is a good sign. He gave me a piece of the toilet paper 'cos it says "Government Property" and said "Now you own a piece of government property!"

4 Thu: Got a letter off Sandra today. She tells me more about her friends and Barry in her letters than she ever did before! I wrote six pages home and six pages to Valerie on my new notepaper. I haven't done any embroidery or leather-work today, aren't I lazy! Still, I wrote those two long letters. Connie is very miserable today, because on top of everything else, her mum is ill (she didn't come yesterday) and she got no letter to tell her in advance. Connie never mentions her dad so I think he must be dead. She never has any other visitors but her mum. She told us once that her boyfriend Neil has stood by her all the time she's been ill. He's never come to see her while I've been here. I wonder if he exists? The way she talks about the men here, he'd be cross if he is real! I sometimes think about having a boyfriend. What I need more at the moment is just <u>A</u> friend of my own age.

5 Fri: Had a history lesson this morning, wasn't very interesting but I didn't yawn. Read a bit of a corny book this afternoon "The new house mysteries" by Elinor Brent-Dyer.[42] I finished it before tea! Started "Wendy's first term" by R.

---

[42] <u>Books:</u> *Elinor Brent Dyer (1894-1969) was a prolific and popular writer of children's fiction (including the Chalet School stories). R. Chatwyn (Pam's First Term) was a similar writer of school stories for girls. I read voraciously, widely, and with little discrimination, including classics, books like these, and many others, some considered 'adult'. The diary does not include all that I read in that time. A list of those mentioned is at the end.*

Chatwyn in 5-6 rest hour. This is a better book. School is not mentioned until nearly half way through so we get to know the family in it first. To think, I once wanted to be at boarding school. Now I know what it's like being away from my family, no thank you. Hurrah, Hurrah, Saturday and Sunday visiting soon! I wrote to ask Scamp to come – hope she can!

6 Sat: Today was visiting day. Mum, dad and Sandra came, and Nannie W AND Scamp as well! Sandra held her outside for a bit and then they brought her upstairs to the ward!! She was awfully excited. I was scared she might wee with excitement like she does when we've been away. I do love her, and I've got her framed photo on the window sill. Mum (and Scamp) went back at 2.15 with dad. I enjoyed today but I missed my private chat with Sandra 'cos Nannie W was here when daddy took mummy and Scamp back.

7 Sun: I got weighed this morning. 5st 11 ¾ lbs. I've only put on 1 ¾ lbs in a month, last time I put on 2 ½ lbs! Gosh, and all the milk I drink! I'll have to tell mummy to bring me even more food on visiting day. Visiting Day Mummy, Daddy and Grandad Salter came. I got a lovely new bed jacket. Its pink quilted nylon with pink wild roses on it. It's beautiful. Mum says it's for "being cheerful". Oh I was pleased! Sally Stevens had "a- farewell-to-the-middle-floor" party. She's been here ages but isn't making progress so she has to have an op, poor thing. I'd hate it to be my mum. It seems to take them ages to decide the drugs aren't working and an op is needed. I hope that doesn't happen to me but does anyone know if the strep IS working? Mrs Stevens seemed very cheerful. She said "At least something is happening". I went down to the 4-bedder – I walked!! - at about 9 and stayed til about 10.30. It was great – and I didn't jive. I really wanted to but kept thinking how cross mummy would be. Lovely things to eat! I had my favourite Babycham –two! Actually, I might as well have jived 'cos mummy would go mad if she even knew I'd been out of bed – AND drinking!! I hoped Helen would be there so I could meet her. Catty Connie said she doesn't come to any parties 'cos she thinks she's too good for us.

8 Mon: French Hmk was horrible, write a letter in French. I just can't do it. It's not that I can't think of what to say – I write loads of letters here – but I just don't have the vocab. And as for those irregular verbs!! I wrote three real letters. Good job they are all in English! <u>Mens requests</u> Nobody was very interested as it was very bad reception. I didn't get any I don't think. I might have done though because I didn't listen all the time it was so faint and crackly. I felt fed up. It's one of the only things I have to look forward to apart from visiting. I wonder if I should send one to Helen? I do so want a friend. If I do, catty Connie will have a go at me. I'll also be hurt if Helen doesn't send one back. She probably wouldn't 'cos I've never heard one from or to her on either mens or womens requests.

9 Tues: For French Hmk I have to redo last night's hmk and answer some questions as well. Ugh!

She's quite rude about how bad my work is. I am determined not to show that upsets me. I don't really care about French but I feel sick inside to think I might have to stay down a year. I am already worrying about going back to school. I want to be there but scared about how I'll manage and which form I'll be in. If I can't keep up my Latin, I can't stay in the A form. I just can't do the Latin exercises Miss Dumbford sent for me. It's a waste of time even thinking about school. Who knows when I'll be out of here. During Womens Requests I finished my pencil case. It's in soft red leather with a fawn zip and I've stitched it neatly, though I say it myself! Amazingly enough, it held everything I had in my box. There were lots of records to Sally Stevens for her op on Friday. I sent her one and one to Mrs Benfield, "Hope you have a good time on your leave." She's been nicer to me lately, probably 'cos she's doing well and hopes to soon be home for good. Mummy said she's put some S.T.s in my drawer in case my periods start. She's asked Mrs Benfield to help me if it happens while I'm here. I do WANT to menstruate so I'll have breasts but NOT until I can walk to the toilet as often as I want to and I can have a proper bath.

10 Wed: Mrs Benfield went home on her leave at about 10.45. She was collected by her son, her husband and their dog in a black Jaguar. Talk about style! I've started using my pencil case today. It's great. I'm going to make one for Sandra for her birthday, I think, with her "black sheep" hankie. She isn't a "black sheep" really but she can be a bit naughty! Anyway, it's the best of the ones I've embroidered so far. <u>Visiting</u> was lovely, just mummy and daddy, I really enjoyed it. We had a lovely little chat, just like at home. Oh I do love them. I WISH I was at home. I must keep being cheerful. Mummy looked tired today so I tried extra hard not to say anything that might worry her. To cheer myself up in the evening, I made a Valentine for John. I'm quite pleased with it. It's funny and clever. It's a matchbox. I've covered it and written on it. There's a match inside. Now I have to work out how to get it to him.

11 Thu: Jill went into her single today. I wish she hadn't. I do miss my red-haired friend. Now we have an empty bed. It means now Jill is not here I've definitely got Mrs Wilson – alone – for a lot of every day. They all went off to be in Jill's single. I always say that in a single company comes to you. They came back for tea time, but as soon as it was over, I had just Mrs W for ages because Connie and Sarah were out and Mrs Benfield is on leave. I had my hair washed today with special stinky shampoo to get rid of my dandruff. Letitia, the younger orderly, did it. It really needs cutting, the front especially. With no Sandra to set my hair, it's wild and frizzy. I wish it wasn't. I'd love straight, silky hair like Judy has. She looks great with it in a French pleat. She tried to put mine in one but the clips wouldn't stay in place. I was actually glad as it hurt my head.

12 Fri: Oh, horrid Friday. Still a break in the monotony in the afternoon. Miss Dumbford from school came to see me. She brought me a lovely basket of fruit. I still can't bring myself to like her 'cos I still hate Latin. Ugh! A new declension, conjugation and vocab to learn and exercises to do. How vile! Daddy brought her but unfortunately I didn't see much of him. Still double visiting tomorrow and Sunday. I suppose she's a nice person but when teaching *!!*? I know I MUST keep up my Latin if I want to be able to stay with my friends but I just can't. We only started in Sept. I'm rotten at languages. And at maths. Oh dear, what am I good at? Only English and NOT even at the grammar in that. Useless.

13 Sat: <u>Visiting</u> today. Hurrah, hurrah. Mummy, daddy, Sandra and Nannie W came. When Daddy took mummy home, he brought Wendy. I was surprised really 'cos we've only become proper friends since 2nd year. Wendy brought me 1lb Dairy Box, some oranges, a box of dates, a Basildon Bond pad, 2 pencils, a steel pencil sharpener and 100 matchbox[43] labels. She'd seen the offer and sent for them for me. She also brought a bunch of daffs,

---

[43] *Match box collecting: I started collecting match box labels when at junior school because both my parents and most adults I knew smoked. Many companies gave away book matches to advertise their businesses. My parents also had friends who lived or were from abroad and they added to my collection. Phillumeny has since become as respectable as stamp collecting and there is a British Matchbox Label and Book Match Society (see phillumeny.com). Now, because of its association with smoking, it's not something children would be encouraged to do.*

narcisses and pink tulips. Wow – the most anyone has ever given me on a single visit! I know she's an only child and her parents are well-off but that's still VERY generous. Gosh all those things. I hope she's never in hospital 'cos I couldn't take her anything like that. Nannie brought some grapes and cakes and my tea. Aunty L sent humbugs and treacle brittle. If I eat that lot as well as the hospital meals AND the milk (yuk) and the food I get on visiting days, I MUST gain weight! By post today I got two unnamed funny Valentines. Probably sent by my family!

14 Sun: Had my usual bird bath today off Nurse Hyman. I'm used to them now. She's a bit brisk and doesn't chat at all so I prefer Dorothy. I'd love to have a <u>real</u> bath. <u>Visiting</u> again. Only mummy and daddy but very nice. I had a lovely delicious tea! Oh, I do love these cosy little chats. Mrs Benfield came back off leave today at 5.00. Unfortunately, she wasn't well, couldn't sleep or eat and felt sick. Also her pain was worse. If she tells Dr Houston about it, she probably won't get her 12hrs tomorrow. I think she should say something 'cos she's had it before and it's probably nothing to do with T.B. Maybe she hurt herself doing stuff at home she doesn't do here. She's awfully sad. I want to go on leave as soon as I am allowed but I bet its horrible coming back afterwards. Connie was made up 'cos she got a big signed Valentine from the faithful Neil AND an unsigned one that she thinks is from 'her friend' in the 6-bedder. It's a change to see her happy for once.

15 Mon: Hurrah! hurrah! Super Sarah has got her date, she's going home on 26 Feb. Lucky thing. I shall miss her. I don't see her much but she is always nice to me. Also she doesn't fall out with people like Connie and Mrs Benfield do. Still she deserves it after all this time. Her life has been on hold now for about 2 years. Mrs Benfield is still not right. She had decided not to say anything but then she had to. She still got her 12 hours today! She cried, she was that happy. Got a gorgeous silk/rayon white scarf with a modern design in green, black and gold off Barbara Seefeldt for Christmas today. All the way from America! Also a 'get well' card. Very cute. I was awfully pleased. If it had come yesterday, I could have pretended it was a Valentine's Day present from my American boyfriend!!

16 Tue: What a surprise I had today – ANOTHER parcel from America! This time it was a stiff polythene folder containing 14 cute little note-lets and envelopes. Or as Barby would say "real neat". Just the job for odd little thank you notes, save me having to think of what to put in a proper letter. I was really thrilled and they are so typically American! Stuck some match-boxes from the ones Wendy gave me in my old books. I've not got room for any more, so I'll have to wait till I get the new book at the weekend before I can put the rest in. I'll have over 300 by then. Catty Connie made fun of me about collecting them but I don't care. I like the different designs. No one makes fun of people who collect stamps (which I do as well but now I prefer matchboxes). There are some really colourful ones in the ones Wendy got. They're easier for now 'cos I don't have to soak them off the backs like the real ones. When I rang for a bowl so I could do some of the old ones, the nurse was really ratty. She said I could only have one bowl a day and only for washing. The ones still on the box are the ones I like best really. I remember who gave each one to me or where I found it. I don't put them in countries, just ones that fit on the page and look nice together.

17 Wed: <u>Visiting Day</u>. Mummy came by herself as daddy had a meeting. He ran her here then came in for about five minutes. Unfortunately he didn't pick mummy up till gone five so couldn't come to see me. It will be the same next Wed as he has to go to another meeting. Poor daddy. Is something up at work? I didn't like to ask. Mummy looks very tired. She was moving like she does when her backs bad. It was the best having her all to myself all afternoon. We had a good ol' natter! I love her so much. Dr Houston didn't come round this morning. Everyone was expecting him. I don't care, I don't think I'll ever move off Bed Absolute. Sister Savage told us this evening that he'd been up to see a patient on the men's side after supper. He will be coming tomorrow so he'd see us then. I hope he does come as Connie's nearly mad with worry. She knows she might have to have another op but if she gets her promotion, then she might not. Poor Connie. Must be awful for her.

18 Thu: Dr Houston didn't come AGAIN so Connie is still waiting anxiously. She got upset and then was cross with Sister Savage for saying he would be coming. Sister Savage snapped back at her. It's not her fault if he changes his mind – it's his hospital. I've felt tired and fed-up all day. I didn't go to sleep last night till gone midnight (last time I looked at my watch). Couldn't be bothered to do anything all day. Tried to sleep in Rest Hour but couldn't, read "Great Expectations" instead. Helped me stop thinking. I know I said yesterday that I didn't expect a promotion so didn't care if Dr Houston came or not, well that's not true. I cannot bear the thought of how long all this is going on for. I do actually get out of bed every day to go in the wheelchair to the toilet. Sometimes I also get out of bed to water my plants or get something out of my drawers. I don't think I'm holding myself back but mummy would say I am not being good. I just wish I was officially allowed to walk to the toilet and to do things in the ward. Sarah and Mrs Benfield sneaked off to Chester, lucky things. They went out as if going for a walk then Sarah's sister met them and took them. Half term Friday and Monday, visiting in between, teeny bit of Mawson Hmk – what a lovely weekend. Of course I got French Hmk.

19 Fri: No Mrs Dumbford today (thank goodness). I'm glad as no Latin and no HMK but still it broke the monotony. No school at all today, yippee! I want to keep up but it is so BORING just me and the teacher. I know I am being lazy and should try harder. I miss my friends. Got dad's wallet off Miss Growcott. It's in soft navy blue leather. I can't start it tonight though as I have no matching thread. I hope to finish it by Wed and I can give it, with the other things, to mummy and Sandra as Bed One celebration – some hope! I have to keep believing I am making progress but until I get a promotion, I don't feel I am.

20 Sat: <u>Visiting Day</u>. Mummy, Daddy, Sandra and Nannie W came to see me. I enjoyed the visiting very much but it was spoilt a little bit because of my strep. My bottie is so sore that I couldn't lie on one side or my back and every time I move the skin stretches over the lump, it's terrible. People send me some lovely things even when they can't come themselves. I was actually a bit glad when visiting was over so Dorothy could give me a bum massage. That helped a bit but it's still very sore and lumpy.

21 Sun: Visiting day again. Today mummy, daddy and Nannie S came to see me. I ate masses! Luverly!!! Sarah's farewell party was very good. She looked terrific in black (as usual) but with a gorgeous red scarf round her neck. Sausages and onions on sticks, chicken sandwiches, trifle and walnut cake to eat, and to drink, sherry, "cherry b", cider and apricot brandy. I had a bit of everything!! It was a super party for Super Sarah! Because it was in our ward, I could be there all the time and still be a good girl and stay in bed. Sarah didn't invite any of the men –she's not like Connie and Judy – but some of the other ladies from the 4 and 5 bedders and singles came. I was SO glad to see Jill again. She's now got long red nails!! Helen came! She sat on my bed and we chatted. I like her. She's from Wales but she sounds more like someone on

T.V. She said she wants to be an actress when she grows up. She's already done some children's radio! I didn't think she'd come 'cos catty Connie told me Helen didn't go to parties. Maybe it was 'cos it was Sarah's and NO men.

22 Mon: No school again today because of half term. Whacko! During Mens Requests I half made daddy his navy blue leather note case. I got a record "To the box from the match". The record was "Why should we both be lonely" by Doris Day. Does he mean it? "He" is John cos of the Valentine I made and sent. I wrote on the box I hoped he was "struck" on me!! I don't think he knows who "box" is. I wish he did and he'd write to me. It's a big clue 'cos I collect matchbox covers! Eh, I'm going like my friends, man mad – corrr!! Now I think I should have had him as the box and me as the match. I could have said "I want to be struck on you" but I didn't think of that before. Ah well! It worked anyway 'cos he's sent a request!!

23 Tue: This afternoon, Mrs Benfield, Connie and I went down for exams. Of course, I was in the wheelchair but at least I was out of the ward. I blew 2,200 this time, 2,100 last time, 1,800 the first time. I hope my "whoof" continues to go up or stay level. During Womens Requests I finished daddy's wallet. I rather like it but the leather is not quite so un-crackable as my pencil case, it is soft though. In the afternoon I wrote to Valerie as I got a letter from her yesterday. Although she's a school year below me, I think I probably am more like her than my school friends now. I couldn't decide whether to tell her about John or not. It's something to say but I know it's not real. I want it to be but it isn't. In the end, I just hinted a bit. She's so pretty, she's already got loads of boys after her. Helen is very pretty too, but dark, Valerie is blond. Helen doesn't join in with the sort of lad chasing Judy and Connie do.

24 Wed: Dr Houston came round today at 11.15. Quite punctual for once. Connie didn't get her other hour – she said she should be on 12 really if she'd carried on without any setbacks. Jill got 1 hour, Judy got 6 hours, I didn't get anything but I wasn't upset at all. <u>Visiting</u> Just mummy as dad had to go to another meeting. We had a lovely little chat and we played O's and X's and dots too. Mummy won. I had 2 home-made potato cakes and a piece of creamy dreamy choc cake she'd made. My very fave. This evening was awful. Connie was upset but being Connie, she didn't cry so much as take it out on us. Me in particular. Apparently, I ruin everything by being here! Why? I can't help being 13! And I didn't choose to be here. I have no idea why she has it in for me. I didn't get a promotion either. I didn't get upset this morning but I am now. WHEN will I EVER start to get better? I want to go home SO much. Mummy says I must be good and I must be cheerful but I don't know how much longer I can be. If I had just ONE friend here it would help.

25 Thu: Last night I finished a 29 ½ "x 9 ¼ jig-saw "Sights of Paris". Wish I could climb into the picture! To-day I started a 20 ¼" diameter one, "Continents". Its round and has Asia, Africa, America, Europe, Australia on. Over 500 pieces!!

Will I ever visit any of them? The other with 350 pieces was bad enough so ….! For the first time, Helen came to see me! She came at 3.00 and we did the jigsaw together for hours. She's already been to France, lucky girl, and says she'll be going to Italy with her family if she's out by the Summer. Boy I felt tired afterwards. So many seem to be getting better but then stop and end up having an op. I can't bear the thought that I will. Helen doesn't seem to worry about that.

26 Fri: Sarah went home for good today at about 9.30. She had piles of stuff and three suitcases, a radio, gramophone and one case which had gone home on Tuesday! Helen and I finished the circular jigsaw puzzle today. It's really lovely but unfortunately 10 pieces are missing and that is rather disappointing. Judy is definitely going to come into our ward – hurrah! She's really missing Sally Stevens now she's had her op and is on the ground floor. It will be lovely with Judy. Perhaps catty Connie won't go out so much now. I hope so. I'm fed up being left alone with Mrs W who gets worse not better. Moan, groan, bedpan – on and on and on! I hope Helen will come in more. Connie made a few nasty comments after she left today. What's wrong with talking 'proper' or about where you've been? At least Connie didn't say anything while Helen was here. Once I'm up, I can go to Helen's single – much better! Can't wait!

27 Sat: <u>Visiting Day</u>. Hurrah! Mummy, Daddy, Sandra and Nannie W came. Aunty Laura came when mum went back. Nannie brought me some black grapes that are nearly the size of plums and I got black grapes off Aunty L as well. It is SO weird how often they bring the same thing! Nannie also brought me a big bag of mixed sweets, banana splits, black currant and liquorice, fondants etc !!!! She definitely won this visit's competition with Aunty L!! I do like fruit but I need to put on weight. No chance for a talk just with Sandra. I wanted to tell her about how nasty Connie can be. I know she can't do anything but maybe I'd feel better it I could tell someone and I know I must not worry mummy.

28 Sun: Bird Bath Day. Today I was "done" by Lettie. She's awfully funny. She's another one who had T.B. in the past. It's good that people like her can work 'cos that means she must be fit enough but it's depressing that they only seem to be orderlies in a sanatorium. <u>Visiting Day</u> again. Mummy and Daddy came then later on Joan (mum's cousin, Aunty Laura's daughter), Jim (her husband) and Derek came on the bike. Derek rides on the back now 'cos he's my age and Joan in the sidecar. I really enjoyed it and they were awfully easy to talk to and funny too. He's a bit shy but we get on OK. I was so at my ease that my temp was a perfect 98.4 after! They brought me some real Turkish delight. Luverly!

29 Mon: I've been here three chart months today. If I don't get Bed 1 on Wednesday I'll do my nut. I hate Mrs Wilson. At dinner time she wouldn't have the windows shut and I was freezing. She's in the far corner, about as far away from the windows as can be. I'm right next to them. When I asked her again she said "Don't you dictate to me" then all other horrid nasty things about me. She said I was an unpleasant child who should mind her manners etc. She said I went round saying spiteful lies about people and I was nasty to her and no one else was. I cried. She brought it up again in front of Mrs B and Connie. They stuck up for me. I apologised politely, but she didn't nasty old woman. It was horrible but at least they were on my side.

MARCH 1960

1 Tues: Today Mave from the 4-bedder went for her op and Judy came to live with us. I am SO glad Judy is here! I hope Connie lets me be friends with her. I don't know Mave but Judy said she was "a right one" and Connie said "a naughty one". Mrs Wilson, although Mrs Benfield said she had to be civil, has never spoken to me or apologised for yesterday (I did, on Mon). When offering things she says "Would you like a biscuit <u>Connie</u> or you <u>Judy</u>, have one <u>Mrs Benfield</u>". Never offered to "anyone want a biscuit" or my name mentioned. Anyway when I sent my record request I named every middle floor female patient (and others, like Sally Stevens, on surgical) except for her. She put me on hers, I bet she wishes she hadn't now. I don't care.

2 Wed: For Lent I am going to do at least 30 minutes letter writing and handicrafts a day. I can't give up sweets because I need the sugar to put on weight and in hospital you get lots of sweets and chocolates. <u>Visiting</u> Mummy and Daddy by themselves, it was lovely. Mummy and I had a lot of time just us 'cos daddy went off to see Jack and stayed there for ages. Sandra couldn't come as she's got 'flu but she sent me a letter. I hope she's soon better. I need to tell her about how horrid Mrs W is still being. I can't tell mummy. She'd worry plus she'd probably say it was my fault 'cos I must respect my elders etc.

3 Thu: Dr Houston still hasn't been. Yesterday he did the first 4-bedder then Mr Temple, the surgeon, came and he was called away. I've been nearly frantic. I do wish he'd come. I want BED 1! I embroidered some of the scatter cushion. It's yellow and round. Mainly stem stitch but with some satin stitch and French knots. I think its lovely (big 'ead).

4 Fri: Oh, I do feel a good girl, in the last two days, I've written to Miss Collier[44] as well as home. I've punched the holes in Sandra's pencil case but I couldn't sew it as I haven't got any grey thread. I am feeling superstitious about it. Once all the gifts are ready, then I'll get my Bed One. Come on Miss G, hurry up with that thread! I did some more of my scatter cushion instead. Radio reception wasn't too bad for once. I was very naughty. Slipped into Jill's to see "Hancock's Half-hour" (B.B.C 8.30). Oh! he was funny, and I wasn't caught. At 9.00 Helen came in to do the jig-saw puzzle with me back in the ward. I think she likes me. She's been here a lot longer than I have. She needs a friend too.

5 Sat: Gave a little pottery ornament in the shape of a basket with artificial flowers in to Kathleen on her

---

[44] *Miss Collier:* *Miss Collier taught me my last year in at Victoria Road Primary School. She was strict, and because I was conscientious and well-behaved, she seemed to like me. We sat in rows, facing forward, in order of how 'clever' we were. However, even if I had been away from school ill (which was often) if I scored low marks in the next set of tests (and we had these very frequently) she would move me into the 'bottom section' (with the children who struggled with school work or the 'naughty' boys) away from my friends in my usual 'top section', so I hated her for that. Quite why she kept in touch with me when in hospital I did not know.*

birthday. She's 21. Judy sneaked it into her single with our presents before she woke up. She was pleased Dorothy told us later. Connie said Kathleen is very very ill and isn't getting better. <u>Visiting</u> Because Nannie was here with Sandra when daddy took mummy back I couldn't have my little private chat with her. I didn't dare say anything bad about Mrs W with Nannie there 'cos they always have a chat and Mrs W is charming with her. Two faced old ***** Daddy went to see Dr Vamar when he came back so he was away a long time. He said my "tiny shadow" was "healing beautifully"! I'm a long time on Bed Absolute because I'm a child he said. I do hope that is true. Catty Connie, of course, had to say something nasty in the evening. She said they wouldn't tell me anything different even if I was as ill as Kathleen. Charming! I am NOT ill, never have felt ill, just happen to have this pesky T.B. at the time of the mantoux test. I will NOT let Connie bring me down. Bed One, here I come!!

6 Sun: Ugh!! I hate bed baths. Oh, to have a real bath for a change! <u>Visiting</u> I enjoyed it very much, just mummy and daddy. I think Judy being here has made things better in the ward. She's such a sweet, gentle person. She makes Connie kinder somehow. Mrs W is probably on her best behaviour to impress Judy. It won't last! Maybe I am being nicer too? I am definitely happier now that Helen has started popping in.

7 Mon: Wrote to home and Nannie W, no one else. Aren't I terrible! Tomorrow I <u>must</u> write to more. During Mens Requests I started Sandra's pencil case. It is in soft grey leather with curved corners. I have stitched her initials "S.S." on an angle on one side. I think it makes it look more professional. Got another record off "The Match" to (me) "the Box". I wish John would write or contact me so I could tell my friends. I know I don't really know him so can't really like him BUT!!

8 Tues: Tuesday is Library day! Today, I got a book called "A daughter of the land" by Gene Stratton Porter.[45] I have never heard of him/her before. I reckon I read at least three books a week! I really like Anya Seaton books at the moment too. I like losing myself in other places and times. Womans Requests Mrs Benfield and Eileen did them. Poor them, it didn't end till 8.30 nearly! Fred (the male nurse from downstairs who Judy likes and Dorothy has a crush on) was on relief. So, for a joke, I rang for a bed-pan and Mrs Wilson asked for a chair. Oh it was so funny!! Judy blushed and so did Fred! It is SO much better here when we have a laugh about something and they let me join in.

9 Wed: Today Dr Houston came round and gave me BED ONE!!!! Isn't it marvellous!!! I've never been so excited since I passed the 11+   Visiting

---

[45] _A Daughter of the Land_ by Gene Stratton Porter (1863-1924). She wrote numerous books for adults and children with a strong 'nature' theme, and was from Indiana, America, a place I lived for a while as an adult, teaching English at a University there. If I could only have known then that life held such possibilities for me, how much happier I would have been!

Mummy and Daddy came. Gave them their wallets and a purse for Sandra and one for Nannie W. Mum brought some lovely fresia. That smell will always remind me of how happy I am to have my first promotion. Walked to the stairs with them when they left! Lettie, Dorothy, Nurse Hyman, Connie and Judy all clapped. I feel I'm on my way home now. I had a gorgeous <u>proper</u> bath to celebrate!

10 Thu: I have enjoyed my "Bed 1" today. Actually it was more of a bed 2 but ne'er mind eh! Helen came at dinnertime and teatime and at night. I do like her. We did a jig saw puzzle then we read some essays she had written. They were very good. She talked some more about wanting to be an actress and what it was like being on the radio twice in Children's Hour serials. Ah! We've a star in our midst![46] And she's <u>my</u> friend! The house she lives in is called Frog Castle 'cos her father has changed it from a dump into a beautiful house. She said it's not a castle but it is big and they have lots of land too.

11 Fri: Went to see " 'ancocks ½ hour" in Jill's again. It was very funny. Helen came down at 9.00 and we did a jig-saw puzzle and (of course) talked. We talk quietly so Mrs W and Connie can't hear.

---

[46] <u>Helen:</u> *I do not know if Helen ever became an actor as we did not keep in touch. I do hope she did. I have searched under her real name (not used here) but have not found her.*
However, if she did fulfil her ambitions, she may have used a different stage name, or married and used that surname.

We aren't saying anything private but I just don't want Connie making any snide remarks. I had a nice Bed 1 walk today as well. Once I'm on Bed Ordinary, and I can go to the toilet as often as I like, I can go to see Helen in her single!

12 Sat: <u>Visiting</u>   Again the girls from school came to see me. I enjoyed it more than last time. They didn't seem quite so man-mad now. Anyway, I got in my bit about the "match" and the "box". I had a nice little chat with Sandra before they came. I didn't bother to tell her about how awful Mrs W has been 'cos she's OK at the moment. We talked about what to get Mummy for "Mothering Sunday" on March 27th

13 Sun: Today I had another bath (<u>Not</u> a bed-bath!) I enjoyed it just as much. <u>Visitors</u> Mummy, daddy and Nannie W. LOTS of food! Mr and Mrs Cooper also called in to see me. They told me about Bethesda and Sunday School. Going to church and Bible class and the craft groups etc. used to be such a big part of my life. I wonder if I'll want to go back when I get out? They all thought I looked very chubby and healthy! Connie got a tape recorder off Neil for her birthday!!!!! VERY generous. He must really exist. He's still not actually been for a visit while I've been here. Connie said he's working away.

14 Mon: Today has been a 'match' day all round! To-night during "Mens Requests" I stuck more of my match labels in. There are some really super unusual ones in the pack Wendy gave me. Tomorrow I will put some more in and soak the others off that daddy brought in. He asks his insurance customers to keep them for me. Mummy asks her friends too. They all are smokers so there are lots of matchboxes around. I got a record off my friend the "match" he said "Isn't it about time you gave me a clue to your identity" So tomorrow I will – I wonder what to put! Once he knows I'm only 13, I bet he'll lose interest. If he actually saw me with my frizzy hair and big nose, he certainly would. Poor (dear) John isn't well so he's still on ground floor surgical. He should be on Bed 1 by now but he has a high temp and he still has fluid on his lungs from the op Fred told us, so he isn't.

15 Tues: Tonight on the "Womans Requests" I sent a record Elvis's "I need your love tonight" to "the match" from the "box". Because of last night I said "Clue. If you want to know who I am, I live on the floor above. Knock on the pipes at 9.00 if you want to know who I am." He did, so we ran round knocking on all the pipes to confuse him. Connie said they can hear them downstairs. I went to the window but he didn't as apparently he's still not well enough to get out of bed even if he was allowed to.

16 Wed: Doc Johnny didn't come round today, but no-one was expecting promotion. <u>Visiting</u> Just mummy and daddy. Really enjoyed it. Poor Connie she was called into Dr Houston's office and told she does need another op. She didn't get upset amazingly even though it's her 30th birthday. She got over 40 cards, some great presents and we had a whale of a party! Her mum had brought loads of food and drinks. We had some during visiting and the rest at night. Jill and Eileen came but Helen didn't. I had Cherry B and Babycham and lots of crisps and sausages on sticks. I enjoyed it as everyone was being nice and friendly. Sister Savage broke it up about 11 and said lights out. I'd had enough by then anyway.

17 Thu: When I woke in the night, saw Connie and Judy come in the ward door. They said next day they'd taken some of the left-overs to the Square[47] and met Kenny and Peter and gone down to the basement! They both looked knackered.   This morning I went to sleep in the 11-12 rest hour (the after-effects of last night) only to be woken by Nurse Evans to go to Exams. I hardly ever actually sleep in rest hour and the one time I do!! Giggling Varmar did it. Blew 2,050, bit less than last time but it isn't that important. I could hardly say it was 'cos I'd been at a party last night! He said my chest is "Very good".

18 Fri: In lessons we did history. I wrote 4 ½ pages of notes. I can't really see the point. I won't be taking any exams here, surely? But it passes the time! Wrote to Susan to thank her for the food and

---

[47] _Square:_ _The Square was the area at the centre of the middle-floor which divided our female side from the male side. As well as where we were weighed each Sunday, it was also where the nurses' office was and a hot water point, where we could make tea or coffee, and where we could collect milk. It was also where both sexes met and flirted. It was forbidden to cross the Square._

for her and the others from school for coming. When I heard "It's only Make Believe" by Conway Twitty on the radio I thought about having a "crush" on someone. Is that love for a person or love for love? I'm not really gone on John. I only want A Boy Friend. As long as he's young and pleasant, I don't mind who. I'm getting as bad as my friends now! From 9.00 to 10.15 I talked to Helen. Best part of the day. We don't talk about boys.

19 Sat: Today was visiting. No Sandra today. When daddy took mummy home, I had no one. That made me think how horrible it must be for people here who don't have visitors. He brought back Wendy plus two other Runcorn friends from school. Wendy was nicest to talk to. I feel she has become a real friend. Janet was too busy boasting and Paula too busy trying not to get T.B. I don't know why they bothered to come. I think they are just nosy and don't want to feel left out. Connie is going on leave from Sunday morning to Tuesday morning. It is pre-op leave. She's excited. It's sad it's not a leave that means she's on her way to being home for good. Poor Connie. She knows what having an op is like as it'll be her second.

20 Sun: Had another real bath today. Wonder when the novelty will wear off? Visiting Nannie W and Nannie S, mummy and Daddy came to see me. Jim, Joan and Derek – some of the easiest visitors I ever have - brought me a lovely 400 piece jig-saw puzzle. Helen will be pleased. Oh, how I hate Sunday night here. I am awfully depressed. I am glad that little things like having a bath or getting a new jigsaw now make me happy but it's also pathetic.

21 Mon: I went for an X-ray today but as Dr Houston is going on holiday on Thursday we won't know the result for a while. Damn! I bet it showed I'm doing so well I should be on Bed Ordinary! Not fair I have to wait 'cos he's on holiday. I'll be SO disappointed if I don't get it next time I see him. During "Mens Requests" I did my scatter cushion. After, I did some more of the jig-saw puzzle with Helen. She cheered me up. I didn't tell her I was miserable because I didn't get a record off John. He didn't send any at all though so he musn't be well. Ah me! I did strict BED 1 again today! I am being superstitious again but I feel if I am good I'll definitely get my Bed O soon! Virtue should be rewarded!!

22 Tues: Connie came back. She had a gorgeous time, but she said she was so excited that she couldn't eat. She looks really tired but kept dashing about and didn't stop talking, even in rest hour. Mrs Mawson gave me a puzzle. You have to sort out the counties and industries then stick them on an outline of Great Britain. I like it. A fun way to learn. She is a kind person. Just not very interesting lessons. Helen and I finished the puzzle in the evening. I sent to the "match" on "Womens Requests". I'm getting a bit fed-up with it now as its pointless but will keep on while John is so ill in case he likes it.

23 Wed: Dr Houston came round at about 1.30. Connie got 4 hours but no news when her op will be. I can't see the point of giving her a promotion when she'll end up back on Bed Absolute after the op. I didn't say anything. Judy got 10 hours. Jill got 4 hours and Mrs Wilson got Bed 1. She's already doing Bed <u>7</u>! That is SO unfair! I am younger and fitter AND I have been here longer AND I don't cough and spit into my sputum cup like she does every day. If she's ready for Bed One I am definitely ready for Bed Ordinary! <u>Visiting</u> Cosy chat with mummy and daddy. I was really good and pretended I was O.K. about not getting Bed Ordinary. Mummy looked a bit worried. Daddy made a joke – nothing 'ordinary about you'. At night everyone else in the ward went off somewhere so I was left with Mrs Wilson. Helen didn't come as she has a lot of homework to do. It will be like this for five days when they go on Easter leave. I cannot bear it. I bet they went to a party.

24 Thu: I feel rather depressed today, especially now (it's after supper). Another long, lonely, "Wilsony" night ahead. Ugh! I don't know what the others are up to. No one said anything about last night. They are all out again. If it's not a party, then they must be watching T.V. in Jill's single. I wish I'd been invited. I know I shouldn't be up but I've been there before for T.V. The only thing I seem to enjoy at the moment is food. For the afternoon, Mr Heel, the head male nurse, pushed my bed and Mrs Wilson's into the bay so we could enjoy the sunshine. Mrs Benfield said sun is bad for T.B. but if it was Mr Heel wouldn't have put us there. Anyway it wasn't very strong sun. Mrs W is O.K. company for a bit. Then she has to go and mention her bowels and that's it. I read most of the time. It was nice but oh it made me so restless. If only I could be out in the sun. Another day without seeing Helen.

25 Fri: This morning I got a letter off Daddy! He did a funny little drawing like he used to in the ones mum showed us he sent from India in the war. Wrapped Sandra's three birthday presents up. 1st 1 hankie with black satin stitch on it in the shape of a lamb. (She's a black sheep – only pretend) 2nd A long l-o-n-g necklace made of dried melon seeds. It took me ages to thread them. 3rd Grey leather pencil case with two pencils. All are hand-made by me (except the pencils of course!) I cannot think of a single other thing about today worth writing about. Oh well, two days of visiting coming up.

26 Sat: I had my bath this morning instead of tomorrow - clean clothes on my clean body! I had a lovely chat with Sandra. For Mothering Sunday tomorrow, Sandra's bought her some talc and I'm giving her the scatter cushion cover. Sandra is so excited about going to Paris. She says her and Carolyn plan to slope off if they can! I hope she enjoys herself. It's meant to be to improve her French 'A' level. Nannie came at 3.30 when daddy came back. We talked about china and ornaments. She brought me some lovely things to add to my collection. If only I could put them on my shelves in my bedroom at home. I enjoyed our chat. Sometimes visiting is hard work but not today.

27 Sun: <u>Visiting</u> <u>Again</u> Just mummy and daddy. I do like it like this and the time simply flies.

Scrumptious food too! Aunty Laura's younger daughter, Rita, told mum she was coming but she didn't so I suppose Teddy was working. I didn't mind. I like her but I don't like Teddy 'cos he thinks he is "funny" when he teases me. I'll never forget what he said when mum told him I'd passed the 11+ "Good job she's got brains, she'd not get far with her looks." He should talk, fat pig. At night I wasn't as depressed as last week (thank -goodness!) because I had enjoyed the visiting AND because I wrote home (the first 4 pages). I also wrote to Nannie and Grandad W. I know there's nothing really to tell them but when I'm happy, I find lots to write. When I'm fed-up, nothing. That's usually true in my diary too.

28 Mon: Another week begins! This is 16th week so it is four (chart) months. It doesn't really seem that long in some ways. In other ways, I feel I've been here forever. On bad days, I feel I WILL be here forever too. A good Monday for once. Helen called in at dinnertime then she came after tea and we had a talk and she was just starting to say the piece she'd learnt for the B.B.C. audition when Connie came in. I was mad. I hope she'll finish it one day for me. I asked her to carry on but she whispered that "some people" here will think she's showing off. On Mens Requests I didn't get a record off the "match" so it is the end of our little "romance"! Ah well, who cares.

29 Tue: Today Connie was told that she is going to Broadgreen for her op tomorrow. What a shock! I thought she'd have more warning than that. Poor

Connie. I do feel sorry for her. She was very weepy for the rest of the day. Nothing else happened today worth writing down. Finished my book "Eight Cousins" by L. M. Alcott that Helen lent to me. I enjoyed it but to read a book is hardly exciting and that was not even an exciting book. I preferred "Little Women". In our ward we talked till after 11.00 after lights out with Connie. She was too upset to sleep. It's too awful to think about. All that time in hospital and still another op.

30 Wed: No Dr Houston, no tension no excitement, no tears, no nothing, because Dr Houston is on his holidays. We saw Connie go off in the ambulance. I think it depressed us all, even Mrs Benfield who is close to going home and Judy who is doing well. <u>Visiting</u> Today I really enjoyed myself. Daddy brought mummy but then he had to go to work. We had our gorgeous cosy little chat. It was just like home! My favourite visiting when it's just us two. I also like it a lot when it's just me and Sandra. Mummy brought me a Flowercraft set. I have to make pictures with coloured sticky paper. Looks fun to do.

31 Thu: Today Nurse Evans told me (in answer to mums request for Friday visiting as she can't come on Sat when the shops are busy this close to Easter) that mummy can't come. She wasn't very nice about it, in fact she told me off and I never asked her, mummy did yesterday! However they can come on Good Friday (special concession), Sat and Sun (ordinary visiting), and Easter Monday, a special treat for all patients, so it won't be as bad as I thought it would be. No news yet about how Connie is. We now have two spaces in our ward. Still only Mrs W and me stuck in bed all day!

APRIL 1960

1 Fri: Two spaces no longer! Today we have Alice and Margery in our ward. Alice is about 20 to 23. She's pretty, a bit plump (well, big bust) with a lovely smile and a soft Welsh accent. Margery, early 30s, is attractive but she's a bit cold and holds herself stiffly. Both are very nice and so now I have company (not just only Mrs Wilson) and Mrs Benfield stayed in more today. That might not last. The new women have had a good effect on all of us. Mrs Wilson has gone really daring and sometimes says quite rude things. She can actually be quite funny now. When she's funny she's funny, when she's not she's oh so depressing! I did a bit more of my "flowercraft". It is quite hard to do. I don't think it will look good enough to give to anyone so what's the point. I am a bit disappointed.

2 Sat: Had a gorgeous bath this morning - all over loofah made me tingle! I THINK my body is changing. Hope so! Will TB slow down puberty? Better not!! <u>Visiting</u> I enjoyed it and it went very quickly. Nannie W came after Daddy had taken mummy to work. Sandra and I had part of our usual little chat in the basement as I went to the optician. I don't see why he had to come on a visiting day. I liked being able to show Sandra what it's like down there though. I also liked being out of the ward – any excuse! He said I don't need glasses after all! Hurrah!! Hadn't been wearing them anyway.

3 Sun: Visiting again, hurrah! Mummy, daddy and Sandra. My favourite visitors (and Nannie W too but she came yesterday). I gave Sandra her presents for the 11th. She wanted to open them straight away. I'm glad she did. She was really thrilled with them. I really enjoyed visiting today, our little family chat. It was very good to sit and natter. Oh, I do wish I was going home! I must try to be brave though. I nearly cried when they were going. I know I mustn't. It's not fair on mummy. The nicer the visiting time the harder it is afterwards but without seeing my family, I'd go mad. I read all evening because I just didn't feel like talking.

4 Mon: Connie is having her op today at Broadgreen. Poor Connie, I hope she'll be alright. She's been there by herself since Wed. She was so upset even with us to cheer her up, I bet she felt even worse without us. I forgot to say yesterday, but when I got weighed I was 6st 4lbs, so in one week I put on 1 ¾ lbs. Whacko! Hope it continues. I'm reading a very good book called "The Colditz Story" by P.R. Reid. Helen lent it to me. It is an escape story book. No tortures or anything like that, just how they tried to escape. I imagined escaping from here!! Not that it is QUITE as bad as Colditz!

5 Tues: Sandra is off to London today ready for her trip to Paris. Connie is "as well as can be expected and her condition is satisfactory". Poor Connie. I keep on thinking how awful it must be for her and thinking it could be me. Womens Requests weren't very clear, but better than last night when they only played a few men's requests then packed up because the interference was so bad. I heard the "Sea of Love" – Marty Wilde. I adore that record.

Makes me feel all swoony! No record to Match!! Or from him. Ah well!

6 Wed: Got a post-card from Sandra in London - photograph of Piccadilly. She leaves Victoria on the boat-train at 9.00. <u>Visiting today</u> Just mummy and daddy. When it is just us three we always have so much to say that it goes so quickly. Yummy food too!

7 Thu: Wrote home. Helen has better books than the library here but got "The Saplings" from there. It is quite funny, but in places it is well indecent. It says things like, "Her thoughts never strayed off beds" + "He took the Times to the lavatory with him."

8 Fri: I have decided "The Saplings" is a super book! I thought Noel Streatfield only wrote ballet books. I've come to some other "indecent" bits! But it is still a good book! In one part it said "The boys after knocking down some of the cottage and smashing the windows cried "Let's wash it!" They then undid their flap and washed the cottage." Cooer! I need something funny on a Friday. Friday is an 'orrible day. Next week is Good Friday so I'll see mum and dad. Hurrah!

9 Sat: <u>Visiting</u> hurrah! Daddy and Mummy and Nannie W came. Then Grandad Salter came. I like him more than Nannie S. No one said why she didn't come as well. I missed Sandra for our little chat, but still she'll be having a marvellous time. I liked just talking to Nannie when dad was taking mummy back to work.

10 Sun: <u>Visiting Again</u> Mummy and Daddy came. I really enjoyed it. Mummy's fresia are awfully pretty, and they smell lovely as well. My happy smell! I do love mummy and daddy and I'm going to try extra hard to get better and not to complain about anything or cry when they're here. I got weighed this morning. I am 6st 6 ½ lbs. 2 ½ lb gain! Yes!! I MUST be getting better. Roll on Bed O! Should be called Bed F for Freedom, not O for Ordinary!

11 Mon: Got another post card off Sandra - L'Arc de Triomphe et etoile. She is staying in a convent – like a prison she says, even worse than Crossley! I bet her and Carolyn are having a great time! No men's requests again. It broke down, then it was supposed to be mended but after a few records it broke down again. I don't look forward to it much now but I like the records. It's something to do while I embroider or whatever. I think the hospital could at least sort it out properly for us.

12 Tue: Got ANOTHER post card off Sandra - painting of the "Moulin Rouge. She's had fun and she said "All we seem to have done is giggle" She didn't say if she'd actually spoken much French. No records tonight but I didn't expect any. Yipee visiting tomorrow! I can't sleep very well. I wish I had a bedside light and was allowed to leave it on to read after lights out. I'm just not tired enough by 10. I feel too fed-up and restless to sleep.

13 Wed: No Doc Johnny! After his holiday he might have come to see us. Instead he went to Top floor. Mrs Benfield said they are cancer patients up there and a lot of them are very old. Sounds even more miserable than here. Helen got her 10 hours anyway. She is thrilled. I am happy for her but that means she'll be going home soon. We have become real friends. I'll miss her. <u>Visiting</u> Daddy and mummy. We talked and talked so the time simply flew by. A lot of it was just mum and me 'cos daddy went to see Jack for a long while. Had a lovely bath in the evening. Think it helped after visiting. Hard not to feel miz on a Wed night.

14 Thu: Dr Houston came round after dinner. He said "Hello Little Nell, how are you?" Me "Very well thank you Dr Houston." Dr H "How would you like an Easter Egg of BED TWO?" I'm awfully excited! I had hoped to go straight to Bed O but Mrs Benfield said once you're on Bed 2 no one is really counting. I could not believe it when Mrs W got Bed 2 just like me! I thought I'd be on it well before she was. The two new ones did ok - Margery got 1 hour, Alice 2. They were promoted 'cos although they've only been in this ward a bit they came from the 5-bedder and on ground floor surgical before that. Connie came back from Broadgreen at 1.20 today. We saw the ambulance. She is now on the ground floor recovering. She does look ill Mrs Benfield said. She'd popped in to see her. She was in pain 'cos they cut your ribs to get at your lungs. Ugh!

15 Fri: Today I got 6 lovely Easter cards. This afternoon mummy + daddy came to see me <u>with permission</u> 'cos it's Good Friday! It was super! Sandra is back. I am SO looking forward to seeing her tomorrow. 3 days of visiting in a row – hurrah! In the evening, Margery told us about living in Africa. Can't remember where exactly. Her husband worked there. She doesn't have any children but she didn't work. They had servants! She said life there is much better than in England. Mrs W didn't like that!

16 Sat: I didn't have a bath. I'll have one tomorrow instead. Something to look forward to. (Yes, I know, pathetic but true.) <u>Visiting</u> Barry brought Sandra to see me. He is very good looking. It was great to see him. I missed just chatting to Sandra though. If he'd not brought her, I might have had no visitors at all 'cos mummy wasn't allowed a long lunch break, they're too busy in the shop, and Daddy only came at 3.50 as he had to do two days collecting to make up for Friday and Monday. Sandra brought me a marvellous soft leather hand stitched duffle-type bag. It smells gorgeous. A necklace in all lovely colours. It is beautiful. A little silver Eiffle Tower + a penant. She's awfully kind.

17 Sun: Got weighed. I am 6st 7lb. ½ lb gain. I thought it would have been more as I've eaten piles this week AND drunk my 3 pints of yukky milk every day. <u>Visiting</u> Sandra daddy and mummy came. I got 10 Easter eggs and off mummy + daddy a very sweet little glass dog. At 4.00 Mrs Cooper came. She brought me a big Sharp's Easter egg from Sunday School. She didn't stay long. When I said goodbye to mummy and daddy and Sandra I didn't cry because it's visitors again tomorrow!

18 Mon: Visiting day <u>again</u>! This is marvellous, 4 days on the run! Yippee! Nannie and Grandad W came with mummy and daddy. I thoroughly enjoyed myself. Mummy brought ice cream in the flask to have with the strawberries. Talk about living a life of luxury! When they'd gone, I felt really sad. I am happy I saw my family for so many days together but that doesn't make tonight any better. Kept thinking about last Easter. Nannie and mummy took me to Liverpool to see "South Pacific". It was brilliant.

19 Tue: Got letter from my U.S.A. penpal. She has such a fun life. I don't know what to tell her back. Today is end of Easter leave day. Judy came back and so did Helen. Judy brought me a cute little doggy brooch. Helen didn't bring anything but I don't mind. I'm just glad she is back. Visiting again tomorrow. Jolly good! I wrote 5 "Thank you" notes today. I have got piles more to do though! Today I've eaten 1 Cadbury egg (large) ½ a Terrys egg (v. large). Loads more to go! Surely I'll have put on a LOT of weight by Sunday!!

20 Wed: No Doc Johnny. Doesn't really bother me I don't want anything, rather I won't <u>get</u> anything. <u>Visiting</u> Mummy and Sandra came by bus. Daddy came at about 4.00. He had to do some collecting rounds he'd missed because of Easter. At least I got to see him a bit and mummy and Sandra went home in the car. Luverly food! Oh! I am terribly depressed now (it is 9.30). I don't really know why, after visiting blues I suppose. Wish I had someone my age to talk to. I know there's Helen but she's in the single so I don't see much of her. She's going to be going home anyway soon and then what? Hell Hell Hell I could cry I'm so miserable!

21 Thu: At 7.45 mummy and daddy came in the car to Crossley. They came and waved up to me but weren't allowed in. They handed in a parcel for me. They brought a present for Mrs Benfield as she's going home tomorrow. It's a lovely modern vase price 10/6.[48] Mummy wanted to spend that much because she thinks Mrs B has been good to me. I suppose she has a bit. I didn't tell mummy about the times she wasn't nice. In the parcel mummy also put new pyjamas for me! They are white cotton with turquoise dragons, a mandrin collar, and shortie pants. And guess what! I don't look skinny in them! Even my arms are well proportioned! Can't wait until I am back to wearing proper clothes.

---

[48] _Money:_ _It is very hard to convey what any of the references to sums of money 'mean' in modern terms. Before decimalisation (15 February 1971) a shilling = 12 pennies (each expressed as 1d); 20 shillings (each expressed as 1/- or 1s) = one pound (£1) but converting 'old' pennies to 'new pence' says nothing about how much a pound was in value. Given that working in a shop or as a clerk in an office could earn as little as £4 a week then, to spend 10 shillings on a present – representing 1/8th of weekly earnings – was generous. Later references to money need to be seen in that context. For example, on 9 May, I say something is to be sold for 5/- (five shillings). I received about half of that (2/6d) pocket money a week at that time._

22 Fri: At 9.45 Mrs Benfield went home. Mr Benfield, her children and the dog came to collect her. She liked her vase. I felt a bit sad as she was very good to me when I was new, and at the end, but a bit doubtful in the middle though. An empty bed. Who will we get in her place? I do hope it's someone my age. Read "The Painted Garden", another by Noel Streatfield. It is very good, Helen lent it to me. We like it 'cos it's about a girl who makes it as a star in Hollywood, playing Mary in "The Secret Garden". Helen might do that one day! It is lovely to talk to someone who you know is not thinking "You're too young to join in." I hate this "Oh dear too many young ears in the ward" business.

23 Sat: <u>Visiting day</u> What a circus it has been! People dashing in and out all afternoon. Mummy, Daddy, Sandra, Rita and Teddy (+ kids, only through the window), Susan plus the rest of the usual gang from school, Aunty Laura and Nannie W in that order. Oh! I was all mixed up! TOO many! Had my new jammies on. I like them. Photo of me taken on Easter Saturday has turned out well.

24 Sun: I got weighed this morning. I am now 6st 9 ½ lbs. Another 2 ½ lb gain! Hope it continues! Good ol' Easter eggs!! <u>Visiting</u> Mummy, daddy and Sandra came. Back to normal today! I prefer it. Dorothy said they are moving people around this week. We don't know who we're getting yet. At night I went in to see Helen in her single from 5 to 9 till 9.25. I daren't stay longer than half an hour. On Bed Two I'm pushing it to be doing anything but a bathroom run. Don't know why but Alice really does NOT like Helen. When I got back she started saying horrible things about Helen being stuck up etc. They are both from Wales but Alice said "Huh, there's Wales and Wales". Oh dear, not another feud starting.

25 Mon: I am depressed today. I have felt like this (apart from in visiting hours) for over a week now. I don't know why but Alice hates Helen. She said she's affected, but she isn't. I'd rather talk to Helen in her room because when she comes to see me Alice joins in with little insulting comments and pulls sneering faces. She acts as if Helen is making up stuff about her life but she isn't. I am still only allowed up twice a day so even if I call in each time I go to the toilet, I can only stay a little while. I hope Alice doesn't put Helen off coming here. I still like Alice too but it is uncomfortable. I know she's missing her boyfriend, Dave. She said to Margery she's been here so long already she doesn't know how long he'll wait. Margery said she doesn't know how long before her husband has to go back to work in Africa again. They both had a little weep. I read "Daddy-long-legs" off and on most of today. Super. It's told in letters. She's an orphan with a mysterious benefactor. Set in France but thank goodness not IN French. Exam. in afternoon. Blew 2,300!! MUST keep thinking I'm doing well but SO slow.

26 Tue: Still depressed, ah well, visiting tomorrow. Alice has been a bit peculiar lately, so I don't think I like her as much now. She is very snappy. She said a few things, not very nice, after I'd said something that was meant to be funny – just a joke remark about sheep in Wales! She said I'm "too big for my boots" and "you think you're funny, well you're not" and "wish you'd know when to shut up". I was actually hurt but didn't want a row so all I said was "You do take things seriously, it was only a joke." She said "Does it matter to you whether I take things seriously or not." She has not spoken to me since.

27 Wed: Dr Houston didn't come. Hell! I am desperate for Bed O so I can spend more time out of the ward. It's become horrible again. Alice can be as nasty as catty Connie was. She was having a go at Margery as well earlier, not that Margery bothered saying anything back, she just ignored her. Visiting just daddy and mummy. Oh it was lovely. Mum is getting me (among other things) a bra when she next goes to Liverpool. Only a 30" one but a start. I'm dying to get it. I can definitely see little bumps under my jama top. Oh Hell Hell Hell It is 8.25 and I'm terribly terribly depressed. I want to cry. I thought Alice was O.K. again. She was saying something then I said something (actually agreeing with her) and she said "I wasn't talking to you." She turned her back to me. I don't like her much at all now. I don't know what I'm doing wrong. I hate this falling out. Horrible.

28 Thu: Dam, Dam, Dam, Doc Johnny came and I didn't get BED O. Mrs Wilson did (and she's only been here 4 months and we both got Bed 2 the same day). I'm sure I'm better than she is. Alice got 4 hours, Margery 2. Poor little me. I <u>am</u> miserable. It doesn't seem at all fair. I know that I ought to believe that if I was ready for it I would get it. But oh! I'm fed up. Alice is very happy with her promotion. Jill got 8, lucky thing. She can go on leave soon. She said she's going to get a professional manicure! Bright red to match her lipstick and hair I bet! Margery is as miserable as ever. She said "this place" is useless and she's "had enough". Instead of being pleased she's getting on she just criticises everything. Had a bath. Didn't feel any better. Went to see Helen from 9.00 to 10.25. And I said I wasn't staying! No night staff around. Today my horoscope in the newspaper said: "LIBRA (Sept. 23-Oct 22) It is not that you will do badly today, but you may not get all you feel you are entitled to!" Very appropriate!

29 Fri: Today I still feel a little upset about not getting Bed O but not too bad. I'm getting used to being disappointed. I know it is silly and unreasonable but I don't think I'd feel this bad if Mrs W hadn't got hers. Can't help it. Finished my marquetry. It was really hard work. It's a scene with mountains and a lake. I don't think I've done it very well. Miss Growcott said I'll be amazed how much better it looks when it's polished and framed. I want it ready for next week as a present for my family in case I get Bed O. I want Bed O SO much. I want it chiefly because A) Want to go to school room for lessons, no more in bed with everyone listening. B) <u>No</u> bed-pans (with everyone listening) C) <u>No</u> more bowls for washing in bed D) <u>No</u> sneaking along corridors just twice a day to see Helen - will go as often as I like!

30 Sat: Read in the morning, a pleasant change from school. Maybe it'll be better when I can do lessons in the school room. I am so sick of being stuck in this bed in this ward day after day after day. Only one bath a week allowed and, if I was doing what I should, only two visits a day to the W.C. and NO popping in to see Helen.   <u>Visiting</u> in the afternoon. I talked to Sandra while mum and dad saw Dr H. I was nervous about why they were both seeing him. Mummy should be at work. Worried it was something serious. It wasn't! Dr H. said: "making amazing progress" I'll be here for less than 12 months from the day I came in. When I go home, I'll be completely cured, so treat as a normal child, not an invalid! Hurrah! When they were here, I felt truly happy. Now, I just keep thinking it's April, I've already been here 5 months, I'm probably not even half way through. HELL!! I just hope THIS version of how I'm doing IS true and not another "you'll only be there 10 weeks" lie to make me feel better.

MAY 1960

Sun 1: Margery signed herself out![49] She's only on 2 hours. She said she was wiping her hands of this place. They used to live in Africa and if she stayed any longer her husband couldn't go back to his job there. Sister Savage was very cross about it. She said "She'll be back, only worse." When they drove past, the car stopped and she got out, took her shoes off and banged them together! We had another surprise today too. This morning Mrs Wilson moved onto the ground floor as she wanted a single. She didn't tell us about it until they came to take her down. Silly fool, said at the last minute she's afraid she won't like it, and cried! I'm not feeling sorry, she chose a single on another floor where she doesn't know anyone. Bliss! without her! Suddenly two more empty beds in here. PLEASE please please make at least one a girl to be company for me. <u>Visiting</u> Mummy and daddy came. I told them about Margery signing herself out. I, jokingly, said I might do that if I don't get Bed O soon. Mummy

---

[49] <u>*Leaving hospital without permission:*</u> *The diary records this and other cases where an adult patient left the hospital – "signing yourself out" - against the advice of the medical staff, and without permission. What happened to any of them, I do not know. It was something that I wanted my parents to agree to at one stage (later in the diary). While it might seem a very unwise thing to do, given that the new drugs were working (if the TB was caught early enough and wasn't of a strain that was drug resistant) perhaps they came to no harm, providing they had the same drugs at home and could still rest enough and have adequate food.*

said "Oh no you won't m'lady." Ah well, worth a try! At about 7.15 Barry brought Sandra up with my washing. Mummy had forgotten to bring it. Sandra looked awfully smart. So did he! We waved and chatted a bit through the window. Got weighed, 6st 10lbs ½lb gain. Bit disappointed.

2 Mon: Lessons – Lessons – Lessons – all morning. Geog with Mrs M. In French I only had a few (for me) mistakes in an exercise. She said "Not frightfully good is it?" Cheek! Would it kill her to say "well done" once in a while. Judy is not well but we don't know what's the matter. I hope it's not a setback. She was doing well. Ha! Ha! Ha! Mrs W (the blood sucker) is back. Boo! I wish she wasn't. Being by herself didn't last long. Everyone kissed and hugged her (I shudder at the thought). I've not spoken to her yet (it is 8.30). I know I should but I can't bear it. I was just about putting up with her but now she's back, it's worse than before. Only now she's noticed, started the same business as before after "the Great Feudal War" (See March 1st).

3 Tues: Judy is ill again, her temp went to 101.4! Wow! I hope she'll soon be better. Everyone seems to think it is strep reaction. Dr Houston came to see her, oh dear hope it won't slow her down. Dr Hughes from Runcorn Hospital came with Doc Johnny to see me. Dr Hughes said "Oh yes your x-rays were really good". He also said I looked well and fatter than when he saw me in November. At night I did part of my Hmk in Helen's room while she did hers. When I'm with her in her single is the only time I feel life here is O.K. It is awful in the ward now. I know I must be nice to Mrs W but it is SO hard.

4 Wed: Dr Houston came round but he wasn't at all generous, in fact nobody got anything. Not even poor me. <u>Visiting</u> Mummy and Daddy came and we had an enjoyable little talk and laugh. I had the only visitors 'cos Judy (much better now, 101 temp though) and Mrs Wilson had none. At night re-did the frame on my silver paper picture. Looks a bit better.

5 Thu: Oh, I'm awfully depressed it is 6.35 but it is all I can do to stop myself from crying. Alice has been beastly to me lately. She keeps on saying nasty things about Helen. Why? I don't criticise the way Alice speaks so why is she so vile about the way Helen does? It is horrid here now, Mrs W dislikes me – it is mutual – Alice squashes me and she is really horrible sometimes. What is even worse, Helen has gone on leave for the 3<u>rd</u> time. I do miss her. I cannot bear the thought that she'll soon be home for good. I'm awfully depressed and I've no one to talk to. I can't tell mummy, she'll worry. I hope I have a chance to talk to Sandra on Sat. Everyone except Helen and Jill (I'm sometimes not even sure of Judy) hate me and neither of them are in my ward where I need friends the most. I wish I wasn't here.

6 Fri: PRINCESS MARGARETS WEDDING DAY. MARRIED TO ANTONY ARMSTRONG-JONES. Jill went on leave this morning. She looked more glamorous than ever. Her red hair is now quite long. I am glad for her but that's another nice person who will soon be gone for good. Judy (on the bed cos of her high temp) Helen, Mrs W and I watched it in Jill's single. It was a marvellous wedding. Princess Margaret was beautiful. Watched from 10 til 1.30 & 4.20 to 5.45. For once we were all nice to each other. I felt less fed-up for a bit.

7 Sat: <u>Visiting</u> Mummy and Sandra stayed all afternoon, but daddy went back to watch the Cup Final with grandad W so they had to go back on the bus. No one supports Blackburn Rovers or Wolverhampton Wanderers so I don't know why they bother. Mum had been to Liverpool and got me a gorgeous pair of 'jamis in white seersucker with pink sweet peas on. Also 3 new vests, 2 nylon pants and a bra! Doesn't fit although it is 30" and I'm 30"! Nothing to put in the cups yet!! She also got me a gold chain with a crystal heart. It is beautiful! She said it was for Easter really but she didn't give it me then because I got so much. She said it's an extra because I'm being a good girl and staying cheerful. Oh dear, if she only knew!

8 Sun: Got weighed. I am now 6st 11lbs. 1 lb gain! Poor Judy, she's really poorly today. She looks ghastly and at 5.00 her temp was 102.2! Dr Shearing told her she's got plurasy. Oh I do hope it won't hold her up too much. <u>Visiting</u> Just mummy and daddy, but I really enjoyed it. We had some good laughs. For tea I ate SO much! Boy am I full! Bet I'd weigh a LOT more if I was weighed now! Quiet evening. I read. No one talked much so couldn't tell who was talking to who.

9 Mon: Blue Monday! Another week of being here. Doc Johnny's last week. Oh I do wish it wasn't. The staff and patients who have known him for years are really upset. He has been in charge here for ages apparently. I like him, even though he has not yet given me Bed O. Perhaps he will before he leaves. Today I finished off a pale blue soft leather pencil case for Sandra's friend Carolyn. It's not a present, I'm making it to order. She is going to give me 5 whole shillings!!! Sandra said she could sell lots for me. I can't make any more yet as Miss Growcott has to finish giving out leather for the Garden Party craft stall first. Cor! 5/- a time! Double my weekly pocket money! I'll be rich!

10 Tues: Ugh! Ugh! Ugh! Met the new head doc today. Dr Erwin is a miserable mealy mouthed ignorant male of the species! This morning he came round with Dr Houston and although we all said pointedly to him "Good morning Dr Erwin" he never answered or smiled to <u>anyone</u> in the <u>whole</u> ward. Oh! He looks a snob. I do wish Doc Johnny wasn't leaving. I'm in a depression through it. Visiting tomorrow thank goodness.

11 Wed: Dr Houston came round today giving out promotions. I am <u>very</u> <u>very</u> sad to write I got nothing. When he looked at me he said "No, not yet lass" Mrs W got 1 hour!! That just doesn't make sense. She's still coughing. I never have. Alice got 6, and Jill 10 hours. Those are the only ones. Jill will soon be going home like Helen. Oh dear. <u>Visiting</u> Mummy and daddy came. I'm afraid I wasn't very cheerful but what with yesterday's horrible meeting with Dr Erwin, today no promotion, and Doc Johnny leaving I couldn't help it. I don't think mummy really understands how horrible it is here. I don't want to worry her but sometimes I can't help it. I am SO depressed. Alice was actually quite pleasant this evening. She's pleased about her promotion. Next promotion, she'll be able to go on leave and see her boyfriend. When I said that she said "I'll be doing more than seeing him!" Judy and her then looked at each other and laughed. They think I don't know what Alice meant. Well I do.

12 Thu: Poor Sandra. She isn't well. I don't know what it is though. I want her to be better for her but also 'cos I'll miss our little chat if she's not O.K. by Sat. Vinny, the Polish man who polishes the floor (get it) did our floor today. It really needed it. I love the smell! He did it quite quick. When he had finished Judy had a discussion about "LOVE BITES" [50] with him. He knows all about them! Cor! I learnt a thing or two!! I think Judy fancies him. She said she doesn't, he's too old, but she was flirting with him more than she does with Fred.

13 Fri: Made a purse in navy blue soft leather for Aunty Laura's birthday. Oooh! I do feel devilish,

---

[50] *Love bites: This was the first I had heard of love bites. At 13, I thought I knew a lot about 'love' and 'passion' from the novels I read, and I understood the mechanics of reproduction from biology, but about what actually went on during sexual activity, beyond hand holding and kissing, I was ignorant.*

wish I could knock-on. No Romantic reasons, just for fun. I think it's 'cos of what Vinny was saying yesterday. Keep thinking about it. Don't fancy being bitten but I do want the love. Wish I wrote to one of the boys. Any boy. It would be something to wait for, to look forward to and to do. I don't want love letters, just interesting ones. I would like someone to hold my hand and maybe kiss me but I don't want a love bite and I definitely do not fancy sexual intercourse.

14 Sat: Had a bath. Put my new 'jamas on, they do look nice –big 'ead! Nannie W and Grandad S came. He is nice but I don't think him and Nannie W together is a good idea. No Sandra, she's still ill. Nannie W has given me a beautiful gold signet ring for Easter. She's taking it back to Browns to be engraved with my initials. She said it was special because I'm being good and she knows it's not nice for me. She didn't say I had to be cheerful but she thinks I am, like mummy does. I have got lots of nice things I probably don't really deserve 'cos cheerful I ain't. Some parts of some days are O.K. but most aren't. I did miss Sandra.

15 Sun: Got weighed. I am 6st 12 ½ lbs! Gained another 1 ½ lb !! 1 ½ lbs more and I'm 7 st !!! Yipeee! Gosh am I pleased. <u>Visiting again</u> This time only mummy and daddy came. Nice as always. I hope I managed to be jolly enough. Very depressed at night, I nearly always feel like this on Sunday evenings. Sometimes writing about how I feel helps. Not tonight.

16 Mon: Oh! Hell! What a week. <u>No</u> Dr Housten to look forward to on Wednesday! Still no BED O! What a rotten week. I feel very fed up. I want to do something devilish. Like, Like – knocking on. Anything that's not being here. In bed. Oh! Oh! Oh! Hell! Got a letter off Valerie and off Miss Collier – why does she keep writing to me! Val's was very nice. Not enough to make me feel any better though. What can?

17 Tue: At 10 to 10 tonight I talked to Peter on the <u>Square</u>. Me! Only for a few minutes though, still it's a start! I can't believe Connie fancied him. He's too young for her. Not very good looking either. Saw John this morning – didn't see me. Only his back-view! I think I prefer him. Not that I have a choice! Feel I'm becoming man-mad. It's my age! Visitors tomorrow – "Jolly Good" as they say. I wonder if Erwin will come round before then. Mummy said in her letter Sandra is still ill, not likely to be better by Sat. Oh dear.

18 Wed: Saw John again. As I only again saw his back as yesterday, I've a good idea to call him the "Faceless One". <u>Visiting:</u> mummy and daddy came and we had a very nice chat and a laugh although I got a little lecture entitled "Do not overdo it" off mummy. She'd go mad if she knew how often I go to the Square or into the other wards now. I think I should have Bed O <u>so I'm doing Bed O!</u> Didn't see anyone decent at night – male! Kenny might be worth having a look at. Judy used to fancy him. Another boring night. Wish we had T.V. in the ward or I was in a single with a T.V.

19 Thu: Finished my letter to Sandra. It is 10 pages, wrote a 2 page one to mummy and daddy as well. Helen washed my hair. It is very shiny but also very springy. Her hair is thick and wavy so she knows what to do. Judy said Andrea in the 4-bedder is trying to go out with Peter. Went to get Judy a glass of milk from the Square (9.10) (excuse to see if Peter and Andrea were there, they weren't). While waiting for the cold milk to come, a nurse I don't know came out and gave me a cake!!! Twas lovely!! But not as sweet as seeing a boy there!

20 Fri: This morning, Dr Erwin, the new Medical Superintendent, Dr Bashray, in place of Dr Vamar, and Dr Shearing came round. This time Dr Erwin was really quite pleasant – bit stiffer than Doc Johnny though – he actually spoke, smiled and joked!! Not that it did much to improve his miserable face with deep frown lines. He combs his thin black hair over his bald head just like dad! He might be quite decent. I hope so. I'll love him forever IF he gives me Bed O!! In daddy's letter he said Sandra is feeling nearly O.K. now and her temp is down. Peter had a suspected appendicitus but it turned out to be over-eating! He ate 1lb acid drops + big Swiss roll among other things! Don't think I do fancy him after all.

21 Sat: Can't have a bath. Well, I could but got no clean clothes. Mum forgot, again, to bring any on Wed. <u>Visiting</u> Mummy + Daddy + Nannie all afternoon. Roast pork bap for tea was yummy. Mum brought the new jamas she made, the ones I started at school. Blue bias binding. Pink stripes. Blue rosebuds on white cotton backing. Shortie pants. Elastic on the legs. I really like them! Sandra's temp is back to 102.0 and she feels rotten again. I missed Sandra but great 'cos for once Mummy was here all afternoon. Happy day on the whole!

22 Sun: Today I feel very very happy. I got weighed and I'm 7st ¼ lbs! I gained 1 ¾ lbs last week, but since I came here I've gained 1st 6 ¾ lbs. Boy! Not even Janet can call me skinny now. I'm over a stone heavier than she was when we were weighed at school. NO one looking at me now could say I look ill. Why can't the doctors see how well I am and GIVE ME BED O!! Enjoyed my bath. New jamies on. <u>Visiting Day</u> Mummy and Daddy came, no one else. I think Mummy is quite worried about <u>Sandra's</u> health. Makes a change!

23 Mon: What a day! Wet and horrid. It started off badly with us all being woken up at 6.00 to have our temps taken.[51] This is going to happen to everyone every morning from now on – Dr Erwin's orders.

---

[51] *Temperature charts: Once I had been there for a while, I, like everyone else, was allowed to take my own temperature each morning and early evening. The mouth thermometer was kept in a pot of some sort of sanitiser on each bedside locker. We put a dot for each one and then joined up all the morning ones in one line and the evening ones in another. When the head of the hospital changed, he introduced a new, stricter regime, and made the nurses take our temperatures and fill in the charts instead, using one line. It wasn't very popular with staff (more work) or with us (couldn't cheat) and my memory is that we soon reverted to doing it ourselves.*

Then our new charts were given out. Black dots, morning and evening temps. joined together, not two separate lines like we've always done. They will do them. They don't trust us! Then at night, so depressed I got under the covers and cried. No one knew. Once I started, couldn't stop. In despair.

24 Tues: Today the weather is much better thank goodness. My temper is a bit sunnier too! No idea why it matters. I'm stuck in bed come rain or shine! This temp-at-6.00 and having-our-charts-done is ridiculous. I hate Crossley. I hate Dr Erwin. I hate BED 2. Hope I'm on BED O before the end of the week. Bet I won't be though. In mummy's letter she said Sandra is a little better.

25 Wed: Dr Shearing came round. I asked him for BED O. He said "You ask Dr Bashray. He will give it to you." So I will tomorrow! I'm not fed-up about it, not yet anyway! <u>Visiting</u> Mummy and daddy came. Sandra is much better, but it definitely is an abscess on her tonsils. Poor Sandra. Enjoyed visiting very much. At least I know I can still feel happy. Just not many hours when I actually do. As fed-up as ever in the evening.

26 Thu: Today I got, off Dr Bashray, BED O!!![52] I am really thrilled and excited. Oh! I am so happy. Freedom to roam!! I went to the school room. John said "Congratulations love." Cor! Had to come back into the ward tho as it was type-writing which I

---

[52] *BED ORDINARY: this meant being free to be up and about so, although in nightwear, a small start to a more normal life.*

don't do. It is GRRREAT being on BED O! Although I didn't know it at the time, this morning I had my last bowl + bedpan! Now I can be out of bed as much as I like and no one can say anything.

27 Fri: Today I am still feeling "tres heureux" about Bed O. Oh! cor!! I feel like doing something I shouldn't. It is the staff barbeque tonight. We, Judy, Alice, and I watched it through the W.C. windows. I don't think they should have parties here, it depresses all the patients seeing them enjoying themselves when we can't. In the Square, after, we went over the line – about 1ft over onto the men's side – and back. Nurse Evans saw us. "Get to bed" she shouted! Cor! I like it when Judy and Alice let me join in. Judy shouldn't really be up at all 'cos she's still not right.

28 Sat: Saturday again. I miss going to the school room (i.e. seeing the boys!) but not my lessons. Visiting Mummy could not come as they are very busy at the shop. Daddy and Nannie W came and stayed all afternoon. I quite enjoyed it but daddy and Nannie W aren't the best of friends. I liked it more when he went off – to the toilet (twice) and to see Jack (for ages). From 2.00 to 3.00 Mr Helsby and Robert were here on behalf of Bethesda. Robert looks much older now. Mr Helsby, of course, talked a lot about Sunday School. I just do not feel that interested anymore. Ah well.

29 Sun: Weight 7st 1 ½ lbs. Gain 1 ¼ lbs. This morning I had an exam off Dr Bashray. So did Mrs Wilson, weird elderly Miss Smythe, Helen and Alice, in that order, me first! He's awful. He doesn't use a stethoscope <u>at all</u>, he mauled me all over, he pressed his hands on my breasts and held them, tapped them and felt them. I nearly died and he did hurt me. He twisted Alice's breasts (they are big) and played with them. We all talked about it afterwards. He was worst with Alice but didn't do much with Mrs W she said.[53] <u>Visiting</u> Daddy and mummy came, great time. Much nicer when it's just them two. Sandra much better – hurrah!

30 Mon: What an awful day Monday is, no visitors after 2 days of them. No good food after all the stuff from the visitors. School again – oh well now I have a change of scenery + faces! I don't particularly like John (now) or Kenny, but it is nice to pretend! Wow! I'm as boy mad as my school friends. Oh well it's too bad! In the evening, Dr Bashray came and asked Judy if she could help him with something later. His flat is opposite our ward. She didn't know what to say. He came back after supper and said "Come now". She went for about five minutes then came back. She said she told him in the corridor she had to go back to bed.

---

[53] <u>*Dr Bashray:*</u>   *This whole episode concerning Dr Bashray (not his real name) may be hard for young people today to believe possible but in those days there was much greater tolerance of this sort of behaviour on the part of men towards women. We were also more in awe of authority figures, especially doctors, and no one liked 'to make a fuss'. While I may not seem to have been upset by it - even apparently welcoming something different to talk about to break the monotony - I do remember feeling afraid and anxious, hoping to be protected by my age.*

31 Tues: Oh dear, today I've got to have my lessons in bed again instead of in the school-room because of typing. I hate Tue and Thursday morning because:- i) lessons in bed again ii) both are maths lessons iii) I can't see John or Kenny. At night Judy and I went, as a dare from Kenny, to the big window on the <u>men's end of the corridor!</u> Kenny daren't come to ours – scaredy cat! I think Kenny fancies Judy. She says he's OK. She went with him at New Year but she'd been drinking then. Good job the night staff didn't see us or don't care. Mum would go mad if she knew. We were just going into our ward when Dr Bashray came out of his flat. He said "Naughty girls!" but smiled and didn't get cross with us.

JUNE 1960

1 Wed: Judy went for an Exam off Dr Bashray. Oh goodness, it was worse than ours. She looked upset when she came back. He felt her (like us) then pulled her pants down and put both his hands right where her legs join her body – ¼" more + he'd have touched her "fanny". I wonder if he's not a real Dr but a sort of sex maniac? We're all talking about it. No one knows what to do. Makes a change from the usual boring chat! <u>Visiting Day</u> mummy and daddy came. For tea I had a hamburger and 2 corn on the cobs, 2 large jellies, and 2 cakes. I enjoyed myself!

2 Thu: Today I am terribly depressed and absolutely fed up! That pig Mrs de H has given me loads of French homework. I hate her – ol' crow. Well, Dr Bashray gave Judy BED O so she's not feeling like me fortunately. I've nearly finished embroidering my garden party apron. Judy got a letter off Kenny asking her to go to the Square. We went, he was there. We hung about and then Dr Bashray came out and saw us. We thought he was going to tell us off! He asked if we'd like to come to see some painting from India. Judy looked like she wanted to so I said I did too. His flat is really nice. He played some Indian music records. He sat on the settee between us with the book on his knee. At first it was ok, but then some of the painting were a bit rude so we left. As we were going Dr Bashray said "Aren't you grateful to me for giving you Bed O?"

3 Fri: Oh, help! Dr Bashray did Jill's exam in her single. As she had been complaining about tummy aches he examined her lower region. He felt all her tum then, with rubber gloves on, he felt her "fanny". All over it he went then he put his hand up her as far as he could go! She said it hurt but he wouldn't stop and she was nearly crying out with humiliation + pain. He thought she'd had a baby but his hand wouldn't go up very far. Isn't it absolutely awful! He <u>must</u> be a maniac. When she told us, Judy said she'd soon be getting her next promotion! I said well I got mine <u>before</u> he examined me!! My signet ring from nan came through the post. It's great. I love the curly style my initials are in. I am going to wear it always.

4 Sat: Had a bath in the morning. Still enjoy it! <u>Visiting</u> Mummy didn't come as they are so busy at the shop. Sandra, daddy and Nannie did. We had strawberries and ice cream for tea. I also ate three balm cakes with lettuce, egg and tomato on them. I then stuffed myself with cherries (1 lb) wafers and at 6.00 I ate 2 packets of crisps! Cor! wonder if I'll gain. I think so as I've also had at least 3 ½ pints of milk a day all week! No chance to talk just to Sandra. I wanted to tell her about Dr Bashray. At night, I went out with Judy again. We hadn't even got to the Square when Dr Bashray came out and asked us into his flat again. I didn't want to go but didn't like to say anything. This time Dr Bashray told us what the Indian singing was about. I felt so embarrassed by some of it. Well rude. We didn't stay long. When we got back, we found Kenny had put sugar in Judy's bed! Hilarious!! Glad it wasn't in mine.

5 Sun: Weight 7st 2 ½ lbs Gain 1lb <u>Visiting</u> Mummy, daddy and Sandra. Good. Kenny has been writing to us again – addressed to Judy but I think it's to both of us. To get him back for the sugar, at night we sneaked across and put pepper in his thermometer pot! We wrote "Was your temp."red hot" Kenny!!" At suppertime there was an awful storm. I felt really excited and couldn't sleep. I think it was partly the storm but also 'cos of the fun I'm having with Judy at the moment. I am sorry Connie had to have an op and is on surgical but it's much better for me when she's not here. I don't think Helen "approves" of what I do with Judy but she's on leave and will be going home soon so I need Judy to see me as her friend.

6 Mon: Oh what a difference to Whit Monday 1959. I love the Whit walks[54] and the tea and fair after! I wish I was there again. This year I am in hospital. We were allowed visitors so it wasn't too

---

[54] <u>Whit Walks:</u> *At that time, where I lived, the Whit Walks were an important celebration of Whitsuntide, a religious festival, as well as a public holiday when everyone came together, whether religious or not, to watch the parade and enjoy the fair afterwards. I had walked in previous years with Bethesda Sunday School, behind our banner (as each church did). We had tea provided for us afterwards – paste sandwiches, small sponge fairy cakes, orange squash – and were then free to go to the fair. It was traditional to have a new dress and shoes. When it was hot – as it sometimes was – the tarmac really would melt and stick to our shoes. Perhaps it did sometimes rain but, as is often the case with childhood memories, I only remember it being sunny.*

bad but the only walking I'll do is to the W.C. and back! Just daddy and mummy came and I really enjoyed myself. Sandra has gone out with Barry for the day. Judy was very fed-up at night. She had a tummy ache so we didn't knock-on. When I went to the toilet at night I was a bit scared in case Dr Bashray asked me to his flat. I would not dare go by myself. I went as far as the Square but no one around.

7 Tues: Alice and Jill came back at 1.15 today, Helen at 5.30. All should have been back at 12.00! Alice brought me two bubble baths and a packet of scented bath flakes. Off Jill I got a little china dog. Helen gave me a bag of cherries. Christmas again! At night Judy and I went to the Square at 9.00. Kenny wasn't there. We hung about a bit. Helen saw me and asked if I wanted to do a jigsaw but I said not tonight. At 9.25 Kenny called to us. As soon as we got to the Square, he smothered me in pepper, Judy in sugar. Well we were ready for him - he got covered in talc! Luckily, no nurses around! They will wonder what happened when they see the mess. We ran to the bathrooms to clean ourselves up before we went back to the ward.

8 Wed: Visiting Day Mummy + Sandra came. Daddy came at about 4.00, before he was catching up on his collecting. I wish visiting was always like this. At night we went to see Kenny. We talked for a bit then came back. We promised a truce on tricks! At about 10.00 we got a letter each off him! In mine he said how old is Andrea? Has she a boyfriend? Cheek! Writing to me to find out about

Andrea! I don't even know her and she's not in our ward. Judy says who cares. She said he's trying to make her jealous.

9 Thu: I wrote to Kenny in the morning to ask him why he wanted to know. I thought it was because he wanted to go out with her. We got a nasty letter back (which I tore up) saying he never mentioned anything about going out with Andrea + we could take it in turns to write to him to save any quarrels. The big headed pig. I told him in the letter that I wouldn't write anymore. I hate him. I won't write again ever! We weren't going to go to the Square again 'cos neither of us want to see Kenny now but we got so fed-up we went anyway. We were so fed-up in fact that if Dr Bashray had asked us into his flat again, we'd have said yes!

10 Fri: Old Wilsony is all moany today again. All day moan, moan, moan, maybe she is ill but it is a case of "Cry Wolf". Well even after the last sentence of yesterday's entry, I wrote to Kenny. So did Judy. We both apologised for our letters. I said I wouldn't mind writing to him, but Judy couldn't be bothered. I wrote at the bottom "Shall I?" I got a letter saying "the answer to your question is no". I wish it wasn't. I wish I'd not written. I bet he only was ever interested in Judy. Anyway, I don't care. He's not that good looking and his letters have a lot of punctuation and spelling mistakes.

11 Sat: Mrs W is quite poorly, it is her heart + so they have moved her into the empty 5-bedder for now but she may have to go to another hospital. I am feeling guilty for not being sympathetic but I am still glad she's gone.[55] Today, perfect timing, I got 1 HOUR off Dr Bashray! I am truly thrilled! That was fast!! If it means I can whiz through my hours he can examine me again!! I'll even listen to more Indian music and look at rude pictures!! Judy agrees!! Now I'm on 1 hour, I went to the garden party[56] and so did Judy (she got 1 hour also). Mummy, daddy, Sandra, Nannie W, Aunty Laura, Uncle Jack, Rita, Ted, + kids, cousin Valerie, Susan and the gang from school came. I wore my new dress. It is flowery blue cotton with a full skirt and short sleeves. I gave the bouquet as I was youngest! Had a marvellous time! When we saw the apron I'd embroidered on sale, Nannie bought it! I am very happy! I didn't feel tired at all. I walked round all afternoon so a lot longer than one hour. At last, I feel I am on my way home!

Sun 12: Weigh 7st 2 ¾ lbs Gain ¼ lb. Must have lost weight yesterday! It was church today and I could have gone for the first time but after my

---

[55] _Mrs Wilson_: _This is the last reference in the diary to having any contact with Mrs Wilson (not her real name). Whether she died in the other ward, or left, I do not remember. It seems I just lost interest in her once she was not in my ward._

[56] _The Garden Party:_ _Each year, Crossley had a fund-raising garden party in the grounds at which handicrafts made by the patients would be sold, as well as the usual raffle, tombola, and refreshments. It was good timing that I was allowed up to go. I was delighted to be the one chosen to give the bouquet. If it was filmed – there is a reference later to the film of the 1959 Garden Party being shown to patients – I have never seen it._

hectic afternoon I decided to stay in bed. I think I still believe in God and I still say my prayers but I don't think I care about religious things as much now. <u>Visiting</u> Mummy, daddy, Sandra and Nannie Salter came today. I got a better chance to talk to them than yesterday. I think Nannie S looked a bit peeved that she'd missed the Garden Party. Of course, that's what we mainly talked about. I ate a LOT for tea in visiting then after, I ate my dinner AND the food mummy left for tomorrow. This being up makes a gal hungry!!

13 Mon: Alice got 12 hrs so she'll soon be going home. She's gone back to being nice so I'll miss her. Connie got Bed O. That means we'll be seeing more of her in our ward I bet. I hope she's not as catty as she was. Now I'm on 1 hour I can get dressed and I eat my midday meal in the canteen. Afterwards, me and Helen smuggled in a kitten belonging to the cats that live in the woods. Poor little thing, it was awfully hungry. It is sweet and has beautiful black and white markings. We call it Oaks. Helen has gone back to being a bit cool with me. I think it's 'cos of the high jinx with Judy. I hate the way you have to choose who to be friends with. I want to be friends with both. I'd like to call into her single more but she's never there. She said she doesn't like coming into my ward because Alice and Judy don't like her.

14 Tue: School in bed today because the school room was being used, so I didn't see Kenny or John. I wrote to Kenny yesterday (to reply to his letter on Friday). I wasn't going to but somehow I miss not writing. I got a letter back so I wrote again. I don't exactly like Kenny but if he tried to kiss me I wouldn't mind! I know it's just pretend. Had a bath at night. Felt a bit upset. Didn't get a letter off Kenny. I should have. I do hope he replies. I feel silly now for having written to him. Dr Erwin came round today. No promotions. He is not as jolly as Doc Johnny was. The nurses say he's a lot stricter with them too.

15 Wed: School in the school room today, thankgoodness, I prefer it 'cos I see Kenny. On the other hand, if no one is in our ward when I have lessons, it's nice to lie in bed and have them, but I DON'T SEE KENNY! I don't feel at all interested in John now. He is a bit weedy next to Kenny. <u>Visiting</u> Mummy and Daddy came. I quite enjoyed myself but I got lectures lectures lectures all afternoon. I am doing too much. I must do as I'm told. I must "wrap up well" when I get dressed. I must stay in bed more. If she knew the half of what we get up to, she'd go mad. Mum says I'm a nasty mean girl now instead of kind and pleasant! All because I had a bit of a moan about a few things and a few people. I am fed up being a good cheerful girl. I want to have some FUN! And if that means being bad …

16 Thu: Lessons in bed - again. At dinnertime, I wore my trews, my navy blue v-neck sweater, and the white blouse I wore at the mannequin parade at school – not baggy now, in fact quite tightish! Cor! My bra really was 35/-worth!!! My tummy is big, but when I pull it in, out goes my bust!! I like having to think about what to wear for my precious one hour a day dressed. Little Oaks came in again today, he really is pretty cute, but he has got very dirty and now smells catty. No one in our ward except me likes him anyway so I'm not letting him in again. Helen said he can still go into her room. She likes animals and has a horse at home. I prefer dogs, Scamp best of all. At night, Dr Bashray came into the ward to see Judy. She was gone for about half an hour. He asked her to help him sort some photographs. She said he is nice, just friendly, because he is lonely.

17 Fri: As Frank – don't know him - is going home, he and Kenny brought tea round! Kenny had a gorgeous red shirt on + fawn trousers!!! School in the school room. Kenny doesn't say much but John does. Maybe he still likes me? (Well, I say still but did he ever really?) Wrote to Kenny and said "Do you still want to write now that Judy doesn't? I will write if you want me to." At about 8.15 I got a letter saying "I'm sorry but I told Judy about one week back that I didn't want to write, as I have a girl now and I write to one girl only. I hope you understand me. Kenny." Judy didn't ask him, she said. I am so cross with myself. I should not have written. WHY why why did I??? Cos I'm a silly fool.

18 Sat*:* This time last week I was at the Garden Party! Bliss! <u>Visiting</u> Just Sandra and daddy came. I had a little chat with Sandra when Daddy went to talk to Jack. I showed her Kenny's letter, she said "he is a big-headed fool". He acts like G G to W (God's Gift to Women). She made me feel better. I also told her about Dr Bashray being "friendly" with Judy and me going into his flat a couple of times too. Oooh! Exam with Bashray tomorrow!!!! I'm sort of dreading it but also kind of excited. Will it lead to another promotion??

19 Sun: Weight 7s 3 ¼ lbs – Gain ½ lb. This morning, even though it's Sunday, I had an exam off Dr Bashray (quite tame for him!) Maybe I'm getting used to his non-stethoscope method.[57] I didn't say anything - and I got 2 HOURS after only a week! Under Johnny, we only got promotions on a doctors round and only with his permission. Dr Erwin seems to leave it to Dr Bashray so he must trust him. Oh! I <u>am</u> happy! I know it might be ages before I get anything else but if I went through weekly ….! Bliss! <u>Visiting</u> Mummy + daddy came. They were very thrilled of course. None of us expected such a fast promotion. Grrrreat!

20 Mon: Helen is in hysterical tizz-wazz today. It seems that Dr Erwin won't give her her going home date + and of course she wants it. He also told her to "go steady" when she goes out, and he talked of break-downs etc, all very, very depressing. Helen overacts a bit but I do feel sorry for her. It must be awful to be held back so near going home. We

[57] *Examining without a stethoscope: Most doctors then (perhaps they still do) used a combination of a stethoscope and tapping with hands (known as percussion and auscultation) which meant putting their head close to the patient's chest, but few would examine only using the latter method and none should caress the patient's skin or fondle her breasts while doing so as this doctor did.*

went on to the lawn at the front of the hospital at dinner time. Judy took photos of us. I hope they turn out well. We also had one taken with Dr Bashray on the balcony outside Jill's single.

21 Tues: Helen is still a bit weepy. Judy and Helen are both feeling very depressed because this morning their charts disappeared, then in the afternoon all the big-wigs (Mr Temple the surgeon etc) came and Sister told Judy they were for "discussion". That is a bad sign. I <u>do</u> hope they don't need ops. Judy's done 15 mths, Helen 16. It hasn't been mentioned before for either. Poor things. I feel sick to think you can get on as far as they have and still be faced with the possibility of an op. Helen has never even been ill once while I've known her. I'd been thinking I was on my way home because I'm on 2 hours. It might not mean anything. I might be told just when I think I'm almost home, I have to have an op. NO, please, no, no.

22 Wed: Oh dear. Judy has been told that she has to go to Barrowmore[58] on Tuesday for a broncoscopy. Judy thinks it means an op especially after yesterday. Helen hasn't been told anything. She said she'll ask her parents to find out what's going

---

[58] *Barrowmore Hospital* *was near Chester. For more information, see separate Note on Tuberculosis (TB) and Sanatoria at the end.*

on. <u>Visiting</u> Mummy and daddy came and we all had a good laugh and a natter. For tea I had THREE salad balm cakes and strawberries + ice cream. I also ate sweets and cherries etc. Scrumptious! Lovely! I must keep putting on weight. I wanted to tell them how worried I am about having a set-back and an op. but I didn't. It's not fair to worry them.

23 Thu: <u>DR BASHRAY SCANDAL</u> At 3.00 Bashray came into our ward + asked Judy to stick a certificate in his book for him. She went to his flat for the book and the certificate and glue. When she came to do it, it needed trimming so she went to ask him if that was ok. He held her hand, put his head on her breasts then kissed her breast then he stood up + kissed her cheek!!! She was quite flushed when she came back but she didn't say anything to us then. When she returned the book later, he kissed her hand twice but when the maid came in with tea, he said "That's all" + dropped her hand. I'd have screamed if he did it to me. He <u>must</u> be a sex maniac! She ran back and told us. We didn't know at first whether to believe her. She said she was frightened but didn't know what to do. Alice said she should never have gone back with the book. She was leading him on. Judy then started crying and said she was only being polite and friendly and he is the doctor.

24 Fri: Dr Erwin came round. He told Judy the bronc. was to find out if the plurasy had turned to T.B. He thought that perhaps there was a lump of T.B. blocking the bronchial tube. If so, the surgeon will cut it out. Oh, I do hope and pray not. He said to the other doctors about me, "Ah yes she's coming on very well." Judy is so relieved that it's not a T.B. lung removal op she has cheered up a lot. It is though still an op so she became weepy again this evening. Everyone in the ward and on this floor is talking about Dr Bashray. The worse so far is what happened to Judy but she's not the only one he's been too "friendly" with. I feel safe as I'm only 13 but I am a bit worried. Some sex maniacs like children.

25 Sat: <u>Visiting Day</u> Daddy, Sandra and Grandad Wakefield came, then daddy took Grandad back and brought Nannie W. I think it's quite funny they prefer to visit separately! I had a lovely little "chin-wag" with Sandra in between. Judy and I told her about Dr Bashray (See 23rd June). She was horrified and amazed! It really is awful though. We both told her not to tell anyone. Judy is worried she might be in trouble for going to his flat. I've been there too. At night we didn't do anything outside the ward 'cos Judy's strep on Friday had touched a nerve and so she still can't walk. She couldn't even manage to go to dinner. I hardly dare go to the toilet by myself at night now in case Dr Bashray is hanging about outside.

26 Sun: Weight = 7st 3 ¾ lbs Gain ½ lb. <u>Visiting</u> Just mummy + daddy came. Although before they came I thought I was going to be "moody", I wasn't so we had a nice time and we laughed and talked - and I ate - almost non-stop. Went to church this morning. I feel I need to pray. I am still worried about people having set-backs when they seem to be getting better. I am afraid that will happen to me. I can't bear the thought of being here for over a year and then being told I need an op. That seems to happen a lot. Judy's still very weepy about the op. She's also fed-up with Alice teasing her about Dr Bashray being her "boyfriend". Alice knows she's upsetting Judy but she doesn't care 'cos she's got her date to go home.

27 Mon: We watched "Hancock's Half Hour" again in Jill's single. It was <u>very</u> funny. At 9.00 we had a bottle of cherry B each. Mine made me feel very happy and "devil-may-care" – but I wasn't tipsy – at least I don't think so. We gave Judy her pennies for good luck for her bronc and we gave Alice her going-home present (table-mats for her bottom drawer)[59]. She was very pleased with them. I enjoyed myself at night. Helen's Eng Lang GCE tomorrow. We sent her a card. She didn't join us. I hope swotting is why she's not bothered to come and see me recently. I miss doing jigsaws with her. She's better company than Judy but Judy is more fun. I want to be friends with both of them but that doesn't seem to be possible. Judy will still be here when Helen has gone.

28 Tues: This morning at 9.00 Alice went home for good. Her father and mother came for her. Boy! I bet they were glad to say good-bye to Crossley. I wish that it had been my mummy and daddy's last

---

[59] *Bottom drawer: it was customary, then, for girls with steady boyfriends to start collecting household goods ready for when they married and had their own home.*

visit, oh well, it will come in time. Judy went to Barrowmore at 9.20. She was quite nervous. Poor her, she had no one to talk to in the ambulance. I have missed my lickle friend but I wasn't lonely because Helen came in after her exam. She showed me the paper and told me what she'd written. I bet she's done better than she thinks. She's not been in to see me for ages. Did she today 'cos Alice + Judy not here?

29 Wed: Had my lessons in the single on the men's side again. Judy came back at 11.30. She said the bronc was O.K. but after it she was awfully sick. <u>Visiting Day</u> Mummy and daddy came and we all had a nice talk. I enjoyed myself. Helen is happy. She's got her date! I am happy for her but not me.

30 Thu: Judy's parents went to see Dr Erwin yesterday. He said "No op!" It could be cleared up by treatment. I am pleased. Mummy also saw Dr Erwin in visiting yesterday. He said I was "improving steadily" "coming on well" and reacting well to drugs. Mum asked whether I'd be out in under 12 months and he said "Yes, definitely". A great surge of excitement went through me! That happy feeling stayed with me all evening but this morning I woke up feeling depressed. "Under 12 months" = 6 MORE months. Why be happy about that? I am SO fed-up and bored. Even Dr Bashray has become a boring topic of conversation. I feel restless. I need a boyfriend!! I haven't written this before but I think I'm infatuated by Kenny. I must be. I don't really like him but I can't stop thinking about him. I wish he'd write to me. I'd love him to kiss me! Cor!!!

JULY 1960

1 Fri: Kenny brought the tea round with another man I don't know who is going home. He had his blue shirt and jeans on. Oh! I do like Kenny! I think about him all the time. I have, even after he said he wouldn't write, been thinking how I'd like him to kiss me etc! I know it's all pretend but it gives me something to think about. At 9.00, as I'm writing this, I feel awfully depressed. There's only Judy who is a friend. I still really like Helen but we're not as close now. Maybe 'cos she'll soon be going home. I don't think anyone likes me much either. I wish I was home. I do miss the little private jokes + the confidential talks about boys etc with my friends. They are all growing up without me. Leaving me behind. SO fed-up.

2 Sat: It's morning and I hate Kenny! I've decided, like in South Pacific, am gonna wash that man right outta my hair! <u>Visiting</u> The best bit was with just Sandra. I told her there's nothing new about Dr Bashray. Judy still hasn't told anyone what he did. Dad went to see friend Jack. He said he was talking to Kenny's mum. Kenny said to ask me "Where's the pepper?" First daddy knew about it but he promised not to tell mummy. I wonder if Kenny sent this message 'cos he enjoyed it and (like me) wishes it had carried on? Jack sent me two bars of choc. (Wonder? Was it from Kenny?) Ooh, I am so fickle. Now I love Kenny again! I go all funny inside when I see him or even think about him. <u>8.30</u> I think Kenny is gorgeous. Little things make me think he liked me a bit too!! Maybe he still does? When I'm feeling happy, like now, I think he does. Tomorrow I'll probably go back to knowing he doesn't and hate him.

3 Sun: Weight – 7st 5 ¼ lbs Gain 1 ½ lbs. Wow! 1 ½ lbs gain. I only need 1 ¾ lbs more and I've reached my goal 7st 7lbs – 2 stones gain! <u>Visiting</u> Mummy + daddy came. We had an enjoyable time and we laughed a lot. Daddy mustn't have told mummy about the pepper or she'd have given me another of her lectures. I still like Kenny but I haven't seen him much today so it's wearing off a bit. He brought the records to the Square when I was in Jill's. I heard him but I was too shy to go. Wish I had! I'm not shy with anyone else. I sort of want to keep liking him so need to see him but I don't really like him so it's better if I don't see him.

4 Mon: Hell! Hell! Hell! Hell! I really could fill the page with them, I'm so awfully depressed. I have been since Friday although I haven't been "madly gay" for ages. I'm not fed-up – I'm depressed which is worse. One minute I love Kenny, the next I hate him. I don't know really what I feel. Went to Grotes at dinner time to collect some leather, he came in, I felt shy but said "Hello". Judy said I didn't blush or look very shy. Is this normal to be so shy? Kathleen came back from Ireland. She had leave – to get married! She is still very ill. She needs an op but isn't strong enough yet. She looked so very ill when I saw her on Christmas Day, I can't believe she's been allowed to go and get married!!

5 Tue: I have come to a decision about Kenny. When I see him I no longer feel excited so I'm going to forget him. If he wants to be friendly, I will be, otherwise no go. Fred said Kenny's new girlfriend's name was on the big tree. So, Judy + I went after dinner. There was KB=AL but this had been crossed out. After supper, when I was on my way back from the toilet, Dr Bashray pushed me into our ward forcibly 'cos he thought no one was there, but Judy was! Phew! He didn't say anything but went to his flat. I thought the Dr B scandal was over. I nearly became a new chapter in it!!

6 Wed: Had lessons in the single on the men's end again. Saw Kenny leaving. We didn't speak. The room didn't smell very nice. Is that Kenny? Visiting Mummy + daddy came. I enjoyed it very much. I neither like nor dislike Kenny but I'm beginning to think he's a bit smelly and repulsive. In the evening, Sister and Fred brought Kathleen round on her bed in her wedding dress!! She looked like a china doll. She is very pale and still has very red cheeks and her hair is very dark. She was happy and smiled and smiled (keeping her mouth shut 'cos of her few teeth) but she didn't say much. It made me think of Miss Faversham.[60] Judy thought it was sweet but it made me shudder.

7 Thu: Today I went to the school room. Whenever I see Kenny now I cringe with embarrassment. Nurse Swift, Fred etc all know about Bashray. Fred said everyone is talking about him feeling up the patients. I hope for Judy's sake they aren't talking

---

[60] _Miss Faversham_: out of Dickens' _Great Expectations_

about what happened to her. She'd be so embarrassed. I know she's told Fred, though. Mr Heels who is in charge of nursing doesn't know yet. Anyway, Mr Heels has gone on holiday for a while as his wife is expecting a baby. In his place will be Mr Myat from the Liverpool Hospital. Because he's new, no one is likely to tell him about Dr B. Fred said he might say something.

8 Fri: Oh! Dear! The School-room smelled really bad today. Worse yet. Kenny – yuk. When Judy and I made tea at the Square we saw Kenny. Ooh! I really do find him repulsive now. We both ignored him. Dr Bashray's game is nearly up. Dr Erwin sent for Judy + Jill who told him all about what happened. Maybe they're the two he did the most to? Fred had told Erwin. Dr E said he had interviewed other people about it as well. We are all now scared Dr Bashray might come into our ward and tell us off for telling on him.

9 Sat: Bashray went away for the day, returned at 11.45 at night. Judy was awake, she heard him come back she told us today. She was terrified he'd come into the ward but he didn't. Visiting First just daddy and Sandra, then daddy went to see Jack (again). Judy + I had a little private talk with Sandra about Dr Bashray and what's happened since our last talk. When Dad came back, he said Jack told him about Dr Bashray "getting into trouble for getting familiar with a Mrs Brown" which shows how rumours spread. We didn't know about her but Dr Bashray was the same with all of us. Daddy asked me some questions but I didn't tell him much. Sandra said mum would have to know about it now it is public.

10 Sun: Weight 7- 7 ½ lbs Gain – 2 ¼ lbs   So I've now gained my goal. Hurrah! I <u>am</u> pleased. Andrea has moved into our ward 'cos weird old Miss Smythe has been awful in their ward. She won't go to bed or anything + she wouldn't go into a single. I quite like Andrea (Kenny's ex). I think she's about 25. She is a bit old for him. She's a bit mousy looking with little eyes.   <u>Visiting</u> Mummy and daddy came. Gorgeous roast. I enjoyed visiting very much and there were no lectures or arguments etc because the main topic was Dr Bashray and what is going to happen next. I keep saying nothing happened to me because it didn't really, did it.

11 Mon: School. Smelly Kenny there before us again. Ugh! **DR BASHRAY** has left.[61] He has been dismissed because of his "familiarity with patients and staff". At 6.30 Dr Bashray sent a nurse for

---

[61] _Dr Bashray: We were told Dr Bashray had been 'dismissed' but no one ever took statements from any of us and no police were involved. I think it therefore unlikely he was prosecuted but instead simply removed from that hospital, leaving him free to work elsewhere, perhaps even within the same area. Shocking as that may be to 21st century readers, it was quite common practice then (and, as we now know, it was also in Churches, care homes, schools etc). It is also worth noting that no one spoke of sexual harassment or sexual interference or sexual abuse but only of the doctor having been too 'familiar' with patients. I have a photograph of this man, smiling happily with me and a few other patients, on the balcony outside the single rooms._

Judy. At 7.00 she came back, crying. Matron was then sent for + Dr Erwin but no one came. Judy said Dr Bashray had told her he loved her very much, and she'd ruined his career + would she write to him. Later Dr Bashray got Jill in + said the same to her (not the love bit). Then Matron came. She said she was going to take Judy to the Nurses Home in case Bashray tried to get her 'cos he'd said he wanted to see her again. Then Dr Erwin sent word that Judy could stay where she was. We hope that means Dr Bashray has gone. He was awful. I'm glad if he's gone for good.

12 Tue: Uneventful day. Still school in the men's single, tomorrow back in the proper school room though 'cos Helen's exams are over. Still smelly. I do wish it wasn't like that. Andrea is quite nice but very quiet and a bit boring. Looks and is mousy. Can't see why Kenny preferred her to me. Maybe he just likes 'em older! She's been here a long time. Helen told me today she is leaving very soon. She says she doesn't want a party. I'll miss her.

13 Wed: Today in the school-room I sat on the lovely, comfortable arm-chair that had been put there for Helen's GCE "sitter-with". <u>Visiting</u> Daddy is not very well so mummy came by herself. Daddy ran her up but then he felt rotten and went home. Oh ho – ill or too much whisky? Jill's Going Home Party. We gave her a vase for a single rose made of amber glass. <u>She</u> gave <u>us</u> little china ash trays, mine has blue round the edge, flowers in the centre. I drank 2 Babychams. We all enjoyed ourselves. I shall miss her and her big red smile!

14 Thu: Lessons in bed. I'm sick + tired of school! Ah well, we break-up on the 20th July! Thank goodness!! Yesterday I read in the Daily Sketch that the world was going to end at 12.44. It didn't!! Hurrah again. Jill went home at 8.00 this morning. He husband collected her. Judy and I were very sad to see our fwend go. Today my drugs were changed from I.N.H. tablets to Liquid P.A.S. and from streptomysin to streptoducin. Not sure if that's a good or a bad sign. My lungs but no one tells me anything.

15 Fri: Doris Martin left today. She walked out like Margery did. I never met Doris 'cos she was on surgical but Connie said she'd been here years. When Margery left without permission, I thought she was mad but now I can see why people do. Oh how I wish I could just walk away from here. The rest of the surgical girls are coming up on Sunday. Finished my library book "Germans Under My Bed", another good P.O.W. escape book. Mmm, wonder why escape books appeal to me at the moment! I got it from the library here. Visiting tomorrow. Good! Today has been a bit boring.

16 Sat: Finished off a jig-saw puzzle that Helen left for me. I did it on the bed-tables which we got on Friday. They are very handy. <u>Visiting</u> Just daddy + Sandra came as mummy had to work. I enjoyed myself + Sandra + I + daddy had a good wee chat!! Sandra did look smart. Helen went home today. She was my best friend here. No one seemed to like her much. Still don't know why. I did. I will really really miss her.

17 Sun: Weight 7st 9lbs Gain 1 ½ lbs This weight is fantastic! I can't believe it!!! That is the ONLY good thing about today. Today Connie + Sally Stevens moved from surgical into the 5-bedder. Judy went to join them. She didn't say she was going until 10 mins before she moved. I was very hurt and upset. I cried as I'll be so lonely. She's a fine "friend" to leave me in a ward alone with strangers. She knows how much I miss Helen. I see now that I was a "make-do" friend until Connie + Sally returned. Angela (20) and Mave (22) are now in my ward. Mave is really pretty. She has creamy skin, green eyes and sort of reddy-brown curly hair, but soft, not frizzy like mine. Angela is taller, short brown hair and a bit ordinary looking. I enjoyed visiting.

18 Mon: Oh! What an atmosphere! We are "all palls together" but the silences are often + strained. Even when someone didn't talk before it didn't feel like this. Nothing has happened and Maeve (spelled with an e she told me today) + Angela are nice, but no one is at ease for some reason. Maybe they don't like Andrea? Andrea's so quiet I can't see her upsetting anyone but she certainly doesn't act like she likes Maeve. They were in the same ward before their ops I gather. They can't dislike me already!! I can't understand it. Oh, I do feel so so depressed. Letter with photos from penpal in USA. She looks older than me and is fatter. Sort of blood on panties, as on Fri. Not strep! Could this be it?? Periods at last!! (No)

19 Tues: Improvement in atmosphere. Don't feel as depressed as yesterday but I still get those icey fingers on my bottom, like I do when I'm nervous or frightened. I think about home and mummy and daddy + Sandra a lot now like I used to when I first came. In fact, it is just like being new. I have no "special" friend and I keep thinking "I can't bear it, I must go home" and "Oh, I do love mummy, daddy + Sandra." Had a bubble bath! The only good thing about today. Pathetic.

20 Wed: Last day of the term. Return on 8 Sept I think. Cor! a lovely long holiday – I was fed-up with school so I'm glad. At dinnertime I walked through the woods to the Liverpool San[62] with Maeve and Angela. It's like a holiday camp there! Visiting Mummy + daddy came, I enjoyed it. We had good fun with Maeve, she is amusing. She said she gets hardly any visitors. She'd not been living in Runcorn long before she got ill. Her family are in Ireland. Cos daddy's family are Irish – and 'cos Maeve is a bit of a flirt – she talked mainly to daddy but me and mummy enjoyed listening.

21 Thu: Lazed about, reading, all morning. Dr Erwin, Dr Joshy and Dr Shearing came round at 11.15. Dr Erwin gave me 4 HOURS. I am very very happy. I went down to Miss Growcotts at 2.00 and she helped me set up the loom. I'm going to make a stole in black + silver lurex thread – cost

---

[62] *Liverpool Sanatorium was a short, pleasant walk through the woods from Crossley. For more information, see separate Note on Tuberculosis (TB) and Sanatoria at the end.*

16/-. Kenny was down there. He looked very smart – but I don't like him anymore. So why am I still shy? I'm not shy with anyone but him.

22 Fri: Went down to Miss Growcott's again today but I didn't stay very long. I'll be glad when Maeve + Angela get 4 hours. I couldn't get it in yesterday, but Andrea moved into the 5-bedder. Reason: she'll be lonely by herself when we're up on hours. No one cared about that when I was all alone (with Mrs W). After what Andrea said about how awful Judy was to go I was really shocked. Well good riddance to you Miss Mousy! You can't trust anyone here. Why wasn't I asked if I wanted to go into the 5-bedder? I bet it's because I'm a child and they don't any of them like having me around 'cos they have to watch what they talk about. Well they needn't bother. I know a LOT from books I read.

23 Sat: Today was my "first-time-dressed-on-4-hrs-visiting day". Daddy + Sandra came. So did SIX of the school gang! I felt better being up with them. I enjoyed it and I got lots of lovely things to eat! Yum! Yum! We went into the day room[63] (all except Dad, off to see Jack as usual). Ol' Irish Eileen was there and said "Will you be quiet!" as

---

[63] _Day rooms and other activities_   There was a T.V. in there as well as table tennis (ping-pong) and darts. Outside, we could play bowls on greens and putting. There was also a swimming pool but it was out of use. The canteen (or hall) was used for films and if anyone came to entertain us (such as the Christmas bell-ringers). There was also a shop.

she was watching TV. It is our room to use as much as hers!!

24 Sun: Weight 7-8 ¼ lbs LOST: ¾ lbs Oh! Calamity! How awful! I <u>do</u> hope I gain next week. I must! I <u>must</u>! Mum + dad aren't worrying. <u>Visiting</u> Mummy, Daddy and Nannie W came. I enjoyed visiting and my tea. Nannie's knitted me a new jumper in pale blue to match my cardi – so now I have a twin-set! Tres posh!!

25 Mon: Today Maeve and Angela got 4 hrs. They walked to Whitbys Café.[64] They invited me but as it is rather far to walk I didn't go. I'm glad I didn't now. They enjoyed themselves but they were tired and coffee (only nescafe made with water) cost them 8d each! Wong is making a hanging basket at Miss Growcotts. He is only about 22. He is a sailor. Tony is too. He's also Chinese. He is 30. They are both sailors who got their T.B. spotted when they docked at Liverpool. I went for a walk in the woods with Wong afterwards. Maeve said she'd heard rumours about our "affair"!! As if!!

---

[64] *Whitby's Café: This was one of several cafes near the various lakes in nearby Delamere Forest, an area that attracted a lot of visitors. I do not know if we were allowed to go to these places but patients certainly did, with and without their families. I seemed to have been shocked at how expensive a cup of coffee was at 8d (about 3p post-decimalisation for a cup of coffee that today would be cheap at £2 and can easily be £3 or more). One of the treats at home was my mother percolating coffee in the evening.*

26 Tue: Today Maeve and I went to the Liverpool San. We went with a nurse from the Liverpool who works here now. We met Mr Myat there and they showed us round. We talked to two Deva patients (male) who seemed perfectly sane![65] We walked back, had a bottle of pop in the canteen + then came back up for tea. I enjoyed it! Maeve is VERY funny and a bit naughty!! Very flirty!

27 Wed: I just laze around all morning now that there is no school – this is luxury. Visiting For a change I did the visiting – I sneaked home!! Daddy parked the car just outside the grounds instead of the car park and I walked out to it. I enjoyed myself. Home looked smaller and shabbier, but I'd like to be back. Scamp knew me, she nearly did her nut. Daddy has done the garden very nicely. My room looked as sweet as ever – how I wish I was in it! Wonderful to eat at home!

28 Thu: Today Maeve + Angela went with two Deva nurses (male) Benny Jones and Don somebody that they know to Chester. It's not allowed on 4 hours. I know I went home but that's not as bad. Maeve isn't speaking to Angela now, 'cos she said all she wanted was a "snoggin" session. Personally, as much as I like Maeve I think she's jealous 'cos she liked Benny + he kissed +

---

[65] *Confusing two hospitals? The diary is transcribed as written. It would appear that either I confused the two hospitals - the Liverpool was much closer but it was the Deva that had mental patients - or perhaps the Deva patients had been transferred to the Liverpool?*

cuddled Angela instead. Just when I thought we three could be friends, here we go again. I don't trust anyone now. I really am becoming bitter + twisted.

29 Fri: Oh! What an uncomfortable atmosphere. I wish they'd speak. If I talk to Angela, Maeve is a bit mad, as I suppose she thinks I ought to back her up. If I don't talk to Angela – it's ridiculous – we've never had an argument!!! Life is difficult! I do wish I had a "fella". I am lonely in that respect + after all I have got TB which causes over-active sex glands etc according to Maeve (and Connie). It's a well-known fact apparently!![66] Ah! Well everything comes to them who wait!!! But for how long??

Sat 30: Nannie Wakefield, Daddy + Sandra came and as Nannie W isn't to know about my "trip" I stayed here. I enjoyed myself - and I ate a lot! I MUST GAIN!! It was a good job I didn't go home again as Mr and Mrs Cooper came on behalf of Sunday School. They are good to keep coming but I don't know if I'll want to go back when I leave

---

[66] *TB and sex: At that time, it was believed that having T.B. increased a patient's sex-drive. This was repeated in one of the talks the doctor gave us later (as noted in the diary) and can be found repeated in most old histories of tuberculosis. What foundation, if any, it is considered to have nowadays, I do not know. It may be that, because of the long stays young people had to have in hospitals, there was a lot of 'fraternising' (as it was euphemistically called by the staff at Crossley) simply because they were young and wanted a normal life.*

here. More drama this evening. Angela told me Tony doesn't speak now to Maeve 'cos she went off with the male nurse from Deva. She said Maeve only wants Tony 'cos she can't have him or for 'what she can get out of him' (?) I think Angela really likes Tony but he doesn't like her as much.

31 Sun: Weight 7st- 9 ¼ lbs Gain 1 lb Hurrah! I've put back my loss plus!! <u>Visiting</u> Just mummy + daddy came. Sandra went out with Barry. We had a super time. I had my tea here then we went in the car through the woods to Hatchmere lake. We met Angela + visitors + Connie + visitors there!! Sputum test tomorrow.[67] I pray it's negative. Andrea, Sally Stevens, Judy, and Connie have all gone positive. Hope I don't. I wonder if that's why Andrea was moved to the 5-bedder and I wasn't?

---

[67] <u>*Sputum tests:*</u> *As mentioned earlier, TB patients had these tests regularly, although the diary mentions them only a few times. I thought, at the time, that patients with positive tests showing they were infectious were kept together in the same wards, but that might have been me looking for an explanation of why some moves were made. I do not remember even those positive patients having any restrictions on visitors but, as I never was positive and I never shared a ward (for long if at all) with a positive patient, I cannot be sure.*

AUGUST 1960

1 Mon: Bank Holiday so <u>Visiting Day</u> again. Today daddy mummy and I went for a run in the country and we had a picnic. I really enjoyed it. It is marvellous to get out. I'm not "over doing" it just sitting in the car or on the grass. It felt normal! To think, a week today, I have an official day out shopping!! From 11-6!! Super super!! We drove around the lanes off the road to Chester + then we went to some caves nearby.

2 Tue: Yipee! Visiting tomorrow! Maeve + Angela went for a walk with Tony + Wong. They're all speaking again now. As it was a long way (and I could tell I wasn't really welcome) I took off my coat + lay on it reading by the big tree. I took sunglasses, a book, a box of sweets, and got pop + a packet of crisps from the shop. I was there from 1.45 to 3.10 it was gorgeous. When they came back, they were all being very hot and giggly. After tea I messed about then had a bath. Maeve and Angela were in a huddle talking boy talk most of the evening. They think I don't know what they've been up to, well I do.

3 Wed: Not a very nice day today, so visiting or not, I've put my trews on! I know mummy likes me to wear a dress but she didn't mind. Mummy Sandra + Aunty Laura came to see me. Daddy ran them here but then went collecting til 4.15 as he's late with his work being bank holiday week. Maeve drove me mad. She didn't leave me alone with my visitors all afternoon. I didn't say anything to her but I will if it happens again. She's only had one visitor since she moved into our ward. He brought her a bag of tomatoes! She gave them away soon as he left. She said she hates tomatoes but it's all he ever brings her and she said it's too late to tell the old fella! She said he's not a relative and not a friend and she doesn't even like him, just someone she used to do business with. Maybe she worked in a shop?

4 Thu: Today I felt very peculiar in dinner so I had to come out (of my own accord) and go back to bed. I had an awful headache all morning but it seemed worse at the table. Went to bed till 2.15 then felt O.K. Went to Swimming Pool for a walk. Saw Wong. We then went to see Miss Growcott. Stayed + talked to Wong and Miss Growcott until time to go back to the ward. At night I fell asleep from 5.45 to 8.00 off + on. Nurse Evans took my temp, it was 101.8 I felt ill. Gosh, hope it isn't pluracy like Judy. Don't feel well. Maeve said I'd caught something snoggin with Wong. I have not. I didn't. I wouldn't. I am NOT like her.

5 Fri: Temp was 101.8 this morning! I don't feel very well. So hot all the time. Whew! Heatwaves!! At night my temp went to 103!!! and my pulse 122!!! What if this is a flare-up? Sweaty like I was when I first came here. In the afternoon Mrs Benfield and Sarah came back to see us! Mrs Benfield looks very well, but she's lost some weight. Sarah looked terrific. Still wearing black! She's going back to art college in September. It was nice to see them again. I wonder if I'll come back to see anyone when I leave? Whenever that will be.

6 Sat: I felt much better this morning, thank goodness. My morning temp was only 98.2 and it was at 5.00 too. Visiting (in bed! grrrr!!) Mummy daddy + Sandra came. Mummy doesn't usually come on a Saturday at the moment but she was worried about me. I wish I wasn't such a worry to them but at least all seem to agree my chest is O.K. so it can't be plurasy or a set-back. (Thank goodness) Maeve left us more alone except she was v flirty with dad (again)! He's as bad as she is even though mum is there.

7 Sun: I didn't get weighed this morning. I'm glad really as I'm bound to have lost a lot of weight I sweated so much. Visiting Mummy daddy + Sandra came again and I enjoyed visiting. My temp was 97.8 at 2.00 + at five it was 97.8! Mummy saw Dr Erwin. He thinks it is gastric flu or a P.A.S. drug reaction. I hope it's P.A.S., it's a shorter time in bed and I can't make anyone else ill. I feel much better now I know it's not a break-down.

8 Mon: Morning temp was:- 101.4 Evening temp was:- 98.0. It was down all day + at night it was still down. Oh! I hope it stays like that. In the afternoon Nurse Evans took a swab from my throat – Dr Joshy ordered it this morning. He thinks it's a virus infection in my throat as my throat is a bit red and inflamed although it doesn't feel sore. Cor, he said 2000,000 virus fit on a pinhead![68] Relieved my sputum test still negative.

---

[68] *How many virus fit on a pinhead*: the diary records what I

9 Tue: I feel very well today + my temp is down M. 97.4 and E.97.6!! Whacko! Alice came back to see us yesterday. She looks fine and she hasn't lost any weight. She says she's enjoying life "outside" + she really does look very well indeed. She hopes to get married soon. Maeve was bitchy about her afterwards. Maeve and Angela had ANOTHER row about "men". Angela said Maeve is "a cheap tart" and Maeve said it's "sour grapes", the men just like her more than Angela. Oh dear. I kept on reading. I do NOT want to get into all that.

10 Wed: Temp wasn't too bad today. In fact it stayed more or less down. A.M. Temp =99 P.M. Temp = 98 <u>Visiting</u> Mummy, daddy + Sandra came. I enjoyed it, but after I felt very depressed and homesick, like I used to. I feel as if I can't bear it here any longer. Oh! I do so long to go home. I love them all + home so much.   Wong gave me a lovely 17" x 13" oil painting. It is a blue bowl of roses on a polished table. He did it himself and signed his name in Chinese on back. He came to outside our bay and held it up to show it to me then Fred brought it up. It is beautiful. I just wish Maeve would stop teasing me. He is NOT my boyfriend. He might want to be but he's too old for me. He doesn't say much I can understand either. She said there's more than talking to having a fella. Yeah yeah I know.

was told. However during the pandemic I heard it said that "100 million viral particles of the novel coronavirus can fit on a pinhead".

11 Thu: Morning:- 99.4 Evening = 98.8 I feel O.K. again today. Really I've been feeling better ever since Saturday. It was on Friday I really felt ill. Dr Joshy has at last decided what it is. He said that by the throat swab they took they can tell I have got laryngitis!! I haven't lost my voice but Mr Heels says that's because the inflammation isn't on the vocal chords! What a laugh! Even laryngitis wouldn't shut me up! NOTHING to do with my chest –hurrah!

12 Fri: Feel fed-up again today. It was awful to watch people strolling round all afternoon when I really ought to be out as well. Still, I'm very, very, grateful that it isn't a chest illness, cos how awful if it was. Maeve, Angela, Connie, Kenny, Peter, dad's friend Jack + I all went to exams off Dr Joshy. At exams, we no longer blow the bag. Another Erwin change. Maeve is hilarious and VERY naughty with the men, even Jack!! Yesterday we all also went to the Theatre for blood tests. No idea why. M:- 98.8 E:- 98.6

13 Sat: Hurrah! Visiting again. I look forward to it even more now that I'm back in bed. Mummy, daddy and Sandra came, then Mummy went and Nannie W came. I was glad that they hadn't brought me lots of food, I couldn't have ate it if they had. I enjoyed seeing them very much. My temp is O.K. After, although we had the T.V. trolley, I felt very, very depressed. Unhappy + homesick. I know I'm lucky it's not a flare-up or set back but I do so want to go home! M:- 98 E:- 98.2

14 Sun: Weight 7st 5 ¼ lbs. Lost:- 4 lbs. Not too bad considering how little I've eaten + how much I've been sweating. Feel fine now. <u>Visiting.</u> Mummy, daddy, Sandra. I enjoyed myself and ate some of the food brought for tea. M:- 97.4 E:- 98.2

15 Mon: It's only 8.00am but I boy do I feel so <u>un</u>happy. And I had a sputum test, so did Angela and Maeve. Pray it's O.K. I'm worried sick. I've been off drugs for a week. Oh, please be negative. I wrote home + 4 more. Got a postcard from super Sarah, she's on holiday in Abersoch, lucky thing. Wales made me think of Helen. She's still not written. Did some more weaving, it's ages since I did. It's growing though slowly. I am shocked by some of the things Maeve says. Worse than in books! She says crude things. She swears a lot too. Not just "damn" or "bloody" but words too rude to write down. M:- 97.6 E:- 98.2

16 Tue: I feel marvellous today + my temp is fine now. Dr Joshy told me I could have 2 hours tomorrow and in 2 days back to 4!! Yippee! Am I glad. That awful catty Connie said at the dinner table "Hum! Why can't everybody be treated the same here. Barbara should build up her hours like Judy had to." How catty and silly. Judy had plurasy. I only had laryngitis. For 30 Connie acts very childishly. Had a bath and washed my hair with smelly antidandruff shampoo. Maeve can be as nasty as Connie but so far not that much to me 'cos I don't get in her way with the fellas like Angela does! I wouldn't like to get on the wrong side of Maeve.

17 Wed: Today I got my 2 hrs back! Yippee! It's super being properly up again! Dr Joshy is leaving tomorrow, but he has left word for me to get my 4 hrs back on Friday. <u>Visiting</u> Mummy and Sandra came, daddy was collecting. (His car broke down on Mon + Tues + so he is behind in his work.) They were thrilled about me getting my hours back so quickly. I really enjoyed visiting, but afterwards I felt oh so depressed and unhappy again. Maeve and Angela were out of the ward most of the evening then Maeve put the screens round her bed. I asked Angela, is she was sick. She said "Yes but not how you mean." After lights out, I thought I saw someone (not Maeve) come in and go behind the screens. Is she ill?

18 Thu: No visiting. I could cry! I'm just like I was when I was on Absolute. I could cry after visiting and when it isn't a visiting-day. I wake up unhappy. In the afternoon Angela and Maeve did a jigsaw + I did my matchboxes while we listened to records. I've got 363 now! People look at me as if I'm nuts when I say I've got 363 match-boxes. "All different?" is the usual question. I wish we had more quiet friendly afternoons like this. Maeve and Angela were out most of the evening, again. Andrea came to see me then. She said she was sorry about how she'd left but she'd moved out 'cos of Maeve. They'd been in the same ward before her op but "never again". She wouldn't tell me why but told me to "be careful with that one". She said it "wasn't right" to put her in with me. More feuds!! I hate this bitchiness.

19 Fri: Up! Up! Up! Up on 4 hrs today again! Oh! It is nice to be back again, I didn't mind being in bed up until Tuesday, then 'cos I felt absolutely normal, fit + energetic, I wanted to get up again! Maeve has stopped speaking to Angela + to me. She won't say why + we don't know. I asked her + she was most rude. When I asked her if she'd been ill the other night she said I should keep my eyes closed and my mouth shut or else. I have NO idea what she's on about. She's a childish little bitch, but she won't tread on me! Andrea warned me. Oh dear.

20 Sat: Maeve still isn't speaking. I said "Oh! Oh! Still in a funny mood?" M: "Watch it." I said "Widdums, musn't make de lickle baby cry." She was blazing and called me an old woman + told me to act my age. I said she acted like 2 not 22. Visiting Mummy daddy + Sandra came. Then mum went + Nannie W came. Susan and the gang from school came in between. They are good to come but they talked amongst themselves about people I don't know all afternoon. I felt very very sad afterwards, I really am out of touch. Maeve and Angela had a big row this evening. Maeve called Angela a "slut" for going with Tony. Angela said "Well, at least I don't charge for it." Maeve then used some very rude words. A nasty slanging match. Ugly.

21 Sun: Weight 7st 7 ½ lbs   Gain:- 2 ¼ lbs. Whacko! I'm putting back my lost weight. As long as I don't go below 7-7 ½ lbs I don't mind. Visiting Mummy, daddy + Sandra came. We went for a walk to the old quarry. It was lovely. We all enjoyed ourselves very much. Mum + Sandra in their high heels got tired before me. Even worse nastiness this evening. Another Maeve V Angela row. I put the headphones on and read. I don't want to get involved. It's all about men and sex. I wish I did not have to hear any of it. Awful.

22 Mon: Last night Maeve and Angela had a right carry-on. Maeve is still not speaking to me! Why? I asked her to tell me what I'd done so I could explain + apologise, but she wouldn't tell me. Their row is something about Tony but what's that got to do with me? Angela told me today Maeve had asked him to come and see her again in the ward!! He said no, because I'm here. Well, it's not fair if Maeve is blaming me! When my family left yesterday, I nearly cried, and I still feel very unhappy. The atmosphere in the ward is awful, even though Maeve is out most of the day and evening. Started to make a tray for mummy today. Angela + Maeve got 8 hrs. Hurrah – maybe they'll soon go home. It doesn't seem fair when I got 4 hours before them, I'm still only on 4 hours and they're on 8 but they had ops ages ago and have been here a long time already. Sputum still negative so one good thing.

23 Tue: I have finished my tray today. It is a yellow base with black beads. I enjoyed making it, but the long canes get tangled up + are hard to manage. It only cost 7/6! It is oblong television shape. What awful, awful weather! Rain! Rain! Rain! St Swithins day prophecy has really come true this year, it has rained every day for 40 days, it ends today. Still fed-up. I am trying to be nice to Maeve but she's still ignoring me. Angela wants to stick up for me but doesn't want to make Maeve angry with her too. Oh dear.

24 Wed: Maeve spoke to me today, so I spoke back. It's easier. I think it is because Angela is going on leave on Friday. Maeve isn't. She doesn't have anywhere to go to. Still, I'm glad she's speaking again, the atmosphere was truly awful. Mummy and daddy came. I'm back to "good eating" now!! I really enjoyed visiting even though it rained + we had to stay in the ward all the time. This evening, Matron came and shouted at Maeve + Angela for "fraternizing" with the men!!!! She said they must not go off with any of the men – patients or nurses! – here or when on leave. She also said Maeve knows she must not go back to her "old ways". Angela started crying. She said she's not like Maeve, she's only been friendly. Maeve's language then!!!

25 Thu: Yesterday Maeve asked for leave. Dr Erwin refused. He said he'd tell her why on Friday. Matron said to Maeve it's because she's got no job + no family here to stay with + nowhere to live when she leaves. Poor her! Angela told me later Maeve was a "pro" and got chucked out of her digs when her landlady found out. I don't know if I believe her. She might just be being nasty. Did nothing very exciting. Went for a walk to the swimming pool by myself that's all. Saw Maeve went off with the Tony then came back and went off with Wong. Maybe she is what Angela said?? I know she goes in the Men's Dayroom and we aren't supposed to. Does she have other 'customers'? I try to avoid her now as much as I can.

26 Fri: Today Dr Erwin came round. He gave me 8 HOURS to start on Sunday. He also gave me permission to go out from 9.00-6.00 on Monday! I'm dying to go! I just hope I'm not ill this time! Dr Erwin said Maeve can't have a leave for a good reason but it wasn't her chest. He didn't say why but said to Maeve "you know very well". Sally Stevens gets 4hrs Sat, 6hrs on Mon, 8hrs on Wed. Judy + Connie are still stuck. Poor things. I feel awfully sorry for them. It was awful this evening. Maeve was horrible, swearing and nasty. I only asked her why Dr E won't let her go on leave. She said it's none of my ******* business! I feel sorry for her if it's because she's got no home here to go on leave to but why take it out on me?

27 Sat: <u>Visiting</u> again! Hurrah!! Mummy, daddy + Sandra came. They were all thrilled with my promotion. In fact, mum was so shocked when she got the letter that she went to work without combing her hair! Nannie W came + mum went. Nannie is very pleased as well. All expect me home soon. I enjoyed visiting very much. No chance to have a "private" chat with Sandra. I want to tell her about Maeve and what's going on. This evening was the worst yet. Maeve put the screens round her bed from 8 and they were still there at lights out. Was it Tony? Not as tall. I thought I could hear voices and other "noises". Oh dear. It can't be happening.

28 Sun: Weight :- 7st-8 ½ lbs   Gain 1 lb   Only about 1lb more to go and I'm back to normal! <u>Visiting</u> Mummy, daddy + Sandra came. We couldn't go out as it rained, so Sandra + I played table tennis in the day room.   Then we all played darts. I lost, my score was lowest. Mum won. Daddy didn't play 'cos he was out trying to get a new window for the car as the other one broke. Enjoyed myself at night - I had a bath. Then I put the headphones on and turned to the wall when I was reading so I would not know what Maeve (and whoever this time) was up to. Awful awful awful. I'm very, very excited about tomorrow!!!

29 Mon: <u>MY DAY OUT</u>   I had a very very happy day – it was marvellous. I've not enjoyed myself so much for well over a year. I love mum, dad + Sandra. Everyone was very kind. I wasn't so very unhappy at night, 'cos I kept myself busy! We came back at 5 past 6 + we had left at 5 to 9! I got new shoes. Oatmeal leather pointed toes. A Sari Peach button up cardigan with a collar. "When will I be loved" – my fave Everly Bros.   I also got some lovely match-boxes. Maeve is in trouble with Sister Savage about something today but I do NOT want to know about it. More men trouble I gather.

30 Tues: 8.5am Feeling a little bit unhappy already, must keep myself busy all day. Wrote to home + Helen this morning. I hope she replies this time. Angela came back. She says she has enjoyed herself very much. She didn't want to return.   This afternoon I was by the pool when Wong came. He talked then asked me to go for a walk with him, I said no, I was tired. I couldn't get rid of him. He insisted on walking round the back to the shop with me. I ran from the shop, said the T.V. show had started. Blow me if he didn't follow + came in to see the T.V. with me in the womens day room. I hope he doesn't think just 'cos Maeve is in my ward I'm like her. I am NOT.

31 Wed: Felt very miz. after visiting as did Angela. Gosh! If I feel this awful after my day out, what I'd be like after a leave, I hate to think! <u>Visiting</u> Just mummy. She got me a lovely new skirt from C&A in Liverpool. It is in cream + fawn checked brushed wool, with pockets with big wooden buttons on. I'm sorry to say I got awfully upset in visiting. I just couldn't help it. Maeve has been nasty again. She said it was my fault she was in trouble about the fellas and couldn't go on leave. I haven't said anything to staff. I hate her sneaking men in and I hate her. I want to go home now. I can't wait 3 months. I had to tell mummy why I was upset. I only told her about Maeve being nasty to me, not about what goes on at night.

SEPTEMBER 1960

1 Thu: Still feel very unhappy. If I can't be with my family, I feel I want to be alone. Went for a walk, Wong met me (accidently!). He said "I have something to tell you." (I nearly died, thought he was going to say "I love you"!!!) He started to say something about Maeve but I couldn't understand. He wanted to go for a walk with me but I said "Bye Bye". He said "You teach me English in the day-room at 1.00 tomorrow." I said "Yes" to get away. I daren't. I'd get into trouble for mixing. I want a boyfriend but I get frightened when boys start to like me. Think Wong likes me but he's too old. Also I think he's been with Maeve like Tony etc.

2 Fri: Today I feel very, very, very, very unhappy again. Maeve is still not speaking – 3rd day! Don't know why! Angela asked her why she'd stopped talking – she said I know full well! She's addressed all her remarks to "Angela" + when she offered sweets around I was left out. She's got a cheek saying it's my fault she's in trouble again. She would really be in BIG trouble if I told Matron what's actually been going on. I HATE MAEVE. I HATE CROSSLEY. I WANNA GO HOME.

3 Sat: Very, very unhappy again. Maeve is awful. She won't speak except to swear at me. Her language is disgusting. Gosh! Am I glad it's Saturday. Visiting mummy, daddy + Sandra came and we went home. I was in a bit of a state. I had to tell them all about Maeve's nastiness and then a bit of the rest came out. I am now afraid to go back. Maeve will kill me when she finds out I've said something. Mum + dad + Sandra are shocked and very cross indeed. Mum says this must not continue. I will go home or go to another hospital. Of course, I won't be allowed to go home for good without permission. Mummy wouldn't let me stay at home even though I cried and cried. It's awful being in this ward. I HATE IT. At night, I put my headphones on and turned to the wall.

4 Sun: <u>Weight</u> 7st-8 ¾ lbs <u>Gain</u> ¼ lb Not much this week. Not surprised, can't eat + I never gain when I'm unhappy. <u>Visiting</u> When they came I was crying, couldn't help it. Maeve was her nastiest ever at dinner + I burst out crying so had to tell Mr Heels. Everyone seems scared to say anything to Maeve. Even the staff. Mum + dad saw Dr Erwin to tell him why they were taking me home. He hates her too, he calls her "Murphy". No one can say a good word for her – I can't either. I was so upset they were allowed to take me home for 3 days. It's lovely at home!

5 Mon: Had breakfast in bed. I slept with mummy last night. She didn't go to work today. Got up about 11.00. Talked for a bit then dressed and had dinner. The weather was nice so we went down town, saw relations. Bed about 9.30. Am trying not to think about what it'll be like if I do have to go back to Crossley. Mummy says she will not allow me to be put back into that ward. I think they should move Mave to Deva – she's sex mad. I am not going to spell her name right anymore. She doesn't deserve it.

6 Tue: Awful wet weather! Still, it's lovely to sit by the fire at home. Breakfast in bed, then up + dressed for 12.00. Didn't go out all day. Did my rest hours and loved it all! No strep tho or other drugs. Mummy said she was still waiting to hear what Crossley is going to do about me. I started crying. It's not me but Mave they should be doing something about. Mummy then got upset, said she should have chosen the children's hospital. I wish she had.

7 Wed: Mooned round all morning, thinking of going back to Crossley. I wouldn't mind if it was a ward like when I first came in I was returning to, but oh! a single on TOP FLOOR! Why? Why do I have to move? Mave should.[69] We all think so. Mummy said this is only temporary. I can't stay at home longer 'cos I'm off drugs here. Arrived back at 6.5. Single is quite nice. Staff had moved up my

---

[69] *Why was I the one moved? It is very hard to understand why I was moved to a single on the 'cancer' floor with all old people when it was Maeve (not her real name) who had made the ward 'unsafe' for me. We did not understand it at the time. I can only assume, as we did then, that she was not trusted to be in a single because she would continue to have men visiting her. Perhaps she could not be discharged because she wasn't at that point fit enough and perhaps no other hospital would accept her as a patient? She had no home to go to or money to live on. To a 21st century mind, it is hard to believe but that is what happened. Was she really a prostitute, or promiscuous, or just a normal young woman who wanted to have sex in her own bed which just happened to be in my ward?*

things. Mummy + daddy stayed until about 7.00. I like the room but it's so, so dark and lonely once they'd gone. It's the cancer floor. Mainly old people. Had a talk with Mrs Sherwin + Mrs Conckling, both very nice, in singles next to mine, then went to bed. Lights out at 9.30, but couldn't sleep at first. Thank goodness it's only temporary till they sort Mave out.

8 Thu: I enjoy playing "house" and straightening up my room + arranging my knick-knacks, but as soon as the novelty wears off, I dread to think what it will be like. Everyone (especially Connie + Judy + Sally Stevens) (except Angela + Mave) are very friendly indeed. They all say it's wrong I'm stuck up here. I feel sick every time I see Mave. She glares at me but hasn't so far said anything to me directly. Mummy + daddy came at night. I was so glad to see them. I'd been waiting to see them all day. I told them I liked the room, but not the dark + loneliness. I'm glad they can sneak in like this but it also makes me scared. What if someone from Deva did?? School started again today. Mrs Mawson was shocked to find out what's happened.

9 Fri: Mummy is seeing Dr Cuthill at Runcorn Hospital today because both herself + daddy (and me!) don't like the idea of me being all by myself so much. It isn't so bad for a short while, but I couldn't stand it for months. I went into the Top Floor 6-bedder – it was horrible. They are all so old. They look very very ill too. Depressing. Yipee! Visiting again tomorrow! Oh! I am glad. In the afternoon I watched T.V. in the day-room + went to Miss Growcotts. I have got three purses to do. I could tell everyone is talking about me 'cos it went quiet when I came in. No one is sticking up for Mave.

10 Sat: Had a bath <u>before</u> breakfast! Gosh! I feel as if I've been back for years!!! <u>Visiting Day</u> mummy, daddy + Sandra came and then mummy went. I told Sandra more about what Mave is like and the men. When daddy brought Wendy I felt embarrassed. I didn't know what he had told her about me being up here. She might not even know what a pro is. Dr Cuthill said he can't do anything, so we'll have to wait until Friday when Dr Erwin comes back. One positive thing - Wendy has saved me a seat on the school bus for when I'm back! I MUST believe I'll need it soon! We (Sandra + Wendy + I) played bowls!!! Gorgeous weather. Went to Judy's birthday party this evening. V.G. Lots to drink and eat!! Mave was NOT invited. Everyone made a fuss of me. Was scared creeping back upstairs alone after.

11 Sun: <u>Weight</u> 7st-8 ½ lbs <u>Loss</u> ¼ lbs I thought I would have lost much more, so I'm pleased. <u>Visiting</u> Mummy, daddy + Nannie Wakefield came. Lovely food and lots of it! As it was nice we went out to Hatchmere + then for a ride round. I love the woods and lakes round here. I really enjoyed myself. Afterwards I felt very unhappy, still it'll wear off I suppose as I get used to things and it is only for now. In the evening, Mrs Sherwin was too tired to talk so I sat with Mrs Conckling for a while. She is nice too but a bit boring.

12 Mon: Another beautiful Summer day. Went out for a walk at 3.30 till 4.30. I would have gone out earlier only I don't like walking alone. I went out, though, as it seems a shame to waste such a lovely day. I'm also nervous about meeting Mave or any of her men. When I'm out in the sun, I don't mind being here, and I think I imagine the loneliness at night, but when night comes I know I don't. Much more lovely weather to come I hope. My night for T.V. in my room! Nothing much on but better than just sitting here.

13 Tue: I've been waiting to see Miss Growcott because I've finished my stole + I want her to take it off the loom + fringe it. Unfortunately, she is off sick. I started it on July 21st, but of course some days I didn't do any at all. Didn't do anything exciting at all. Watched T.V. in the dayroom, then came to bed, + wrote my diary (is 10 to 9 now). I wish I could have T.V. in my room every night. It passes the time + I like it. When Helen was in a single, I wished I was too. Now, I hate being by myself. I am SO lonely up here. No one pops in like they would if it was on the middle floor. The old ladies up here are nicer than Mrs W was but they are very old and very ill and just stay in bed.

14 Wed: <u>Visiting</u> Just mummy + daddy came. I enjoyed it very much, just chatting together. We were trying to decide what to do if I can't go home. I was undecided then but, as I write this at 6.20, I am sure I could not bear it here much longer. I feel awfully lonely + it seems ages until Saturday when I see them again. Erwin comes back tomorrow so (I hope) by next Wednesday I may be home. Somehow, I don't think so though. Awful weather now, cold + wet. Last night, I was woken up again by noises in the corridor and the lift.

15 Thu: No room yesterday, but I wore my new yellow thick batwing sweater that Nannie knit. It's a lovely sweater + everyone admired it very much. I had an awful nightmare about the War last night. I was absolutely terrified. When I woke up I was crying with fright. I was hoping the night-staff would come in but they didn't. I didn't like to ring the bell it sounded so silly to say "I've had a nightmare, I'm scared". I went to sleep but kept waking up again. A nurse told me today that someone had died and was being taken down to the basement, that's what I'd heard the other night. I hate it here.

16 Fri: Hurrah! Hurrah! Hurrah! Visiting tomorrow. I only live from one visit to the next. Mummy's letter said they have an appointment with Dr Erwin for 2.30 on Saturday. Oh! I do hope he lets me go home. I felt very unhappy + lonely all of today. It's cold so I got into bed after dinner till tea, then after tea till supper. No one comes in, and so unless I visit other wards, I don't see anyone. There is no point going into any of the wards on this floor. I'll go mad if I'm here much longer. I like Mrs Sherwin but I'm afraid she's going to die, she looks so ill. At least she's still OK in the head.

17 Sat: Visiting Mummy, daddy, Sandra came. I enjoyed visiting, especially when it was just Sandra and me. Mum + dad are very cross with Dr E because he didn't even take them into his office, they were just in the corridor. He won't let me leave or do anything about me being up here. When mum said she thought Mave would have been moved he said "Don't tell _me_ what to do." They saw Matron after + she was very nice. She doesn't approve of me being alone up here. She said she's very sorry but it's complicated. Dr Erwin cannot tell us what is going on, he's not allowed to. Felt very, very lonely at night even though I had T.V. I cried at night, couldn't help it.

18 Sun: Weight 7st-9 ½ lbs   Gain 1 lb I think that's wrong, my wrists are thinner, I can tell by my watch + I've hardly eaten or drank milk. Visiting Mummy + daddy came + we went for a little run out. We just went round the country lanes but I enjoyed it. For a change the weather was nice. I'm sorry to say I got upset in visiting 'cos nothing seems to be done. However I've promised to be good + wait. I do not understand why Dr Erwin is being so horrible to me. Why can't he tell mummy and daddy what's going on? Mummy said she won't sign me out so I can only leave if Dr E agrees. She won't allow me to go back on the middle floor if Mave is still there. I'd be scared in a single there if she was.

Mon 19: Ugh! Monday! The beginning of another dismal, lonely + miserable week. I know now I'm here until I leave. I've promised to stick it + so they'll never see at home how much I hate it here. When I get out I may tell them but until then I couldn't, mummy worries so much. Daddy takes it in his stride. I've been back 2 weeks on Wednesday, seems like 2 months at least. I HATE IT HERE. I will NEVER understand why Mave is still on the middle floor and I was moved. Mrs Sherwin said it's probably because they can trust me to behave and they can't trust her. That's not fair. I am being punished for being good!

Tue 20: Messed round all day. I didn't do anything special, just passed the day waiting for mummy + daddy to come at night. It was lovely to see them + we were all happy + I didn't get upset at all. I somehow feel much more resigned to it now. One advantage is now they can come ANY time they want. No one seems to notice or care up here. Tomorrow mummy + daddy are going to see Matron to see what she has arranged. She promised on Saturday to do something. Mummy said not to give up hope but I have. Mrs Conkling was very upset this evening. Something about her family but she didn't want to talk about it.

21 Wed: <u>Visiting</u> Mummy + daddy + I went out for a little run only about 1 hr from 2.30 to 20 to 4 Had to come back in time for mummy to see Matron. She got nowhere. Matron's very sorry, it's not right – just like she said before – but it's "out of her hands". Mummy and daddy are furious. I just feel fed up. Why won't anyone do anything? Daddy said they probably daren't let Mave be up here by herself. Gave mummy her present for her birthday tomorrow. Table mats in a kind of cane + I put alternate black + yellow tassels along two sides. She liked them very much, I'm glad to say. Felt very miz. at night. Watched Tribute to Oscar

Hammerstien on T.V. It was very good, made me sad cos it reminded me of home + before I came here. Me, Mummy, Nannie we like musicals. "The King and I" best of all.

22 Thu: To "Frere Jacques" tune: "I hate Crossley! I hate Crossley! But who doesn't? But who doesn't? Wish I was at home! Wish I was at home! Hark don't you? Hark don't you?" That's just how I feel but without the jolly tune. Oh, I promised to stick it but it is hard hard hard. I feel so very, very, very lonely + miserable all the time. After visiting + at nights it's worse. Wish I was home especially today 'cos it's mummy's birthday. I can't bear to think of how sad and worried she'll be when she should be happy today.

23 Fri: Thank-goodness it's Friday again! Oh! I do so wish I was at home. I had good news this morning though. Mrs Mawson is going to see the Education man about my lessons, so she had to find out how much longer I would be here. Dr Erwin said "She should be home within the next month or two" Oh God, please make that come true. I hate it here cos everyone hates everyone else I think. After dinner Judy said everyone knows what Mave is but the hospital can't prove it, even though there were complaints about her before. Andrea said now you know why I wouldn't be in her ward again. I know Mave's got no family here or a place to live so they can't chuck her out but why don't they send her to another hospital?

24 Sat: <u>Visiting</u> Mummy + daddy + Sandra came. Then mummy went + Nannie W came. Mummy got a lovely underskirt off Nannie, a tin of talc from Sandra + daddy gave her money for a tea-set or whatever she wants. She liked my card + present as well. At night I was watching a film "She couldn't say no" with Jean Simmons + Robert Mitchem + the TV tube went. I felt so upset at the thought of the lonely night + how we were meant to be watching it <u>together</u> (them at home + me here) I cried.

25 Sun: Weight 7st-9 ¾ lbs   Gain ¼ lb   <u>Visiting</u> I went home for the afternoon. It was lovely. For tea we had chicken'n'chips'n'peas, chocolate cake a la Salter! It was absolute bliss! About 50yds from our house on the way there we had a puncture, so after dinner daddy had to mend it. Good job it didn't happen on the way back out in the country. Felt very very sad at night as well as homesick. I am now resigned. I will be here until I leave. It IS unfair but nothing I can do about it. Mrs Sherwin said it'll all be all right in the end. Mrs Conckling said God's ways are not for us to understand. I don't even understand Dr E's ways!!

26 Mon: Quite a pleasant day really. I haven't mentioned these thoughts recently but for the last few weeks – last week especially - I've been thinking to myself "14 nearly + never been kissed by a boy". I would love a boyfriend. I think I'm getting a complex. I rather like Dave (16) a boy in the office here, but I haven't got a crush on him. I just feel too full of love, and if I had a boy he could have some. I am SO lonely. Mrs Benson in the other single died yesterday. I didn't really know her but I'm still sad. I HATE hearing the trolley and the lift at night and wondering who'll not be here tomorrow.

27 Tue: T.V. is now mended. One day more – one day less! Today went quite quickly really, but I am still, as usual, a bit depressed. I was especially upset this morning as in French we did some work out of the present French Book instead of Revision work, and I realised how much I had forgotten. After, I cried + cried as I was getting ready for up at 12.00. I long to be out and back at school but now I know I am too far behind to be in the form with my friends. I am in despair. I do not really like Dave, I just did yesterday for something to think about. At night saw film of 1959 Garden Party + Rose Fete, in the dining-room. I wish I could see a film of the 1960 one 'cos I'd be in it giving the bouquet! That was a happy day!

28 Wed: Mrs de H came again. We did 2 ½ hr French nearly! I did a little Latin at the end, but I think I'll never catch up in it now. No A form. Oh well. I feel much more confident about my French today, I could remember quite a bit. Must keep hoping. <u>Visiting</u> Mummy came (on the bus) to see me. I really enjoyed it. Oh I do so love mummy + daddy + Sandra. I pray I can go home soon. Mrs Conckling reminds me of Nannie Salter (thin face, doesn't smile, religious and a bit grim) and Mrs Sherwin reminds me of Nannie Wakefield (silver hair, lovely smile, likes me and is good company).

29 Thu: Last night mum + dad came up to tell me that dad is no longer a Pru Agent, but now he is a

Cargo Checker at Runcorn Docks. He likes it very much. I thought he liked being an insurance agent. Oh dear, has he been sacked aga again? No one is saying.[70] This time last week was mum's birthday. I am so fed-up with Crossley. I do so want to go home + be with people I love. Oh! I do love mummy, daddy + Sandra so much.

30 Fri: I had very good news in a letter from mummy. She rang up Dr Erwin + he said that definitely I will be home within 2 months! Oh I am happy! Only 9 weeks, or about 60 days! I will be glad to leave this hateful place. Also I can have leave from Thursday morning to Friday evening, wish I had longer. Still I'll be home for my birthday. He also said that my x-ray had improved very much indeed. I have decided that I will stay up here in my single even if Mave leaves and Dr E says I can go back to the middle floor. I don't have

[70] *Dad's change of job: When my parents told me dad had left the Prudential Insurance Company to work as a checker on Runcorn Docks, I was not convinced it was his choice. Why would he want to leave his sociable job as an insurance agent, travelling by car, to work outside in all weathers, for less money? It certainly did not give him the freedom to bring my mother to see me on Wednesdays as his old job had. I suspected he had been sacked, yet again, but it was not presented to me like that and I chose not to ask questions. Because my dad had promised God that he would stop drinking if God would make me better, I think there was a part of me that feared that if he did not stop drinking, I would not get better, so I really was afraid to know the truth.*

any friends here now so I might as well be by myself anyway.

OCTOBER 1960

Sat 1: <u>Visiting</u> Went home for a meal – fish + chips! I enjoyed it. Nannie came up at 3.00. She said she liked to "visit" at 58 Vic Rd rather than at Crossley as well! Mummy is off work, she's worn out and she's been overtired + unwell lately. I feel as if it's my fault. I hope it isn't. Daddy likes his new job, I'm glad to say. I'm so depressed now (8.25). I've been crying off and on all night. Mave was nasty to me again in the canteen. Why won't she leave me alone? I thought she'd have had her date by now. Maybe all that carrying on has set her back. I know I've only 2 months to do, but I still feel awfully unhappy.

2 Sun: <u>Weight</u> 7st 10 ¾ lbs <u>Gain</u> 1 lb It was church this morning, 6 of us went, all female. If Mave had been there, I'd have left. <u>Visiting</u> Mummy + daddy came. I didn't go home because Sandra's doing her homework. It was a good job we hadn't planned to go out as it was very cold and wet. I enjoyed visiting very much indeed. The only time I am happy. I am really looking forward to Thurs when I go home! <u>Didn't</u> get miz. at night!

3 Mon: Messed around all day. It was rather cold + drizzly, so after dinner I got into bed + read the third Whiteoak[71] book "Young Renny". It was

---

[71] *The Whiteoak Saga by Mazo de la Roche: I was obsessed with the characters and their exciting, passionate lives. Throughout the diary, there are references to them as I steadily read my way through all 16 novels.*

super. I couldn't stop reading it. Each one I get I like more! Went down to Grotes after tea. Judy was there. She said Tony's left. Mave is back to one hour. I don't care if she's had a setback but I wish she was well enough to leave. I'd finished two of my purses and Miss G put press studs on them for me. The day passed quite quickly + happily for once. I enjoyed the T.V. at night very much indeed. I like "River Boat", set in old America – sort of "Wagon Train" on water! Now I have a T.V. in my room all the time, I find the evenings easier.

4 Tue: Today it is rather warm. When the sun goes in it is chilly though. Oh! I am looking forward to going home. Dr Kirkpatrick said that instead of going home on Thursday morning, I can go on Wed evening as soon as I've had my PAS. Yipee! Roll on tomorrow. I suppose it is because I feel more content now that I know I'm going home, but the days go quicker and I'm happier again.

5 Wed: Mrs de H came again. I will have to learn my French (+ Latin) very well to catch up with 3A. How can I? I must not think about what that means. Visiting Mummy came but not until the 3.00 bus. We were so excited about my leave that we could hardly talk! Mum went back on the bus then, at 6.30, daddy + Sandra came to collect me! When we got home Barry was there. He says I look so well he'll go out with me instead of Sandra! We all talked + played records till 9.00. Very nice!

Thu 6: Woke up at ¼ to 7! Had breakfast in bed. Went to Liverpool on 10 to 10 train with mummy + Nannie. I got a new dress in greens, blues + mauves with ¾ sleeves and a full skirt. It is a winter dress, but it is made in thick cotton. It had a blue belt with it so I wear that or a gold belt I got off Gran + G'dad S (for my birthday). Had hair cut at Andre Bernards[72] (as did mum). Washed it + Sandra set it. Looks v. nice. Mum dad Sandra + I went to see "Who was that lady" at Empress. Very good, we all laughed at it a lot. Can't remember the last time we ALL went to the pictures together. Super day.

Fri 7: MY BIRTHDAY! I am 14!! Breakfast in bed. Went to nans at 12.00, had dinner, saw all relations. Wore my new shoes. Very pointed, in black leather. Only a low heel, but it is shaped. They are lovely! So many people came in the afternoon with presents for me. After school, Susan plus EIGHT other school friends + cousin Valerie, all came to see me! Had an informal party. Lots to eat and drink – but no alcohol like in Crossley!! I

---

[72] _Andre Bernard was an expensive and well-regarded hairdresser in Liverpool (with, I believe, another place in Sheffield, and, it was rumoured, in London). I was always taken there to have my very thick, very curly hair cut, even though it cost a lot and meant a journey by train to Liverpool, because my mother was convinced that it was a cheap, local, hairdresser's cutting of my sister's baby curls that had left her with just wavy hair. In fact, my hair would have stayed frizzy and wild, whoever cut it. Even when I paid to have it straightened (twice) at Andre Bernards when a student in the late1960s, it remained very very curly. One claim to fame Andre Bernards had was that in about 1963, Ringo Starr, who had just joined the Beatles, was filmed having his hair cut there and fooling around with shampoo suds._

was dressed up (new dress + shoes + hair) they were in uniform. I felt the grown up one for once! Had a marvellous birthday. Really enjoyed it. Got 34 cards. Returned to Crossley at 8.30. My newspaper horoscope for week of 5th to 12th said: "LIBRA – Sept. 23 to Oct 22 Little if anything interferes with your programme. Home incidents that please you are indicated, and some unexpected happy occasion may well be in the offing. A gift, news and a romantic tinge about your week. Lucky birthday, 7 Oct." All true so far so who knows the romantic bit might be by the 12th!!

8 Sat: Can't list all the things I got, but I loved them all!   Visiting Mummy, daddy + Sandra came. I enjoyed it + although it was my first day back off my leave, we weren't very depressed. We talked about my leave + I think everyone enjoyed it as much as me. It was perfect! Watched T.V. at night. It was quite a good programme. Wasn't too upset at being back. I'm used to it now.

9 Sun: Weight 7st-8 ½ lbs Lost 2 ¼ lbs. Oh! Oh! I lost. Never mind, I'll soon replace it. Visiting Just mummy + daddy came. I love it when there is only my family, no other friends or relatives. The weather is bitterly cold + up here it is very cold inside because the radiators on the corridor aren't working. I woke up with a cold last Thursday so I didn't get it at home, but today it is much better. Yesterday it was quite heavy. Wore new clothes today.   I collected lots of compliments in the canteen (except, of course, from you know who).

10 Mon: School again! We did Geography, Canada. I'd like to go there. Sometimes I think I'll never catch up at school in Biol + Chem + Phys which I haven't done here at all. Oh! Well! Too bad! Now that I'm in a single, we do all my lessons here. I miss not going to the school room but at least it means I don't have to worry about bumping into Mave when I'm by myself. I got into bed after dinner + had my tea in bed! It's very cold and anyway I'm trying to get rid of my cold. Read a book called "The Feast of July" by H.E. Bates. It had a good plot (about a young woman who is "seduced" by an older man (!) so love and tragedy) but it wasn't well written. In the evening, went to the film "Baby + Battleship" it was a bit silly – you couldn't really hide a baby on a ship – but funny.

11 Tues: I got the next Whiteoak book "Whiteoak Heritage" out of Crossley Library. Went to bed in the afternoon + read it. Finished it now! It was great! Wish I was a grown up and in love! I also had to do some of my French Homework. I left it a bit late this week with going home + I couldn't quite finish it. There was a very good play on T.V. (I.T.V) tonight, called "The Pets" by Robert Shaw. I thought it was terrific. The mad German kept two RAF pilots locked in his cellar for years and didn't tell them when the war was over! It made me wonder how I'd feel if I found out I'd been locked up here when I needn't have been.

12 Wed: Mrs de H came once more. It's a hard morning's work, but in a way I quite enjoy it! She's nicer now also! Mummy came by herself on the bus. We had a lovely long chat. I like it when we natter all afternoon. I do love mummy + daddy + Sandra. I do so hope that I can go home in 6 weeks. Now after Wed visiting, there is something to take my mind off how unhappy I am. Dr Erwin gave his first talk on the earphones about T.B.[73] from 5 to 6. It was very interesting. He said in the past we'd all have died out with T.B. so by keeping us alive he might be interfering with evolution!! Charming! Film in the evening – "Spanish Gardener" Dirk Bogard – very good. He is very handsome. No wonder the young boy enjoyed spending time with him rather than with his dad. Cold has gone.

13 Thu: Hurrah! Hurrah! Hurrah! Only 6 more weeks to do now, providing nothing goes wrong + Dr Erwin keeps his word. I haven't got 10 hours yet + it worries me in case I don't get out on time. I must! I must! If I didn't I'm sure mummy would make herself ill with worry. As long as I'm out for Christmas, I don't really mind much. Must just wait + see!

14 Fri: Feel rather fed-up today because I keep thinking "This time last week I was at home." I try

---

[73] *Dr Erwin's talks on TB: These were no doubt well-meant attempts to educate us about tuberculosis but to start with telling patients that he had moral qualms about making us better was odd. I remember he said that by making us well enough to leave and perhaps have children of our own, he was contributing to damaging future generations as 'natural selection' meant the weak should die out and the strong dominate.*

not to, but I feel miz.! Did some of my matchboxes. Read a bit of "Sherlock Holmes" then went for a walk. It's the first time I've been out for a week. Did not see anyone. Visiting tomorrow. Good! We've got two new patients – Mrs White (65ish very ill) and Mrs Kirkpatrick (77, not v. ill, an "amenity patient" whatever that is). She is Dr Kilpatrick's mother! Got a letter from Wong asking me to write to him. Don't know what to do. I don't really want anything to do with him 'cos of the Mave business, although it was mainly Tony then I think. Would be nice to have a boy to write to though and a friend here to walk with.

15 Sat: <u>Visiting</u> Mummy, daddy + Sandra came + because they ran out of petrol it was 2.30 by the time they got here. I don't really know why, but I couldn't be bothered to be nice + they all irritated me. They asked me why + somehow they thought it was because I hadn't got 10hrs. Perhaps it was. Sometimes I just run out of the energy to be positive and pleasant. Anyway I felt terribly sorry and ashamed of myself afterwards + I've written a letter to them which I'll give them tomorrow. I went to see Mrs Kirkpatrick - Mrs White is too ill to see anyone - but I didn't stay long. She thought I was her granddaughter!

16 Sun: Weight 7st -10lb Gain 1 ½ lbs Church today. Only 4 there this week. I prayed for God to help me be more cheerful. <u>Visiting</u> Mummy, daddy + Nannie Salter came. We all enjoyed visiting I think. I know I did. I am awfully sorry about yesterday but my wonderfully kind parents are pretending it never happened (well, at least while Nannie S is there). I was chatty + pleasant. (I wish I had been yesterday.) Nannie liked my new shoes, dress + hair. I <u>feel</u> great in them + everyone says I look it! (Big 'ead B.S.!) At night I thanked God for helping me. I am happier when I am nice. I will try hard to be cheerful in every visiting.

17 Mon: It was pictures tonight "The Black Tent" starring Anthony Steele - I enjoyed it - romantic in parts! He is quite good looking. I'm glad Judy likes films too. I look forward to sitting next to her, with Connie on her other side of course. I have kept a note to Wong in my pocket but couldn't give it 'cos he wasn't there. It says "Sorry I will not write to you as I am already writing to someone else hope you don't mind etc." I'm not writing to anyone but that's what Kenny said to us. I decided not to write (a) might get into trouble (b) think he wrote to Judy also (c) he went with Mave (I think) (d) his English isn't very good (e) do not even like him (He's 23!)

18 Tue: The day passed quite well on the whole. I read "Whiteoak Bros" all afternoon + at night. It's a great book. I love them all in the saga. I only watched Emergency Ward 10, then I turned the T.V. off + listened to the Everley Bros on Mrs Sherwin's wireless. She is my favourite and only friend here. Finished my book at 9.30. (Then wrote this!) Today I've been in a "wish-I-was-in-love" mood + I've felt dare-devilish. (Nothing happened!) I think I do like Dave from the office + even in a group when he speaks he looks at me!

19 Wed: Mrs de H came. We did LATIN from 9.00 'till 11.25! Then French 'till ¼ to 12. <u>Visiting</u> Mummy + Nannie W came on the 2.00 bus. I enjoyed visiting very much + we all had a good chat. I got a new, lovely yellow teapot to match my birthday yellow cup + saucer. I make tea for "my ladies" in the singles as well as for me most afternoons. At night I went to the pictures. "A Man without a Star" starring Kirk Douglas was on. It was a cowboy + not very good really. Hurrah! Hurrah! Judy told me Mave has left! Don't know if she's gone home or to another hospital. Don't care. Dr Erwin 2nd TALK on T.B. Very good. Called "Environment" About how you get and catch and spread T.B. I enjoy them. No one else does! We're all supposed to listen but Judy said they don't in her ward.

20 Thu: Oh! Today was a long day. It seemed about two days, not one! Not sure why. I thought I'd be happier now Mave has gone. Actually, it makes no difference to me now. I'd rather stay up here till I leave. I am reading a book set in old China called "Pavilion of Women" by Pearl S Buck. It is very good + I am enjoying it. Especially as it's about China – Wong etc! Not that I like him but I wish I could ask him about China. Went out in the afternoon for a walk by myself + didn't see anyone else at all. I hoped to see Wong but only to explain why I'm not writing as I haven't had chance so far. IF his English was better, I'd like to talk to him about China but he might think I am being "friendly" like Mave was and I do NOT want that.

21 Fri: Jack, dad's friend, went home, so he + Kenny came round with the tea! I wondered who they were + where I was, being woken by men's voices! (Yes, I'd nodded off 'cos I was in bed reading!) They don't usually come to the Top Floor. They did it just for me! Dr Erwin did his round + I got 10 HOURS! In four weeks I will get 12 hours then I'll go home, he said! He was awfully nice + chatty. I still don't like him though, especially since the Mave business. I feel much more certain that I am going home in about 6 weeks now. Very pleased.

22 Sat: Got up at 10.00 and went to the shop – lovely to be up in the morning, but I don't feel like getting up at 10.00 back at 11.00 for rest hour, up at 12.00 again though! <u>Visiting</u> Just daddy + Sandra came + we all enjoyed ourselves. We played ping-pong! Sandra won 2, so did I, Dad lost all. I'm glad visiting wasn't like last week. I wrote + apologised about it + they all accepted my apology but I still worry about it. I showed Sandra Wong's letter, she agreed I better not write.

23 Sun: Weight- 7st – 12lbs Gain 2 lbs (Cor! I'll soon be 8st!!) <u>Visiting</u> I met the car + went home! It was great! For tea I had chips 'n' chicken which I love. Saw Sandra before she went out with Barry at 2.30. I'd already had a talk to him while he was waiting. Gave daddy his (part of) present – a casket of matchboxes made by me, to put cufflinks in, like a little chest of drawers, covered in wood effect Fablon. It's dead easy to use 'cos sticky once you peel off the backing paper. Between us Sandra + I got him a tie to go with his best suit. Mum gave him shoes + got his watch mended.

24 Mon: Geography! Test on Wednesday! I do find it hard to learn now, I've nearly forgotten how to! I am making a lampshade in black + yellow raffia. It will go with the mats I made for mummy's birthday. Also I am knitting a tea cosy cover to go over the old stained one. The stripes go smaller to the top + it will be drawn up by a string. It's my own pattern! Film "The Kidnappers" at night. V. good. The boys accidentally kidnap a baby cos they can't have a dog!! I can't wait to be with Scamp again! Daddy's birthday. Wish I was home for it.

25 Tue: This morning for the first time we did biol – PHOTOSYTHESIS! Ooh! It was complicated, especially as it's nearly a year since I did any! Sandra had her interview at Sheffield Training College last week. Mum said on Sunday it was so awful Sandra couldn't face going to Speech day when she got back on Friday. She wasn't expecting a prize or due a certificate so it didn't matter. Last year at Speech Day I got the Prize for Progress – "1066 And All That". This year I'd be getting the Prize for LACK of Progress!!

26 Wed: No Mrs de H as she's on holiday so Mrs Mawson gave me a Geog + a Hist test – both long and hard. I got 95% for History + 98.6% for Geog! I was pleased! I don't think she marks as hard as the teachers at school. <u>Visiting</u> Just mummy came on the 2.00 bus. We had a gorgeous chat + a "cuppa" out of the new pot. Poor mummy, she was very cold coming and it was even colder when she left. Dr

Erwin talk (5-6) was about "Symptoms" of T.B. I felt quite sick as he discussed coughing, sputum, blood spitting, sweating + vomit!!! I am SO lucky not to have been really ill at all. Just a bit sweaty at first.

27 Thu: Today when we were waiting to go into dinner Dave went past + he said "Hello" looking <u>straight</u> <u>at</u> <u>me</u>! It's funny but he always looks at me even if I'm in a gang. I do like him, not soppy-fied just "I-wish-he'd-take-more-notice-of-me-ish" I've nearly done half of my tea-cosy cover. The lamp-shade is awfully difficult! It's sending me scatty. I gave up with the other raffia one I tried. Try, Try + Try again!!! Hope mum will like it!

28 Fri: Mrs Conckling went to her nursing home today at 2.00. She will get there at about 5.00. It's a long journey by herself. She gave me a ½ lb box of "Weekend" and a silver spoon. She was sad. She hoped she was going to live with her son. I do like Dave. He spoke to me two times today! Going into tea Wong was talking to me (first time since letter). He acted as if he never sent it. Then he went into the Men's Door. Dave then came along + he spoke to me – my two (imaginary) boyfriends within minutes! I sat with Mrs Sherwin for ages at night. She is very upset about Mrs Conckling leaving. They were proper friends. She said Mrs C didn't want to go. I felt very sad for both of them.

29 Sat: <u>Visiting</u> Mummy, daddy, Sandra + Nannie W came. We had a good chat, then mummy + Nannie went back with daddy. I liked my chat just with Sandra. Valerie returned with daddy. A visit at last! It was nice to see her again after all this time. We had a good talk. She is very pretty now + her eyes are gorgeous – really blue – and she seems more grown up. At night I felt a very low and lonely but I shook it off. I don't really know why I did as it was visiting and again tomorrow and home in about 6 weeks. Mrs White died. Good job I didn't get to know her. Another trolley.

30 Sun: Weight 7st-12lbs Gain 0 Loss 0 OK my weight stayed the same. <u>Visiting</u> I met the car and went home for tea. We had my favourite chicken'n'chips'n'peas – gorgeous! Mummy's friend Mrs Fenton called in with Tracy (now 7). I felt really glad that no one is worried about young children near me anymore. If they were listening to Dr E's talks, maybe they still would be!

31 Mon: Half-term! I finished my tea-cosy yesterday and took it home. Mrs Sherwin is very fed-up today. I think she misses Mrs Conkling a great deal. I'm not much company for her, I'm too young. Also she has still not heard whether she will need an operation on her gall-bladder. The film was "Brothers-in-law" starring Ian Carmichal, Terry Thomas and Richard Attenborough. Funny bits in Court but I've seen it before. Hallow e'en – nothing happened. So many have died even just since I've been up here, I'm surprised the corridor wasn't full of ghosts tonight.

NOVEMBER 1960

1 Tue: Mrs Sherwin is still very very cheesed-off. I think she misses Mrs Conkling more than she admits. She is also very worried about her gall bladder op. There is no point getting to know people here. They leave or die or you do. Nothing special happened today, in fact it was a pretty rotten day altogether. Listened to the Everly Brothers again tonight on Mrs S's radio. They are on every week from 8-8.15 with Connie Francis (ugh!) Fortunately they play more Evs than F's. I love Don + Phil!! Mrs S thinks it's funny how "gone" I am on them but she says she was like that at my age. I like her very much. I do hope she doesn't die while I'm still here.

2 Wed: Mrs de H came. I think I've gone and forgotten everything again! I was pretty hopeless this morning. <u>Visiting</u> Mummy came. We had a lovely visit. I think since the Saturday I got worked up, we have enjoyed visiting much more. Two weeks today mummy is going to see Dr Erwin to see when I am coming home, definitely! Not just "a few more weeks" but a specific date! Film – "It's a Wonderful World" Rotten film apart from James Stewart. Stupid story I just did not believe it.

3 Thu: I'm sick and tired of this place. Still it won't be long now. 5 weeks more, if Dr Erwin keeps his word and I'm out on Dec 7th – one year to the day since I arrived! 4 wks if I'm on 12 hrs for only 2 weeks. I hope it is the fastest one that will come true, naturally! Oh! these last weeks seem like years! I must be patient, just think only a few weeks and I'll be home! I pray every night that this will come true. Even this close, some people have a flare-up or a set-back and are told they have to have an op after all. PLEASE don't let that be me.

4 Fri: Hell! Hell! Hell! I'm as miserable as anything today. They have left me out of the Bonfire preparations. I've not been given any fireworks. Connie is having one of her "catty-to-me" doos. I wish she'd stop it! She acts as if it's my choice I'm up here (well, it wasn't at first). Said I'm a snob! And other nasty things. How she can say I'm getting special treatment, I do not know. I came up from dinner + had a good cry to relieve my feelings. We've got a new patient, a German woman, Mrs Bracks, she is 58. She's had her lung out. (Cancer not T.B.) She looks awfully ill. I feel sorry for her but I don't want to risk getting to know her. It's too late.

5 Sat: Visiting Sandra + daddy came. I had my hair ready washed + Sandra set it for me. By 2.30 it had been set, dried + brushed! We had a lovely time, talking fast + furious! In the evening, they had a big, big bon-fire here + very expensive fireworks. They gave everyone toffee + 2 fireworks! Including me! I quite enjoyed myself. Talked to Wong for a long time! Judy was with catty Connie so I stayed well clear.

6 Sun: Weight 7st-11 ½ lbs Lost ½ lb Visiting Mummy + daddy came. I thoroughly enjoyed the whole afternoon. We (=they) have decided I am not going to go home unofficially until I go home for good officially, as the weather is too chancy + I may get caught in the rain. But we still went out! After the delicious roast dinner they brought we went for a ride around the forest "switch-back". It was great! I love it when daddy drives really fast up and my stomach flips on the way down! Like the fair. We didn't get out. We were only out from 3.15 to ¼ to 4 then we came back + had a cup of tea.

7 Mon: Dr Erwin came to see Mrs Sherwin this morning to tell her that she could go home on Friday, + that she doesn't need an operation on her gall-bladder. I am very pleased for her, but I really shall miss her. Just think – no one at all to talk to! I'll really go mad!   The film was "Blind Date" a thriller starring Hardy Kruger + Stanley Baxter. H K is a dream – he's great! I thought I liked dark hair best but maybe not!! No wonder she had him as her lover!!

8 Tues: Today I heard that Sally Steven's husband has died. Sally went home for good only about a week last Friday + he died last Saturday. I think it is an awful shame. She has been in hospital 18 months, had two serious operations and has just been waiting to go home and then when she does, this car accident has to happen. Their poor children. I do not understand why this should happen as she + he are both very, very nice good people. It makes me doubt that God is good. We collected for a wreath. Judy and Connie are especially cut up about it as they are all close friends.

9 Wed: Mrs de H didn't come so I had to do the work by myself. She wrote to tell me she wouldn't be coming + set me work – quite a lot as well!

<u>Visiting</u> Mummy came. I had to sell poppies for Remembrance Day in visiting by going round all the wards so mum went to see Dr Erwin. He said I am to ask him for my date when he does his rounds! I hope he soon comes round. He also said when I go home I'm to act as if I'm on school holidays. Not ill or convalescing! He shook hands with mum + said about the chest clinic + I can go to school after Christmas! I wish he'd do a round tomorrow! He also said I'd still be out in about 2 months from when he said. So I've only got about 2 weeks more to do! Yipee!!! Film "Long Arm" thriller starring Jack Hawkins. About safe-breakers. V. good! I didn't think Judy and Connie would go because they are still both upset for Sally but they did. Catty Connie is O.K. with me again but will it last?

10 Thu: Tomorrow is Mrs Sherwin's last day. I thought she'd be really happy to be going home. She said she is glad she doesn't need an operation but she knows she'll never be really well again. At least she's going to her daughters to live, not into a nursing home like poor Mrs Conckling. In the afternoon I went in + talked to her. I stayed for ages. Gosh! I shall miss her.

11 Fri: Mrs Sherwin went at 11.00. She gave me ½ lb box of chocs (also ¾ pkt Lux soap + some sugar she had left!). I gave her a lovely brooch, a bird in sort of marquesite Mummy chose. She got a bit upset when she was going because everyone told her how much she will be missed because she is so nice. I think she was sad to leave all her friends here. I was upset she was going. She's been here 18

months! That's a long time for a TB, but AGES for
a non-TB. I think cancer must be as bad but in a
different way. No one with it up here is young so
maybe only old folk get it.

12 Sat: <u>Visiting</u> Dad and Sandra came. Sandra set
my hair, as last week, + while I was under the dryer,
I ate 3 hot dogs! They were really tasty! They were
pleased with what Dr Erwin said and of course we
are now waiting impatiently for him to come round!
The television at night was very good. I watched the
"Remembrance Festival" on T.V. I always watch it
with mummy so I was a bit sad I was by myself this
year but it was still good. Also the Bob Hope show,
a skit on U.S. elections (John Kennedy, a Roman
Catholic, got in) was funny. I cannot bear the
thought of next week without even Mrs Sherwin for
company. I managed not to cry about it in visiting.
I did in the evening. I am so lonely and I miss my
family so much.

13 Sun: I haven't been weighed. No one came for
me. <u>Church</u> Only Connie + I went. She was nice to
me! <u>Visiting</u> Mummy + daddy came. Nannie Salter
was going to have come but they said not to as it is
very cold and it's a long way from Widnes without
a car. We like our little chats together best. Boy!
We talked non-stop from 2.00 until 4.40! Nannie S
sent a <u>home-made</u> malt loaf! I wish I could share it
with Mrs S. I was going to see Mrs Bracks the
German lady but Sister said she was too poorly so I
couldn't.

14 Mon: Mrs Mawson told me today that a male
maths teacher came on Sat to teach me, but he went

to Kenny + Judy instead! Fancy Judy not saying anything about him! When I mentioned it at the dinner table + that I was supposed to have lessons catty Connie set on me. "Judy has got as much right as anyone (sneer) to have lessons" etc "He's too advanced for you" etc Ooh! I hate them. To work off my temper I did 2 maps + 1 graph for geog. Then 2 Latin exercises! Film in the evening was a rotten cowboy - lousy! Sat by myself. Not happy.

15 Tue: I felt really fed-up after dinner, and I had a good cry. Then I wrote two letters to cheer myself up. At about 2.10 I went for an exam from Dr Kirkpatrick. He said I was "as fit as a flea" + he gave me my 12 hours (which I was due for) + I start them on Friday. I am making a lampshade in yellow raffia for Sandra's bedroom. It is chimney shape. Mrs Bracks died. I don't want to know anyone anymore, not this near to going home.

16 Wed: Mrs de H came. She always leaves me depressed, I don't really know why! I think it's 'cos she tells me how bad I am at French! Mrs Mawson is probably too soft on me. Visiting Mummy came. Nannie had sent me my tea, which was 2 pork chops, and 3 potatoes in their jackets! Delicious! I was absolutely famished as well because the food here is even worse now than when I first came. Plus I don't eat much in the canteen when Connie is having one of her goes at me. We had a lovely visiting but in a way we couldn't settle because we were wondering when Dr Erwin would do a round! Still, we had a good chatter + I enjoyed it. "Rainbow Jacket" was the picture tonight. It is about a young boy who becomes a jockey and the man who trains him. V good. Once it started, I didn't mind being there "by myself" cos I was so worried about what was happening to the lad.

17 Thu: Dr Erwin did a round this morning and he said that I can go home on DEC 10th providing my final x-ray on 6th Dec. is all right + as the others were, there is no reason to believe this one won't be! Yipee! 3 weeks more, but boy! am I thrilled. I got the office to ring home + tell them I was fed-up + could they come up + cheer me up! They came at 7.10 – worried! When I told them, they were thrilled, but, like me, a bit disappointed at in 3 weeks time, until we all realised how lucky I was. I AM GOING HOME!!

18 Fri: Started my 12 HOURS today!! Today I am still more or less riding along on the crest of my "going-home-on-10th-ish" wave! I finished my lamp-shade. I finished it on Tuesday really, but I undid some of it. It is quite hard to make it straight. I also at last made a red purse that had been waiting to be sewn up for about 2 months! I'm reading a great book at the moment "A Town Like Alice" by Nevil Shute. It's super. Really sad about the Japanese in the war but a lot of love and passion too. Three meals in the canteen now! Actually, I think I prefer breakfast in bed!

19 Sat: Up for breakfast again. I don't mind getting up really, just so long as someone remembers to wake me up! If not! Oh! Dear! What a rush OR no breakfast! Visiting Sandra and daddy came. Wendy was going to come but she got a cold + I don't want to risk it now! For tea I had 2 potatoes cakes, 2 bowls of soup, 2 apple slices and a custard. I <u>did</u> enjoy it!!! Must keep on putting on weight. The T.V. at night was good. "Perry Como Show" + Fabian, Frankie Avalon + Shelly Burman! It's better than just sitting here but I can't wait to watch T.V. at home with mummy! P.C. is one of her favourites (not mine but I do like Fabian!).

20 Sun: Weight 7st-12 ½ lbs Gain ¾ lb No church or I'd have gone to give thanks. I spent the whole of the morning packing a case to send home (I'm not sure whether it's the 3rd or 4th one! Plus a cardboard box full!!) <u>Visiting</u> Mummy + daddy came. We didn't go out, it is too cold now. I enjoyed visiting very much. I had my usual delicious roast. We are all looking forward to Dec 10th. Yipee! Roll along Sat 10th Dec at 9.00!!!

21 Mon: Mrs Mawson didn't come today. I do hope she is not ill. I miss her. I look forward to talking to her even more since I've been up here and since Mrs Sherwin left. The day has gone very slowly, mainly because of no school, even though I did some lessons alone. Also I have finally finished all my handicrafts and I don't want to start anything else. This time next week I'll be able to say This time next week I'll be able to say - home next week!!!! "I'm All Right Jack" Peter Sellers, Ian Carmichel etc V.V. good V. V. funny! "Russia - all cornfields and ballet in the evening"!!

22 Tue: Still no Mrs Mawson. I did some more lessons by myself. I wonder what is the matter with her? Nothing serious I hope. It's a bit late but now I am wanting to work hard there's no teacher! I didn't feel a bit like writing any letters today, but I wrote home and (as I'd put it off yesterday) to Nannie W. As always, I felt better when I'd written. Telling them I'm fine makes me feel fine! Visiting again tomorrow, thank goodness. It seems weeks since I saw mummy and daddy + Sandra! Each day is like a month.

23 Wed: Ooh! Ugh! Ugh! Ugh! I feel rotten today. I've got awful diarriah (on the toilet for 20 mins at one time!) + I feel sick + fainty. I couldn't go down to breakfast, couldn't get up. Mrs de Hout came but we couldn't get much done I kept feeling ill. I do hope it's only P.A.S. but I've been on it for ages already. If it isn't . . . .   I've seen other people doing well then really close to going home have a set back and be told they have to have an op. Please God no, not that.   <u>Visiting</u> Mummy + Nannie W came. I felt awful at being unable to eat the dinner they'd brought but I just couldn't. I hope mum doesn't worry. Dr Erwin's taken me off P.A.S., so it must be that. Didn't go to the pictures. Dr E's talk today was: going home, adolescence (cor – the sex stuff is true!) + "the future".

24 Thu: Calamity! When I woke up at 7.20 + took my temp it was 100! Then I had some more diarrehha . When I came back to bed. at 7.35 it was 99 and at 8.00 it was 98!! Boy was I relieved. Good job I'm allowed to do my own temp. up here! I was scared I was really ill. I went to meals for the company not food but got into bed in between. I feel better now, though I've got bad tummy ache still. My T.B. is in my lung like everyone else's here but Dr E said in his talk that you can get T.B. anywhere.[74] What if it's gone to my stomach or bowels? If it's spread or it's flared up in my lungs I might have to have an op and be here for months and months more. I'm back to worrying if I'll die. Mrs Mawson came but I wasn't fit for a lesson. Her two kids had had tonsilitas so she had to stay + look after them. Now I'm the one who is ill. At night Mummy + daddy came up as a surprise! I enjoyed seeing them but I'm so sorry I am worrying them. They left at 10.00 + no one saw them come or go! Temp at night was 99. I was honest and put it down. No one bothered about it. Thank goodness.

25 Fri: I feel fine today, I'm glad to say. My temp is normal. I've still got slight diarrhae but my tummy ache's all gone. I feel a bit hungrier as well! I'm back to thinking I am still on track to leave! I did lessons from 9.00 till 11.00 with Mrs Mawson. We got quite a lot done. This afternoon went by quite quickly. The T.V. was good at night + I watched until 10.30. No one bothers about lights out up here. I would really go mad without the T.V. to keep me company at night. I usually watch til late.

---

[74] _Other forms of TB:_ _This was the first time I realised that TB was not just a disease of the lungs and could also affect more than growth. The thought terrified me. The NHS website says that TB infections are much less common outside the lungs but can occur in the lymph glands, the bones and joints, the digestive system, the bladder and elsewhere._

26 Sat: I had maths lessons with the new Male Maths Master. Not TOO bad. What a lot of maths I don't know! <u>Visiting</u> Sandra, daddy + Wendy came. Then Susan + the school gang arrived at about 3.15. They looked very old, and were all smartly dressed in tight skirts. Wendy looked her age more so more like me. It was nice to see them but I missed my little private talk with Sandra. They left me, as usual, feeling depressed, with an inferiority complex + sure I will never catch up in school work.

27 Sun: Weight 7st 11 ½ lbs Lost 1lb (A lie!) I'm really only 7-9 ½ but I didn't dare tell! Good job they leave me to weigh myself up here now. It's because of my diarreha + not eating. No one checks. <u>Visiting</u> Mummy + daddy came. I feel fine again today but not awfully hungry still. We went out for a little run in the car in the afternoon. I enjoyed visiting very much. I do love them so. Just think! In 13 more days I'll be with them at home!

28 Mon: No Mrs Mawson again. I wonder why? I hope she hasn't got tonsillitis now! Or caught my tummy bug. I have felt rather fed-up all today. It is because I realise how different I am from the girls at school + I'm miles behind in my school work. They are self-confident + have boyfriends. I'm shy + I've never had a boy. They talk about people + things I don't know but I musn't talk about the hospital or I'll bore them. I feel really frightened to face school + everything now. I must just think once I am home my family will back me up. Film "Blue Peter" was very good. Made me think about how people overcome horrible experiences – he was a P.O.W. – by helping others.

29 Tues: All today I have been thinking about going home + to be quite honest I have been a bit worried. You see, I'm sort of frightened to face all those people. I know they mean well, but I'm awfully shy. Also I don't think I'll ever catch up at school, or be in the same groove as my friends. I noticed how different from them I am. I don't like the same things + we don't have anything in common anymore. Also, I worry if I'll stay well when I'm leading a normal life again. People have break downs and end up back here.

30 Wed: Mrs de H came. We got an awful lot done and I could remember things better + she said my homework was good! It must be the effect of no drugs. I've been off them for a week now. <u>Visiting</u> Just mummy came. We had a nice chat but I had to tell her what was worrying me. (See Tues) She has set my mind at rest a lot. She said if I could do this year, I could do going back to school. Plus I never had T.B. very badly and I've done well to get better so quickly. I hope she is right. Pictures – "Quartet" 4 plays by Somerset Maughan were on. I enjoyed them. Felt so sorry for the musician who found he wasn't good enough to fulfil his dreams.

DECEMBER 1960

1 Thu: Dr Erwin did a round this morning. He was very nice and chatty and said "Not long now" etc. In the afternoon I just read "The Loving Spirit" by Daphne du Maurier – another family saga - and messed about generally. Thank goodness I can lose myself in a good book. I also like the Emily Bronte poem mentioned. All day I have been thinking "wish it was this time next week". I feel very impatient, but happy all the same. Excited but scared too. I enjoyed the T.V at night, "Citizen James" is funny. He was in Hancock before.

2 Fri: Oh, as the days go by I feel very, very, very, very, very excited! Yipee! This time next week it will be my <u>last</u> day! I made my bed here for the last time with clean sheets! Yipeeeeeeeeeeeee! I did some homework in the afternoon and read. After tea I cleaned the gramophone with a damp cloth and DAZ. It looks much better now. I played some records this afternoon. I used to like it when we played records in the 6-bedder with super Sarah. Now, I enjoy playing just for me.

3 Sat: Last <u>SATURDAY VISITING</u>! Daddy + Sandra came. Sandra set my hair. I really enjoyed it and we all kept saying "Next week we'll be at <u>home</u>!" Oh! I <u>am</u> excited. I sent home a lot more things as I don't want to have to take a lot with me when I actually go. As I watched T.V. at night, I was thinking - "This time next week – " Couldn't concentrate!

4 Sun: Weight 7st-11lbs Lost ½ lb Still a lie! I gained 1lb, I'm now 7st-10 ½ lbs but I'm not telling them (last time I'll be weighed). Last <u>SUNDAY VISITING</u>! Mummy and daddy came and we had a jolly good chat – mostly about 10th Dec! Natch! Ooh! I am getting excited – only 6 more days! Yipee! I sent home all my plants, another case of things and the bookshelf. We should be O.K. now, just one case on THE DAY.

5 Mon: The day dragged like hell! "Time goes by so slowly etc" Sure thing! I keep on singing "Unchained Melody"! I made three little red leather photo frames out of a pencil case that I had meant to make for months and had forgotten I even had! Anyway, I got fed-up with it and decided to make something different – my own design! They are quite nice really. Oh! I can't settle to any school work at all! Or reading. Or watching T.V. If it wasn't so cold, I'd walk and walk.

6 Tue: The film last night was "Aunt Clara". It was a peaceful kind of film, but slow. It was a comedy – but we ended up crying! One bit was about a brothel. I wonder if Mave is working in one now? I sat with Judy. She still doesn't know when she can go home. Neither does Connie. They were both here when I arrived. No homework done yet for Mrs de H. Naughty me! Today I have been very, very, very, bored and restless! I cannot settle to do anything (like yesterday!) and my Latin + French homework <u>still</u> hasn't been done. Had my (I hope) final x-ray today. Fingers crossed while she did it. Plus a prayer to God.

7 Wed: 12 months ago I became a T.B. patient in CROSSLEY. (3 more days to go + I'll no longer be a T.B. patient at Crossley). Mrs de H wasn't very cross really, she understood about the homework + my excitement. <u>Visiting</u> (For the very <u>last</u> time!) Mummy came + we had tea together. It was frosty + crisp and the sun was out so we then went for a walk. The grounds here are beautiful. I wish I'd seen them in snow just once, like in my dream before I came. Just think – next time I see her, I'll be going home! Roll on Saturday. In the evening, "The Card" with Alec Guiness + Petula Clarke. Very good. A funny film. Although the hero is a cheat and a liar he ends up happy and successful. (My last film here!) Connie said Pet Clarke had T.B.[75] – and look at her now! A good sign!

8 Thu: ONLY 2 DAYS TO GO! I started on PAS/INH cachets today. 10 a day are needed. They are bigger than a penny. They are made of rice paper. I have to dip them in water then swallow them whole. That makes them slippery. Fortunately, I don't find it difficult. I'm glad in a way I'm still on drugs, it makes me feel more secure. No more injections!! Oh! Roll on time! Somehow it doesn't seem real. Daily life here (naturally) is no different from any other day. Oh! only two more days now!

---

[75] <u>Petula Clark</u> told me on 24 Oct 2021 she did not ever have TB as I had been told. I'm glad for her but as I took great comfort from how lively and successful she was and it gave me hope for my own life ahead, I'm glad I didn't know that then!

9 Fri: THIS IS MY LAST DAY AT CROSSLEY! I am awfully happy! This is my happiest day for 12 months I'm sure! I even got my last wish – it has snowed. I went out in it, threw it, held it, washed my face in it. I am so happy, happy, happy! Life is great! Yipeeeeeeee! I don't care I'm not having a farewell party. Helen didn't and I can see why now.

10 Sat: HOME! Yipee! The snow was very thick up here, but at home there was none so they got here on time. Oh! I can hardly believe it – it is so marvellous! Home by 9.30., a cup of coffee, lunch and then in the afternoon we went down town to see the relatives etc. I am so very HAPPY! We managed to get everything left into my case but as we drove past the front of the hospital, Dorothy ran out – under the bed I'd left the old cardigan I sleep in! We had to stop and mummy went to get it. It spoiled my triumphal drive past but it made us all laugh.

11 Sun: Woke up in my own bed! Bliss! Stayed in all day as it is bitterly cold. I re-arranged the ornaments on my bedroom shelves. I have a lot of new ones to fit on but I don't want the old ones to feel rejected so took me ages. In the afternoon we watched T.V. (a change from visiting at Crossley) + afterwards mum + I emptied out some of my drawers. If I hadn't I would have been living out of a suitcase. I have grown out of ALL the clothes I had before Crossley. Anyway, they're too childish for me now. It is SOOOO lovely to be home!

12 Mon: In the morning mum + I went to Dr Staunton to get a prescription for my P.A.S./I.N.H cachets. In the afternoon I went to Valeries. We had the usual beans and sausages for tea. I enjoyed myself very much, it was "just like old times". Valerie is away from school at the moment with an abscess on her finger. It must be awfully painful for her but good for me she is at home. I think we still feel like good friends. I hope we are.

13 Tue: We set off to go to Liverpool but the fog was so bad we didn't go. Instead, in the afternoon mummy went to work + Daddy + I played "Kan-u-Go". I am managing to take my cachets all right – so far so good! The T.V. was good + "Whacko" was funny. I'd rather have Jimmy Edwards than Miss Bird in charge of our school! I am just starting to believe that I really am home for good and actually going back to school.

14 Wed: Today mummy, daddy + I went to Warrington in the car. We had a lovely time and we got most of the Christmas presents for people. This year, I will be home for it! The shops look very beautiful. I am VERY glad that I am not in hospital this year. At night we watched the T.V. warm + cosy round the fire! I went to bed early because I thought I was tired but got up later as I couldn't sleep. I am too excited!!

15 Thu: Mummy, daddy + I went for dinner to Nannie and Grandad Salters. I enjoyed the ride to Widnes! It was a delicious HUGE roast dinner. She is a good cook. I especially love her rice pudding! I ate the lot and lots of it. Waited an hour for the transporter bridge on the way back, there was such a long queue.[76] Home + T.V. at night. It is lovely to be here!

16 Fri: Today we (mummy, Nannie W + I) went to Liverpool. It was quite a nice day, but the trains were over 45 mins late even though no fog! Had my hair cut, not much, but it looks a lot better. We didn't really buy much. One important thing we did get was a pair of tan leather laced school shoes (size 7!) Another x-ray but this time in the shop and just of my feet! They are very nice even though they are school shoes! SCHOOL – yes!!

17 Sat: Mummy went to work. Sandra + I didn't go out at all, just lazed around. Sandra + Barry have had an argument so she didn't go out at night. I hope she makes up soon or I can see us not going to Barry's 21st party + I do want to. He rang her twice. She is hard-hearted!

---

[76] *Transporter: The Runcorn-Widnes Transporter Bridge linked the towns by crossing the River Mersey and Manchester Ship Canal. It consisted of a large platform, carrying cars, with a cabin for passengers down one side. Once loaded, the whole platform moved across the water, slung on cables from the overhead construction. It often broke down and, with its limited capacity, that led to long queues of vehicles waiting to get across. It also – I was told as a child – led to accidents when people, unused to the concept of a bridge that moved, drove on and off the other side into the water. How often that happened, I do not know but I remember playground talk at junior school that some American G.I.s from the base at Warrington had done just that.*

18 Sun: In the afternoon, Sandra, mummy + I went to a Carol Service at Bethesda. It was very good + we all enjoyed it. The church choir was very good and so were the soloists. Everyone was very nice to me + seemed genuinely pleased to see me. Mr Cooper announced (from the pulpit!) how glad they were to see me and (miracle!) I did not blush! I just said "Thank you" (I hope) graciously!

19 Mon: Got up quite late in the morning. At 12.00 I walked down town with mummy, she went to work + I went down to Nannies. I went shopping with Nannie + we picked up her Christmas Box to me – a white 50yd net can-can underskirt![77] It's lovely. I took Scamp with me + by the time we got home she was exhausted. I wasn't!

20 Tue: I went to the Christmas party at school. I got the 10.20 bus by myself which arrived 20 mins late + broke down on the way. When I arrived I saw Miss Bird, the Head Mistress, in the entrance by her study. She didn't speak to me and I was too shy. I then sat with the "gang" in the hall + watched a film about Norway. After, went to a French lesson. Sag (Miss Sanders) didn't notice me until half-way through! The party in the afternoon was great + everyone was very pleased to see me. I wore my birthday dress. Carol Service – very good.

---

[77] _Cancan underskirts:_ *In that period, it was the fashion to have a very full, net underskirt to hold out the gathered skirts of dresses with tight waists. The more yards the better. I later had a 100yd underskirt.*

21 Wed: At the Carol Service at Helsby last night I met Mrs Mawson. She told me that Kathleen from Crossley had died. I was awfully shocked and upset. Mrs Mawson said her family knew she was dying when she got married in the Summer. How awful. Her poor husband. Went to Vicky Rd to see Miss Collier. She was very nice but goodness she is a typical school marm – poor thing. She has been very good writing to me and sending the things. Mummy wanted me to go to see her so I did.

22 Thu: Sandra is on holiday today. We got up quite late, lazed around, and then had dinner. In the afternoon we went down town + got the rest of the presents. It was very Christmassy + we felt all jolly! I am looking forward to the party tomorrow but I feel nervous as I'm shy. I imagine Barry's "little" brother Billy to look like Richmal Crompton's "William". (He wasn't! He's nice.)

23 Fri: Barry's 21st Party. We went at 8.00. Sandra had her new sophisticated dress (black) and mummy her kingfisher one + I had on an old one of Sandra's, yellow nylon with black spots on it. Had my 50yd can-can underskirt on (off nan W). I looked lovely I was told –dress + figure + hair + me. Brother Billy (5th Form at Helsby Grammar School for Boys) danced every dance with me. I like him. Dark hair and blue eyes and a bit taller than me. He is very nice – no crush! Home at 12.00 to bed. Oh Had a marvellous time!!!!!!!!!!!!

24 Sat: Yesterday I went to see Dr Hughes with mummy. We waited from 9.30 to 12.15! However it was worth it as he told me that I can go back to school next term! Yipee! I am so pleased. Next check-up 27th Jan. I got up at 11.15 today. Morning after the night before! In the afternoon Sandra, daddy + I went delivering and collecting presents in the car! Lovely! At night two good films on T.V. "Gunga Din" with Carey Grant (fighting but interesting cos set in India) and Bing Crosby in "Bells of St Marys" (a nun and a priest try and stop a school closing but sort of a love story really). Daddy might have enjoyed them - war + India + R.C. priest and nun – but, of course, he was out. I've smelled whisky a couple of times but its Xmas.

25 Sun: I really enjoyed Christmas. In the morning I went down to Valeries to see her presents + to wish all the relatives a "Merry Christmas". In the afternoon, after lunch at home, Valerie came up for tea, so did nan + G'dad W. I enjoyed having them here. At night Barry came. Billy really does seem interested in me – they told him I was on the phone + he flew to it! When he discovered I wasn't he was very de-chuffed! Good!

26 Mon: Got up at 11.30 – only woke at 11.20!! It was lovely! We just lazed round until about 4.30 then Daddy + Mr Fletcher came back from the rugby match and we had tea.

27 Tue: I did nothing all day! Got up at about 11.15, got dressed at 2.00! At night we all went to the Barry's dad's farm. I enjoyed myself as I think we all did. (I wore my new brushed turquoise wool V-neck sweater + reversible pleated skirt.) I had a good talk to Billy. He is nice but shy. I haven't got even the tiniest crush on him. He is interested in me (so I heard) but he's so shy (as I am) it is hard to tell!

28 Wed: Up very late again! Did nothing all day long! Mummy was off work in the afternoon and we sat and sat! I like doing this because I'm with my family at home – not at Crossley! Still, I prefer going out though as I've had 12 months of "lounging". I think about Billy quite a lot, I hope he likes me + asks me to go out with him. I haven't got a crush on him but I like him. He's nice!

29 Thu: Once more we rose late and lazed around. In the afternoon we went shopping. (Sandra + I, I mean.) I got a Gala "Slim Line" lipstick "Orange Floss". Sandra got it in "Sea Coral". Both great colours! I went to the opticians. He said my eyes have got much worse + I should wear glasses all the time!! I said "no" so we compromised. If in 6 months my eyes have improved, O.K. If not, I will agree! I prefer the optician at Crossley who said I don't need glasses at all (although I know I will for blackboard work when I'm BACK AT SCHOOL!!!)

30 Fri: Up early (for me!) at 10.30! Went down to Valeries at 2.30. We went down town. I got a v. pale orange nail varnish – "Orange Fizz" matches my lipstick!! I hope that on Monday Valerie and I are going to be allowed to go to the teen dance at the Scala. Yipee – am I looking forward to it! I had a great time at Valeries. We are as good friends as before. I took our records down + we played them on her new record-player.

31 Sat: Got up at 10.30 again. I went to Wendy's in the afternoon for tea. I enjoyed myself very much. We talked until tea, then, afterwards we played "Cluedo". I won all three games! I'd like that game. <u>New Years Eve</u> Enjoyed it! Best ever! Had chips + sausage rolls for supper + cider! Mum + dad + I had a lovely time. First time dad has ever stayed in with us on New Year's Eve! Poor Sandra came in crying, Barry + her have finished for four weeks.

JANUARY 1961

1 Sun: Dull day. Sandra was miz. over Barry + the quarrel, so we couldn't go to their farm as planned + I did want to see Billy. Didn't go to Church but Mr Helsby brought me a prize "Pride + Prejudice". I felt awful 'cos I hadn't been and I looked a sight.

2 Mon: Another uneventful and unmemorable day. Wendy came to tea. Daddy was at work but mummy was on holiday. Sandra really wants to make up with Barry but won't so he'll "be taught a lesson". Better evening. Sandra + I went to Scala teenage dance.[78] Valerie was meant to be going but her dad said she was too young. Had a great time. A boy called Raymond asked me to dance and then for a date! He's 18! I'll see him on Friday! Not great looking – a bit square – but a boy and a date!!!

3 Tue: Oh! What a day! Wish it had been as uneventful as yesterday. After tea at night mum said "Your fathers got something to tell you." So daddy

---

[78] *The Scala, Runcorn, had, at one time, been a cinema, but then it was a ballroom where dances were held, including teenage alcohol-free 'hops' on weekdays. In October 1962, there to celebrate my 16th birthday, the week "Love Me Do" came out, I saw the Beatles. As I recall, they had been booked when they were still unknown and had honoured the date. We paid the usual low price to see them. They were four scruffy, tough-looking lads from Liverpool. They sat and had soft drinks next to where we were sitting but we didn't speak to them because they looked a bit too rough for us Grammar School girls! We did, though, think their music was terrific – far better than the groups that usually played there.*

said "I'm in serious trouble." Oh! It was awful. It seems that Daddy has been systematically forging documents of the Pru to get money. He was sacked. That's why he's working on the Docks. He is being prosecuted. What I hate is that it has all been spent on whiskey. So much for his promise to God about me! I HATE HIM NOW.

4 Wed: We felt really fed-up all morning because daddy was "on trial" today in the Magistrate's Court. There are <u>16</u> charges against him, and he has swindled £118 (less 1d) Oh! It is terrible. Poor mummy has known for over 3 months. He doesn't seem sorry.[79]   Sandra + I went to Warrington to cheer ourselves up. Mum didn't go, she felt too miz. We just had to get away for a bit. Got 34" bra for me!! Sandra + Barry friends again – hurrah! More bad news. Tonight mummy told me Miss Bird said I have to stay down in the 2nd year because I've

---

[79] *The case against my father: The diary tells the story well enough but I'll add a bit of background. The sum stolen may not seem much to modern eyes but, then, it was a considerable sum (when a good salary was £1,000 a year and decent houses cost hundreds not hundreds of thousands of pounds). The Pru decided to prosecute, rather than just dismiss my father, because he had stolen directly from customers, having taken money out of amounts due to them. As there were 16 charges against him, it was systematic theft over a period of time, not a singular, sudden, impulsive act. His area was rural, payments were made in cash, and he was liked and trusted by his customers. He also decided to plead Not Guilty at the first hearing at the Magistrates Court, which meant that he had to be sent for trial to the County Court. (See newspaper extracts at the end.)*

missed so much. I cried. Mummy said she'll try to get Miss Bird to change her mind. I want to be with my friends even though I know I won't be able to do the work in 3A.

5 Thu: Today I went back to school after 13 mths. I am glad to be back. Everyone was very nice to me, and no one mentioned T.B. But oh! the situation with dad is even worse today than I'd realised. There is an article in the paper about HIM. Reporters were in Court yesterday. When I came home, I saw it's in all the local papers. Looks bad enough in the "Runcorn Guardian" + "Runcorn Weekly News" but even worse in the "Liverpool Echo". I'm dreading school tomorrow. Now everyone will know. I HATE HIM. I am so ashamed. All that time when I was in Crossley, I thought I'd be so happy to be back at school. Now I dread going again tomorrow. Mummy managed to persuade Miss Bird to agree to at least let me start off with my friends but she won't say for how long.

6 Fri: School. Not as bad as I expected, in fact no one said anything about HIM. Gosh! When I think of all the time he was coming to Crossley being a "dear Daddy", he was no better than a thieving alcoholic. He expects all of us to forgive him but for at least 7 or 8 years he's broken his promises to us + has made our life miserable. He couldn't even keep the promise he made to God about making me better. I didn't want to go out but I'd agreed to meet Raymond outside the pictures at 6 so I went. He turned up but said he was a Roman Catholic so had to go to church. He wanted another date but I said "No". Dad is R.C. and rotten.

7 Sat: Me and Sandra speak to daddy as far as "Good morning Good night". That's all. Somehow he doesn't seem a bit sorry. I can't bear to look at him. Mummy and I went to Widnes market by bus to get some material for me. It was a hard job to find what we wanted but we've got some lovely, thick wool, turquoise + brown herringbone design. It was 12/6 a yd – I bought it with my Christmas money. Mum says it was worth 25/- a yard. She's going to make a pinafore dress or suit for me. Yipee! Dad went out at night (good riddance) and Sandra was out with Barry (lucky her). Just me and mum watching T.V. (Lovely!)

8 Sun: Went to Sunday School. I didn't want to go because of dad. Mummy said we can't stay at home forever. I'm in the "top class" at Sunday School. Mr Cooper takes us, in the little hall. We are talking about some interesting things. I like it. Came back and took Scamp for a walk 'cos dad was here. Very cold out. Had a lovely tea, roast potatoes, sprouts + lamb. It was delicious! I love home cookin'! Gosh! I'm always famished (like Finch in the Whiteoak Saga). At night I got upset about school tomorrow. I showed mummy my timetable. Dr Cuthill said I can't do P.E. outside yet. I can't do the Latin but I have to do it to stay in the A form. It's an awful problem. Mummy said she'll write to Miss Bird about the Latin and the P.E. and she'll give me a note to excuse me from P.E. tomorrow.

9 Mon: Oh! Dear! It's getting awful! I just can't sleep. No matter what I do, I can't. Only when I have a sleeping tablet do I get a good nights rest. Dr Staunton has given mummy some for her and I can have a half. I thought Crossley was a nightmare. This is worse. I am worried about school and dad. I am glad I am at school all day though. The atmosphere at home is awful. Even worse than some times in the 6-bedder 'cos these are people I love. No one has said anything so far at school but they all know. The Chemistry Master said I don't have to copy up, just start from now. All very complicated to me because I've not done what they've all done before. Anyway, I may be down in 2A by next week. It's hard enough that I feel "old" and "odd" with my friends. How will I bear being with girls so much younger who don't know me but will know about my dad?

10 Tue: I enjoy being at school, but it is rather disheartening to find out what I <u>don't</u> know, all the time. Here is my list of how things are: <u>Maths</u> – I'm at sea! The Male Maths Teacher at Crossley was too little too late. <u>French</u> – Could be better. Despite Mrs de H's best efforts I just can't seem to remember the irregular verbs. Better on vocab. My best subject is, of course, <u>English</u>, 'cos I've read a LOT, much more than any of my friends but missed a lot on clauses! <u>History</u> – O.K. as it's just facts I can learn. Just a pity what I did with Mrs Mawson turns out not to be what they were learning. No time charts. <u>Geog</u> – Generally O.K. and, again, I can learn facts. No maps though . <u>Biol</u> – copy up the lot and learn might be good enough but, of course, I've done no dissecting. <u>Phys + Chem</u> – I'm at sea. I've missed so much basic theory and practice in both. <u>Latin</u> – err, NO. Only did a tiny bit in Crossley so no way can I catch up. There's no way I'll be able to stay in the A form. <u>Religious Knowledge.</u> – yes!! That is a subject I do know a lot about – well, the Bible anyway, thanks to Bethesda. I don't know what's worse, being in this form with my friends but not being able to do the work or being in the year below without them but maybe better at the work? At the moment, I just want to be with them. I don't care about low marks. I LOVE not having to do P.E. Makes Miss Dale SO mad she can't make me!

11 Wed: At night I lie awake thinking about how awful everything is. I thought I was going to be happy again. I am glad I am with my friends but they talk a LOT about boys. In bed, I try thinking about Billy + what it would be like to be kissed by him! I wanna be loved, kissed, hugged + petted. I don't want a "one-sided" love affair - I want passion. In other words – I wanna BOY! School was hard work today. I feel a fool almost all the time. Mummy has talked to Miss Bird. She has agreed I can use the Latin and P.E. periods to copy up in the library! She said I can stay with my form <u>for now</u> but if I have not caught up by the Summer exams, I will have to stay down a year. Mummy isn't sure if that means I'd start again in 3A or 3B (no Latin) or 2A. I could not bear not going into 4A. I MUST catch up.

12 Thu: Oh! Every week it gets worse! In the Weekly News there were <u>10</u> columns about Daddy. The sums of money taken added up to £118-0-0. He has stolen from a lot of people. I feel awful about going to school. I hate him even more now. He still expects us to forgive him. He "left home" but returned at 9.30. I wish he'd gone for good. On the bus a few people looked at me in a funny way. I sat with Wendy. She didn't say anything. I can't concentrate in lessons. I keep wanting to cry. I am glad I had two periods today by myself in the library.

13 Fri: In Art we had to do a design using a culinder, teapot, mop + wine bottle. The teacher said mine was very good! Sweet music after so long of "can't do it". No one said anything about dad but by now they must all know. I felt really miz all day. I didn't feel like laughing with my friends but I had to. I don't know what's worse, being at school or at home. I am unhappy in both.

14 Sat: Daddy has gone to stay with his parents. Hurrah! Hope he stays there. Now Nannie Salter can see what her precious son is like. Poor Grandad S, for his son to do that in his old company in the job he got for him. Went down town in the afternoon despite fog. Wore black-watch pants + Sandra's (no longer!) pink short coat. I went to "El Capacino" and had some frothy coffee. I love coffee bars – wish I was a beatnik in London. Made me think of super Sarah, our Christmas artist. Bought a goose that lays eggs from the market! (It's blue plastic!) Silly! But I wanted it + it was only 1/-. For so long, I wanted to grow up but now I think I'd rather be too young to know how rotten life is. In Crossley I learnt you can't trust people. Now I know you can't even trust your own father.

15 Sun: "Too cold, damp and foggy to go to Sunday School" mummy said. I was going to go, but I didn't mind not having to. I just messed round all afternoon + then watched the last episode of "Pathfinders to Mars" it was great! Not as good as "Quatermass" though. I love space serials! Anything to be out of this world for a bit! Dad back from Widnes at night, worse luck. I am still not speaking to him more than I have to. Mummy said I have to be polite. Sandra won't speak to him at all.

16 Mon: School once more. Today was the first time anyone has ever even referred to me having had T.B. After lunch a girl said "Why aren't you doing hockey? Aren't you strong enough?" Ooh! I could have hit her! I said she should think of me in the warm library when she was running round the cold field! Dr Hughes didn't say I couldn't do gym, just outdoor sport in Winter, but we've told school it is all P.E. I can't do yet. One thing good to come out of Crossley! More boy talk at lunchtime. Oh I wish I had a boyfriend, so I can join in! Hope I'm not sex-mad, like they are, but I do long for some boy to kiss me! I wonder what they'd say if I told them about Dr Bashray. They probably have never been felt up by a man. I didn't like it but it must be different with a boy you love.

17 Tue: School was O.K. It is easier now with the free periods. I cannot believe how much I have to copy up in all subjects – including Chemistry he now says - from partway through November 1959 to the end of December 1960. I am also finding most of the new work we're doing difficult. I went on Valerie's school bus into down town Runcorn so I could go to the library. I got "Finches Fortune" out. I love the "Whiteoak" books! I wish I knew a boy like Finch! I want a boyfriend! Mmm! I'd love a nice boy to kiss me long + mean it! I try to imagine how different boys kiss, but then when I meet any I feel embarrassed! After tea, I went to bed and read and read. Then I remembered I had to do some homework!!

18 Wed: Oh! An awful thing happened! Billy's bus passed us + instead of me being serene + ready to wave I had my hat off + was drinking milk out of a bottle! What will he think? I do wish he would ask me for a date. I haven't got a 'crush' on him! Another hard day at school. My face aches with "smiling" as they all talk about their boyfriends etc. I wish the teachers wouldn't ask me questions. I sometimes don't know even when I put my hand up.

19 Thu: Hurrah! At last a Thursday with nothing in the papers about dad! Oh well, monotonous as it is my thoughts have been mostly about "wish-I-had-a-boy" again! Beats thinking about dad! I don't tell anyone, not even my best school friend Susan, but I do so long to be in love + have a boy kiss me + mean it. I wish life was like at Jalna! Barry took Sandra to Hereford for an interview for Training College. She wanted to be a teacher since she first went to school. I think she'd be very good. She taught me to read before I was at school! She told me she doesn't want to leave Barry though.

20 Fri: Exams started today for everyone else. I didn't do any but it was terribly boring just copying up all afternoon + morning. Ugh! There's another week of it. At night mummy + I went to see "Let's Make Love" starring Yves Montand, Marilyn Monroe + Frankie Vaughan. I thought it was a rude title about sexual intercourse but it was really about courting, although it was a bit sexy in places. MM is gorgeous looking. We went upstairs for a treat + had sweets AND ice cream! I enjoyed myself a lot.

21 Sat: Washed my hair. What a mess of frizz. Went to Sunday School Party. Too childish but I enjoyed looking after the young kids. Only Robert Helsby and me there over the age of 13. He's improved with age but not boyfriend material. Can't stop thinking about Billy. He didn't kiss me or anything when he had the chance but he seems to like me. Sometimes I feel I love him and feel the need of his kisses, others I just 'like' him as a friend. Wonder how he feels about me?

22 Sun: Went to Sunday School. Mr Helsby gave us (top class) our lesson. It was good, about how much we should obey our parents. I wanted to ask him, what if your parent is an alcoholic thief who tells lies? Of course, I didn't. He is a very nice man + a good speaker. In this class we are told how to live our lives more than just about the Bible.

23 Mon: <u>School</u>. I did the English Language exam in the morning. I enjoyed doing it + it was just the type I like – plenty of vocab + metaphors + similes plus (of course) essay + comprehension. There was only one grammar question on clauses + as I haven't learnt those I couldn't do it. Unfortunately, that will bring down my overall mark. French for the others. SO glad Miss Saunders agreed I did not have to do it. Billy's bus passed ours! A good day!

24 Tue: I will not be doing any other exams than the English Lang. one I've already done. I would have done the Art one on Friday but I have to go to see Dr Hughes. Hope "all is well" on Friday! Should be, I feel really fine + as I feel good so I eat good, piles + piles of food! I bet I've put on weight. Ah well, at least I'm getting a LOT of copying up done in the exams. When I'm in the library I do read a bit too. I know I shouldn't. It's like when I was in Crossley I knew I had to work to keep up but couldn't. Now I know I have to copy up or I'll be kept back and lose my friends which I couldn't bear but instead I read.

25 Wed: I read my Whiteoak book ALL morning during the exams, I can't leave it alone! It is called 'Master of Jalna'. In the afternoon I managed to keep my book closed and copied up some Chemistry and Physics - even the experiments I wasn't there for! My mind was still on the Whiteoaks though. So much more interesting. Oh! for the kiss of a boy like Finch! Maybe copying up would be easier if I understood more of what I was copying. I'm using mainly Liz's books as she is the cleverest in the class.

26 Thu: I finished copying up Chemistry since September in the morning and in the afternoon I started copying up Physics! Ugh! It really is boring just copying up by myself all day. I stopped praying after Thurs Jan. 12th because I can't understand why God wants to punish us all for what dad has done. On the other hand, I am glad that God still let me get better even though dad broke his promise. Maybe if I start again life will be better in future.

27 Fri: Dr Hughes. 9.30. Weight 8st-3 ¼ lbs. Gain 4 ¾ lbs!!! Dr Hughes was very pleased with me, and he praised me highly! I had an x-ray and that was "very good"! Yipee! I am pleased. He said that the ideal bed-time for me was in bed by 9.00, lights out by 10.00! Good!! Mummy had been saying I should be asleep earlier. Didn't go back to school in the afternoon but did some copying up. Mummy + I went to see "Lost World" (exciting and scary but not real!) + "Man who never was" (also exciting but actually true!). Both v. v. good. Friday night at the pictures is our special treat! Plus T.V. with sweets on Saturday.

 28 Sat: Got up at 10.00. Went down town in my red coat, nylons, black heeled shoes! Dead respectable! Bought a second-hand poetry book "The Golden Treasury of Modern Lyrics". It was only 2/- and it has all my favourite poems in it. It's great! A lot of poems are about death or love. Most of them are sad. Well, so am I, a lot of the time. But love might be just around the corner!

29 Sun: Today it is very, very windy! I went to Sunday School and then came straight home. I did some more Physics copying up in the afternoon. Ugh. We had Yorkshire pudding roast potatoes, carrots + roast beef. I really enjoyed it, especially as dad, for some reason, didn't join us. (He was at the pub and ate his later.)   Sandra is not well.

Mon 30: Sandra has got 'flu and laryngitis, poor ol' thing!   Some exam results were given out today. I enjoy school very much most of the time. Very often in a lesson I suddenly feel deliriously happy to think I'm here and not at Crossley! Then I remember dad and down I go.   But I am SO glad to be well and with my friends at school.

Tues 31 Billy's sister Christine saw me today and said that Billy had never stopped playing the jazz records I lent him. Maybe he really does like me? Big sisters are teasers I know so could be her idea of a joke to say that.

FEBRUARY 1961

1 Wed: This morning I got three things in the post:-
(1) "Readers Digest" Mrs Mawson bought me an annual subscription for Christmas. Very good! I like the "increase your vocab" tests. (2) Letter from U.S. penpal, Barby. They have had deep deep snow. (3) Chinese calendar from Wong. It has a large Chinese picture on each of its 6 pages, 2 months to a page, and it is written in English + Chinese. It's from a Chinese restaurant in Liverpool. It's great! Mummy said it's ok to write and thank him but not to encourage him. I hope his English is so bad he couldn't read the Liverpool Echo about dad. What if he did and he's sent this out of pity? I hate thinking about people like Mave reading about dad and laughing at us.

2 Thu: Sandra is much better today and in the evening Barry came to see her. Liz's average mark is 83!!! She's definitely top of the class. It is utterly fantastic! Not big headed, pretty, terrific at sport. Must be wonderful to be her! Today I felt really miserable because all the girls at school were discussing their boyfriends and I haven't one. I'm not surprised. I'm not clever or pretty or sporting. I try to be nice but I am not always.

3 Fri: At night mummy and I went to see "Solomon and Sheba" starring Gina Lollobridgida + Yul Brynner. I enjoyed it, it was "spectacular" and quite sexy in parts – there was an orgy!! Mummy said she's had a few nasty comments in the shop about dad but most people don't say anything. He is still working and out most nights. The less I see of him the better. If he'd stolen for us, I'd forgive him, but not for whiskey.

4 Sat: Today I've got a rotten cold. Didn't get dressed all day. Sandra + I made some Potato Janes for dinner. Just baked potatoes mixed with cheese but they were delicious!   In the afternoon Sandra + I played Cluedo before she went out with Barry. T.V. was good. Troy Donohue in "Sunset Strip". Mmm … think I'm starting to go for blond boys!

5 Sun: I did not go to Sunday School as I want my cold to be better by Monday, at least enough to go to school. The T.V. was good at night. Adam Faith was on the Paladium. I like him a LOT. Troy Donohue was on T.V. again, this time in "Hawian Eye". He's grrrreat! Wouldn't say no to either of these blonds!!

6 Mon: <u>School</u> Last night Mummy didn't really want me to go so we struck a bargain, if I was no worse, I could go, if not - BED! I was O.K. so I went. My cold isn't really too bad. Yet another of our gang announced she had a boyfriend. He is 15-16, goes to Balfour Sec Mod. and is "good-looking". She is so little and cute and cuddly, no wonder she has a boyfriend. I'm too thin and tall and not sweet enough I know.

7 Tue: Cold is still quite thick. I found school awfully hard today. Maybe I should have stayed at home and got really better. At night mummy told us that on Thursday dad is on trial again. If he had pleaded guilty at the Magistrates it would be over but he pleaded Not Guilty so it's going to be at the

Crown Court at Chester. Why didn't he just admit it? He did it. Oh! It's so awful! I can hardly bear it. In bed I couldn't stop thinking about it. I wish I had a boy to love me and kiss me. It would be a comfort to me. Someone who would love me whatever my dad did.

8 Wed: He didn't go to work as he "had things to do". Sandra said he stayed in all day + didn't go to see Reston the lawyer till 20 to 6 so lost a day's pay for it. I HATE the PIG. He makes a very bad situation even worse. He is so selfish. Mummy is worried sick about tomorrow. Went to Susans birthday party straight after school as she lives in Frodsham. It was great. We jived, played 'beetle', pass the parcel + darts! Lovely things to eat. Marvellous time. Really cold coming home on the bus. I was the only one from Runcorn so I was by myself. I wish I hadn't had to come home at all.

9 Thu: All day at school I felt awfully worried wondering how they are getting on at court. Hope he goes to prison because it would mean he wasn't here and he deserves it. Found out when I got home they didn't even hear his case today! Hell. I had hysterics at night in front of him. I told him I could kill him + I hoped he went to Prison. He said some nasty things also, too horrible to write down. Mummy said after he didn't really mean them. Why does she still stick up for him? He doesn't seem a bit sorry. We are all so so miserable. When will it end? Being in Crossley I was unhappy most of the time but sometimes I was O.K. Now I'm more unhappy than ever but I'm still glad I'm at home with mummy and Sandra and I am well and at school. If it had happened while I was in Crossley it would be even worse. I just don't think I'll ever be able to forgive him. I can't help it, I hate him.

10 Fri: The case was heard today at Chester Crown Court. Sandra + I went to school but we came home in 2nd lesson. It was best for both of us + we decided we had to. Miss Bird agreed. It's so awful. A girl in Sandra's year is at Court today taking notes for work experience. I hate him. Mummy wasn't here when we came back so I guessed she'd gone to Court. She had. He was found guilty. He has gone to Liverpool prison for 6 months.[80] Sandra + I (and I think mum) are very glad but also very ashamed. Peace at last.

11 Sat: We all stayed in. We couldn't bear to go out and see people although they don't know the verdict yet. I wrote to Barby (my U.S. penpal) in the afternoon. I did not tell her about dad. I am too ashamed. Just like those last months at Crossley, I don't know how I'd manage the evening without T.V. Sandra said Barry is being lovely with her. She is so lucky. I wish I had a boy who really cared for me.

---

[80] *Sentencing: Had he pleaded Guilty initially, there would have been less publicity, it would have been over sooner, and he would probably not have received as long a sentence. Whether he was wrongly advised by his solicitor, or he was too stubborn to listen, I do not know.*

12 Sun: I didn't go to Sunday School, I just couldn't. We all stayed in all day again. I did out the toy cupboard. I want to keep my favourite old toys forever. I have lots of books and more games than I thought we had. Sandra went out with Barry tonight. We've all felt pretty miz. today.

Mon 13: <u>School</u> Ugh! I thought it was going to be awful, but no one said anything and no one enquired very deeply as to why I left on Friday, thank goodness. I managed to shake my feelings of sadness off and enjoyed school. Felt much better today than on Friday. Yesterday, I thought I'd never want to go out again but this evening I went to the United Nations Association Ball with Paula at the Memorial Hall. It's only just up the road and people don't talk much at a dance. It was very nice, bit childish but good. They crowned a Queen. I didn't like Paula the one time she came to see me in Crossley but she's alright.

14 Tue: I got 3 VALENTINES!!!!!! I was awfully shocked and thrilled!!!!!! Are they from my family?? Or from someone in Crossley? Wong?? I don't know! One (the nicest) is (I hope) from Billy. I don't really know but who else is there? The verse fits, and the writing is how I imagine his. Barry is very romantic with Sandra. She was made up by the roses and his card.

15 Wed: Only ONE other person in our gang got a Valentine! Goody! I got 3!! Nannie Wakefield came to tea. I didn't feel like talking but I had to 'cheer up' mummy said. Nannie never liked dad. How right she was! I don't know why mummy feels she still has to stick up for him. I felt all "boy-friend-wantish" today. The worse things get at home the more I want to be out with a boy, any boy. Gosh! I can't last much longer without a boy!

16 Thu: On the bus in the morning they had a "Weekly News"[81] and were passing it round. It was awful. The girl chosen as Queen at U.N.A. Ball on Mon was on the front page but the headline was "Insurance agent goaled for theft and forgery". I nearly died. In the "Guardian" it is inside but quite a lot of it. This is the worst day yet. People were whispering and looking at the paper then at me. Wendy was really sweet and kept chatting all the way. I wanted to be sick. Once I got to school, it was O.K. No one said anything. I wonder if the teachers know? I wish half-term had started today. I keep on thinking what Nannie said – today's news is tomorrow's chip papers. At least this is the last week he'll be in the news.

17 Fri : Half-term! NO school!! Sandra and I went to Liverpool to have our hair cut at Andre Bernards. Mine is short + forward, Sandra's is shorter but still the same style. In the evening Nannie Salter came, wept + told us how hard we were. We told her how

---

[81] *Newspaper reports (see at the end of the book) refer to mitigating circumstances – the official travel allowance falling short of his actual expenses – and Mr Helsby, from Bethesda Sunday School, mentioned earlier, appeared as a character witness. However, I was firmly of the view then that the theft was to pay for his whisky, even though I read those reports.*

rotten her precious son was. It was awful. Nannie S seems to think we had the money so we should stand by him! She will not believe it was all for his whiskey. When she left, mummy was shaking and I was crying and Sandra was really angry. I could not sleep for hours.

18 Sat: I'm very pleased with my haircut, but he has cut the sides wrongly for Sandra so she was a bit upset. Went to Wendys for tea. Her parents must know but they didn't say anything. Had lovely time. Played "Cluedo" "Jacks" "Kan-u-go" + "Faraway Tree" (my fave since I was 9). For tea there was lettuce, tomato, ham AND salmon, jelly AND ice cream AND fruit AND choc. cakes AND biscuits! Wendy's mum seems to think she has to feed me up! Well, that's fine by me!! I like being at Wendys. It's like being with Helen – no boy chat.

19 Sun: Sandra + I went to Barrys for tea. I was nervous about going but Sandra said they know about dad and not to worry. We went at 2.30. and stayed until 11.10! In the afternoon we played Billys guitar, + then went round the farm. Billy was working all afternoon with his dad but after tea he came in. Talked till about 8.00. then Sandra + Barry went out. Watched T.V. with Billy and Christine then Chris went to bed + Billy + I watched alone 10.00 till 11.00! We're both shy so we didn't actually say much but it was lovely. Had a marvellous time! Got on well with them all!

20 Mon: Got up at 11.45! Worn out after yesterday! Sandra said it's after watching "Hawian Eye" <u>alone</u> with Billy. Little does she know we hardly spoke and he never even touched me. Wish he had. I would have let him. Gosh, I long for him! Stayed in all day. Helped Sandra tidy her top drawer out in a.m. She gave me some make-up she didn't want and a bracelet. Couldn't sleep at night. I wanted to think about Billy but kept thinking about dad. I wonder what it's like in prison? I bet he's sorry now. Went to sleep about 1.30.

21 Tue: School! Everyone was suitably impressed with my accounts of Sunday! I feel sorta awful because Susan said "All day it's what Billy said + does" She even said "Did he 'do' you?" I just blushed and blushed although he didn't even touch me. Still who cares! I want Billy to want me. I want his kisses + his love. I'd rather be teased about Billy than anyone talk about you know what.

22 Wed: School was as usual. Two horrid Maths lessons. Awful. Can't do Maths at all. Billys bus passed us on the way home, he didn't see me. I love him so much. He looked depressed + tired. He hates school. Mmmm I'd love to be able to kiss away his frowns. At home, life is better without dad but mummy is really worried about money so she's a bit ratty. All I want is Billy, but no-one knows I like him like that. Got 9/10 for English!!

23 Thu: Got 8/10 for French and 9/10 for a map in Geography. Yes! I wonder if the teachers are marking me kindly? Christine told Sandra that Billy had pretended not to see me, then had looked out + watched the bus for as long as he could. Yipee! Perhaps that means he's shy like me which means he feels like me! I think I love him. Barry came to see Sandra for about 30 mins as a surprise. He's awfully nice + good. We could have a double wedding!!

24 Fri: Billys bus didn't pass us. Oh. I do love him and wish he was my boyfriend. Chris said to him "Why don't you ask her to the pictures" and he blushed like mad + said "I'll thank you to leave me to make my own arrangements." Sandra said that if he wasn't Barrys brother + me her sister he'd probably ask me for a date. Oh I wish he would. Mummy was too tired to take me to the pictures tonight. Maybe we can't afford it now?

25 Sat: Got up at 10.50 so I had 12 hours 20 mins deep sleep last night! Boy! Did I need it! Still long for Billy. Oh! If only he'd ask me for a date. I love him in a way, not sloppily, just truly. Billy Billy I want to keep on thinking about him and nothing else. More bad news. Mum told us tonight that Dad had a 'fancy woman'. She's got a letter from her to dad. Oh, this is worse than ever. I was just starting to feel sorry for him in prison. Now I hope he never comes out. Sandra said she hopes mum won't be soft enough to let him come back here when he is out. I hope so too. [82]

---

[82] _Fancy woman:_ *Whether my mother read us the letter or just told us about it I cannot remember. As a child, I knew my father was considered charming and he was a flirt (as he had been with Maeve in the hospital) but it had not occurred to me until then that it ever went further than that. For me, it was the final straw: he had stolen not just to pay for his whisky but for his other woman as well. I was enraged he hurt my mum.*

26 Sun: Got up at about 12.00. I didn't want the day to start. I couldn't face Sunday School. I like it once I'm there but just couldn't be bothered. I've felt suffocated all day. Not hard to breathe but as if I'm wasting my life. I waited so long for Crossley to be over then look what happened. I feel as if I can't live with myself the way things are. Maybe if I had this craving for demonstrative love quenched, and Billy is the one to do that, I'd feel better. Oh! Wish he would. Messed around all day feeling a bit cheesed off. Did my hmk. T.V. at night.

27 Mon: <u>School</u> I've hardly thought about Billy today. But only because I wouldn't let myself. Oh! It's torture. I long long long for him. To feel his body next to mine would fill me with divine ecstasy. I <u>want</u> him, I need him. God! How I need him. I've even prayed for a date but so far to no result. Here is a list of the test results so far: Eng. Lit 13/20 (disappointing). Maths 10/10 (unbelieveable!) French Dictation 7 ½ wrong (so 12 ½ right!). Chem 13/20 (v pleased with that). Am I doing enough to be able to stay with my form? What if they're marking me easy now 'cos they feel sorry for me but when the exams come they mark me like everyone else and I'm not good enough? I could not bear staying down a year.

28 Tue: In the afternoon we had a concert in the hall. A man and a woman played an oboe, a cor anglais, a violin and a piano. We had a good laugh but we weren't meant to. I felt like one of "the gang" today. Lovely! The boys from their school came. I wonder if Billy was there? I've felt +

thought a lot about him today again. Oh, for his kisses. I feel terribly unhappy. I always seem to do things wrong. I am (sexually) frustrated. Is it my age or 'cos of the T.B. like even Dr E said? I feel I must must must love Billy, or another boy. I feel that I must be depraved my longing for kisses is so passionate. And yet sexual intercourse is repulsive to me, even after marriage. I feel so mixed up.

MARCH 1961

1 Wed: NO school – teachers marking 11+. Mummy Sandra + I went to Warrington. We were quite reckless! I got a girdle (!!) cos the suspender belt digs in. In the evening, mum + I went to see Albert Finney (he's great!) in "Saturday Night and Sunday Morning". It was an X. I really enjoyed it. Sexy man! Mummy wouldn't approve if I had a boyfriend like him!!

2 Thu: School once more. I'm off cachets today because I had such horrible stomach ache. Mummy said I could stay off until Monday, + then I'll go back on them + see if it was them that had given me stomach ache. I worry about not being on drugs in case I have a setback. That would be even worse than not being able to stay with my form. I bet I'd lose all my friends for good if I went back to hospital. I could not bear being ill and away again.

3 Fri: In art I did some more to my "Clown in his Dressing Room". I rather like it, and although it isn't very good, it's good for me. It makes me think of daddy though 'cos when he'd had too much to drink he'd sing Pagliaci about a clown crying. I have decided to pretend not to like Billy anymore because I couldn't sleep for thinking about him + perhaps if I pretend it will come true. Anyway he doesn't seem to like me or he'd ask me for a date.

4 Sat: Lovely day today! In the afternoon Sandra + I went down town. Sandra got a new slim button through dress in white straw cotton with blue + green flowers on it. It's lovely! I got the next two

Whiteoak books from the library "Return to Jalna" + "Rennys Daughter" The T.V. was good at night it was the "Adam Faith" show. Grrrrreat! Another blond boy!

5 Sun: When to St. Michaels church in the a.m. with Wendy. I quite enjoyed it, C of E but rather Catholic, really felt as if I've been to church. Prefer it to Bethesda.[83] In the afternoon took Scamp for a walk up the Hill. Should have met Wendy but we missed each other. At night we went to church again. I prefer evening service. Afterwards I met Mrs Cooper as I was walking home. I had to tell her I'd left Bethesda! Ooh! I felt awful but I just don't want to go back there. More friends go to St M's.

6 Mon: School. I wish people wouldn't ask me what I think of their boyfriends. I usually think they are foul but don't say so. Gorgeous weather. We ate our dinner on the field. We had a good time fooling around. I'm getting better at that! Sat facing the cinder track so I could watch the boys on the other field but didn't see Billy. Boo hoo!

7 Tue: <u>School</u> Looked out for Billy's bus on the way home. Didn't see him. Ah well! I am getting on

---

[83] _Sunday School:_ _I seem to have changed my allegiance from Bethesda to St Michael's. Nothing in the diary explains why but perhaps it was peer pressure, just preferring to go where my friends went? Or perhaps it had to do with not being able to face the congregation that knew about my dad's crimes? But then so did a lot of people locally. Reading my diary now, I am shocked by how easily I cast aside the good, kind people of Bethesda._

quite well at school I think. I cannot do Maths at all, but that is the worst. I have copied all the work I have to now, except some 2nd form Biol. I pray by the end of term I will be told I can go into 4A with my friends AND I'll be dating or at least had A date with Billy! Bliss!!

8 Wed: When I got on the bus at night I saw Billy. He was on his bus (alone). I was on ours (alone). We just stood there, looking at each other. Gosh did my heart thump! Then someone got on his bus + we sat down. I'm telling people that I've gone off him, when they start teasing me, but really I still like him very much, but as he hasn't (+won't) ask me for a date, what's the use? Went to Confirmation Class with Wendy[84]. It was good.

9 Thu: This evening when I went to the toilet after tea, I happened to notice my panties and I saw they were covered with blood. So I presume I've started my periods! Good! now I'm a woman! I put on my

[84] *Confirmation Class:* *Maybe I started going to Confirmation Classes at St Michael's Church of England just because my friends went, in much the same way that I had joined Bethesda when younger because my cousin Valerie went. Also, in 1961, I visited St John's Presbyterian Church which, like St Michael's, was conveniently within walking distance of where I lived and friends went there. I was christened Catholic, and my mother had agreed the children would be brought up Catholic, but my lapsed Catholic father and Church of England mother left me free to decide for myself. Perhaps, faced with what was going on in my life, I was looking for some spiritual home - I certainly still believed in God then and prayed – but felt closer to my mother's brand of religion.*

"sani-pants" + I didn't feel scared, just excited. I am not using a sanitary belt 'cos it would cut into me like the suspender belt did. The plastic in the pants rustles a bit if anyone pats my bum. Just hope no one does! About 2yrs ago I started praying for 3 things a boy, a bust + to menstruate - now I only need the first one!

10 Fri: I finished my "Clown" in Art. Mrs Sheaff said "Oh! I like that. I really do! Isn't he funny!" I was pleased. I think he's sad too but she didn't notice that. Another gorgeous warm day! I love sitting on the field, laughing with the others, and eating our dinners. No sighting of Billy. Boo hoo.

11 Sat: Sandra and I went down town. We were going to buy mummy some flowers for Mother's Day but they were 4/9 a dozen, so we got her 40 cigs (6/4) instead. We had our tea in a coffee bar. I did enjoy it! It was like being on holiday somewhere! At night I got the usual 'I-wish-I-was-going-out' feeling, but I didn't show it. I know I used to long for T.V. with mum on Sat night but now I'm bored. I long to be out with Billy.

12 Sun: MOTHERING SUNDAY We got mummy breakfast in bed. She liked her cigarettes very much. At night Wendy called for me and we went to St Michaels. I like evening service ritual best. It went awfully quickly + I had hardly settled down when it was 7.35 + time to go.

13 Mon: SCHOOL. We had another test in Chemistry. Last week, I got 6/20, this week 6/30. I really did learn it but somehow I can't grasp the chemistry symbols. Oh! Oh! Oh! Went to bed early at night again. I love going to bed with a hot water bottle, a cup of cocoa, and a Whiteoak book."Renny's Daughter".Super!

14 Tue: Had dinner down on the school field again. It's lovely to be out there with my friends. I try not to let not seeing Billy spoil it. Went on Valerie's bus to the Dentist[85] after school. Had 4 teeth filled. Ugh. Needles hurt, but that's all. NOTHING after all that strep!! I have kept to my rule (8th March) but on Sunday I didn't, that's why the service went so quickly. Tonight I couldn't sleep again for thinking, thinking, thinking about Him! Him! Him! Him!

15 Wed: Warm! Went to confirmation class at night with Wendy. I enjoyed myself and we had a good laugh. I like going out, even though it is only confirmation class. I put my new pinafore dress on

---

[85] *The dentist:* *There are numerous references to going to the dentist. Like many children of my generation – especially if you were poor and Northern – I had bad teeth. Although the dentist was kind and, being at the bottom of the street where my Nannie Wakefield lived, easy to get to, I was not taken regularly by my mother when I was young because she had a fear of dentists. She had had all her teeth out in her 30s, which was a common occurrence then, because it was thought false teeth were preferable to the bother of keeping real ones in good shape. While in junior school, and with my mother's consent, I was hypnotised by 'young Mr Powell' (as he was always referred to as) and it worked. After that, I went by myself and was not troubled. Valerie and I liked Mr Powell because when we were younger, he sometimes gave us mercury to play with in a matchbox. Again, that seems beyond belief now, given that mercury is poisonous.*

that mummy made with the wool herringbone material I bought after Christmas. It is great. I saw Billy as I passed his bus. He waved, smiled and looked pleased to see me. Yipeee!!

16 Thu: Very Very Hot! It's fabulous! Summer in March! I walked past Billy's bus again tonight but when I got up to it, I didn't dare look! Dang!! I daren't think about him at night, if I do I can't sleep. Not sure if its frustration not going out with him or excitement at the possibility of doing so!

17 Fri: Hurrah! I saw my "Clown" on the Art Room wall. Cor! Was I proud! In Art we did a portrait of Janet in pastels. Mrs Sheaf said mine was good – I thought it was awful. I keep resolving to stop thinking about Billy as it makes me so restless and miserable but I find it so hard.

18 Sat: Today Sandra + I went to Liverpool. We had £20 to spend from the "Helping Hand Fund".[86] The ONLY good thing that's come from dad being in prison. We spent about £17 of it! I got a lovely new coat (leather buttons, cream hairy stuff) - I love it! – and some 'jamas. Sandra got a mack (blue

---

[86] _The 'Helping Hand Fund'_ was, I assume, a charity, perhaps for families of prisoners. £20 would have been a lot of money then. I am not sure the charity would have thought we had spent it wisely but I think our mother must have thought we needed to have some pleasure so gave us the freedom to spend it as we liked on clothes. The diary entry suggests I felt only glee at having money to spend, with no shame about it being from a charity. My poor selfless and long-suffering mother was left with only £3 for herself.

poplin, pocket flaps) and a chunky cardigan. Had a lovely day + am pleased with my buys!

19 Sun: Went to church morning and night with Wendy. More time to think about Billy, even though I know I should try not to. In the afternoon we went for a walk round the park.

20 Mon: Very Very cold + windy + wet! What a change from last weeks lovely weather. Had to take a letter to the Boys School today. Didn't see Him. After school, went on Valerie's bus so I could go to the dentists for a polish. The boy I used to be crazy about for two years in juniors 'cos he looked like Elvis was on the bus. Mmmm … he was gorgeous and dark haired too, just like Billy, but now it's Billy only for me!

21 Tues: Another day at school. Another day wishing I had a boyfriend. Another day hoping Billy will ask me for a date. I don't know whether to write "Hurrah!" or "Oh Dear!" as today Billy's bus passed ours. He's friendly at a distance but that's not enough. He smiled (oh! he's handsome) + later when were held up at the swing bridge,[87] he kept turning round to our bus! I felt as excited as ever + I'm afraid my reserves of strength against thinking about him have ebbed very, very low. Oh! To be kissed by him!

---

[87] *The swing bridge was between Runcorn and Helsby, over the River Weaver. Most of the time, it was a normal road bridge but sometimes it was swung aside to let boats through, which could lead to long lines of traffic.*

22 Wed: After tea Sandra was going on about wanting to get married + how she was wasting her life not being married. Mummy was getting upset. She wants Sandra to go to university. I said something (which I meant to be funny) about me keeping Barry happy while she is away. Sandra took offence + started weeping, so naturally I got blamed. Oh dear. I won't bother to try to help lighten things up next time. Confirmation class. Went with Wendy.

23 Thu : Sandra isn't speaking yet. She's very cool + says the bare necessities. Tomorrow I am going to see Dr. Hughes. Hope everything is O.K. I feel fine so it should be. I pray it is. Today I realised that I will never go out with Billy + I felt awfully sad. I cannot forget him, although I try so very hard.

24 Fri: Went to see Dr Hughes. He was very pleased with me. I had an x-ray, it was O.K. He said I can do games, sun-bathe + go in water! I didn't think I'd be able to yet! He said I'll be on cachets until about March next year!!! That does NOT thrill me. At night Mum + I went to the pictures to celebrate. We saw "No Kidding" starring Lesley Phillips, Geraldine MacEwan. It was very funny, about a summer holiday home in a big old house for some very naughty rich kids. I'd like to have a holiday there!!

25 Sat: It is 1.45pm. I am fed-up. I should go to St Michael's Youth Club tonight but oh! I can't. I'm so shy. I'll die meeting all those people especially the boys. I've got nothing to wear + mum has got the wrong nylons. I wish she'd listen when I tell her something. Well, I went to youth club. Had a marvellous time!! Didn't feel shy when I was there. Met a nice boy called Nevil, he's 17 + dark +lean + hungry. He talked to me for quite a while. Wendy said he's after me! Goody!! Goody!!!

26 Sun: Got up at 12.00! In the afternoon I washed my ornaments and re-arranged them. At night went to Church with Wendy. Sat on the back row with the two tough girls from my junior school who used to pick on me who go to the sec. mod. Now I'm really "in" with all this church gang! Wendy told me that Nevil asked her who I was etc + said "Where's your friend?" He's nice! Hope he takes me home soon!! Thought about Nevil not Billy in Church + bed! HOUR SPRINGS ON.

27 Mon: I had a letter from Mrs Mawson today. She said Crossley is nearly empty of T.B.s + now they are doing minor ops. there and more old people. Connie is still there, poor her! She didn't mention Judy so perhaps she's gone home. As Mrs M seems keen to tell me bad news, I think she'd say if she'd died (like Kathleen the doomed bride did).

28 Tue: I vowed today to give up boys until I found a boy I liked who liked me. It's better than being tortured by longing + thoughts.

29 Wed: LAST DAY OF TERM In the morning we had a lovely Easter Service. After break we had a smashing concert! The staff, U.VI + L.VI did items. Oh! They were all so funny! In the afternoon we messed round until "Dismissed Service" Got a good report – phew! Surely the teachers wouldn't pretend I'm doing ok if I'm not? I'm very happy. Maybe my prayers are coming true about staying with my form! Hope they do for a date with Billy!!

30 Thu: FIRST DAY OF HOLIDAYS   Last night + this morning I did some gardening   I've removed most of the dead braken + dug part of the side so far. It's a mess. Dad used to do it. Mummy can't 'cos of her bad back.   Horrible weather! Hope it improves for Easter. Sandra + I carried mum's grocery order home. Boy! Was it heavy! Finished "Wuthering Heights" (4th time of reading). Ah Heathcliffe … another dark man. Emily Bronte died of TB. A lot did.

31 Fri: Read "Sea-Wyf and Biscuit" today. She's a nun but he doesn't know and they fall in love in a boat lost at sea and he can't forget her. Very good but sad. Heard the play on the radio a few years ago and made me cry then too. Sandra said she'd finished with Barry "forever" this morning. He came this afternoon, but he only stayed for about 15 mins + she's still finished with him. I feel sorry for him, but Sandra said she just doesn't love him. I bet she does really! If she finishes with Barry, will that help me with Billy or make a date even less likely?

APRIL 1961

1 Sat: Went down town with Sandra in a.m. Saw Barry in his old 'pick-up'. When we got back he'd sent her some tulips and irises. Bet that cost a lot. Must be lovely to be loved. Went to Youth Club. It was O.K. but a bit dull. Just my luck - Nevil is queer everyone says. And simple. He must be to have liked me. I didn't really like him but I might have done.

2 Sun: EASTER DAY I got 2 eggs + 2 boxes of chocolates! Yummy! Not as many as last year but rather be here! Did some gardening in the afternoon. This is my 3rd bash + it looks pretty decent. The dead stuff + weeds have been cleared away, it's been dug, raked + some bulbs (found in garage) planted. Went to Church at night. Wendy didn't go. Barry came to see Sandra at about 8, went at about 11.00. Friends once more! Have to stop myself asking him about Billy. If Billy doesn't like me I don't want him to know I like him.

3 Mon: EASTER MONDAY Sandra went to Wales with Barry and his sister Chris + her boyfriend. Wished I was going with them with Billy! Mummy, nanny + I went to see "Pollyanna" with Haley Mills at the Plaza, Widnes. It was great! Funny and sad! She always tried to find something to be glad about, like I do although I don't always manage it. Got home about 9.00 + we had chicken + chips for supper – my fave! I enjoyed today very much indeed, just being with my family. Made me so glad I wasn't at Crossley watching a film by myself. Would be even better to be watching with Billy!!

4 Tue: In the afternoon Sandra + I played cards and "Pick-a-stick". Then she swotted + I did some painting. I enjoyed it. We should have gone to the dance at the 'Scala' but it rained + SNOWED! Oh, I'm awfully disappointed. Every time I arrange anything, something happens. I bet we can't go next week. I feel awfully miserable.

5 Wed: Mummys back is bad.[88] In the afternoon I sorted some drawers out, I painted + Sandra sorted some beads out. Tomorrow we're going to make some necklaces! Day passed uneventfully. Sandra + I do all the housework now nearly, as well as doing the cooking. I shouldn't mind but I do.

6 Thu: Went down town by myself. As usual with me, my plans went hay-wire – Valerie couldn't go to the play tomorrow. Her dad won't let her. Hell! Yet another disappointment. I would have lost 2/- so I asked Wendy to go. She could! Miracle – after 7.00 she's usually not allowed out.

7 Fri: Wendy and I went to Helsby to see "Puss-in-boots". Susan was the king in it. She was good. She's got lovely legs! It was good for an amature

---

[88] _Mum's back:_ _The entries about my poor mother being prostrate in bed with a very painful back are quite shocking to my adult eyes for the lack of sympathy shown by 14 year old me. I should have been much kinder and more concerned for my mother but, with the teenage ability to see everything primarily through the perspective of one's one needs and wants, I was not. I am sure that we were not as slave driven by cleaning, shopping, cooking and looking after her as the diary makes out!_

pantomime. Afterwards Wendy + I went for chips + ate them walking home. Wendy slept at our house. We had some good fun. She's like me, she'd like a boyfriend but is shy and hasn't got one (yet).

8 Sat: Went to Youth Club. Wendy practically ignored me all evening! She went round arm-in-arm with Janet from school. My god, she's changeable! I enjoyed myself very much indeed though. I went round with Minny. She's new to our school. She's moved here 'cos her dad is working for Janet's dad. I beat one of the boys 20-21 in table-tennis! All that playing in Crosslcy!! Ncvil cried for some reason. I think he was being bullied. I'm glad I don't go out with him, it would be embarrassing. I felt sorry for him but I didn't say anything though I know I should have. I hate myself for being a coward.

9 Sun: LOW SUNDAY Very, very suitable – that's exactly how I've felt all day. I haven't had such a black mood for ages. Mum's been in bed since Friday – her back's gone again. It's getting on my nerves. I know I'm wrong, but I hate to see her in bed. She used to tell me to be a patient patient. Well, she complains + is always shouting things down to us. I'm sorry but I still feel cross and fed up. Mummy can't be the ill one. I'm sick sick sick of doing housework. I'm sick of church. I was bored tonight.

10 Mon: Mummy has been in bed since Saturday with a bad back. The doctor said it was lumbago, but because she ignored it (we told her not to) it is much worse now. Sandra + I went to the Scala. I love the atmosphere. Raymond was there. I've not seen him since the date that wasn't on 6 Jan. After the first dance he put his arm round me + tried to kiss me! After his cheek, I wouldn't dance with him again but he bothered me all night. He even asked to take me home! I do really want a boyfriend but then when anyone shows interest, I get scared. Anyway, I don't like him enough to let him kiss me. I know I can't hope for Billy but I can't help it. He is the only one for me. His kisses – yes please!!

11 Tue: Sandra's birthday (18). I bought her a long green pearl necklace. She got a lot of presents. Went to Wendy's for tea. Sandra went out with Barry. Another boring day for me.

12 Wed: Yesterday Wendy lent me her Monopoly, mum + I have been playing it. It's good! Stayed in all today. Mummy is a hard patient to please! I didn't think she'd be the demanding type. She is in pain though. Sandra + I are nearly worn out, washing, cooking + cleaning. She's always saying "Bring me so + so please, it's downstairs". Keeping us fit!

13 Thu: This afternoon I went downtown. Not a pleasure trip, but a shopping (grocery-type) spree! Took Scamp with me. She is being good lately. She keeps to heel when we go out, and comes when I shout her, so I make a fuss of her, groom her + take her for walks! I wish when I'm good I was rewarded that quick!

14 Fri: I've felt so tired all day + I've had a bit of a sore throat + stomach ache + back ache (from the floor scrubbing) + head-ache. To cap it all I have about 8 small but puss-headed pimples under my arm through using Buto hair-remover. I've a good mind to tell them pesky people who made it.

15 Sat: Ha! Ha! Ha! I might have guessed that after yesterdays entry, I am now in bed with a temp of 100! I don't feel cheerful. Despite the fact that my throat hurts a lot Dr Staunton says it's not important, it's the under arm that's making me ill! So now I'm on penicillin tablets.

16 Sun: I'll go to school tomorrow as I feel fine! Got up after dinner. No temp! Dressed + sat on lawn in gorgeous warm sun shine. Before I was awake (10.00) Barry, Mr Field + <u>Billy</u> came! He came for the ride, Sandra said, but she thinks to see me as he was sorry I wasn't up. DAMN!! They dropped Barry and their lawn mower off and Barry cut the lawn. Garden's nice now. The cut grass is the finishing touch to my hard work.

17 Mon: Back to school. Not for me! After a somewhat sleepless night because of my 'killing' throat, I am not at school. I wish I could have gone. Dr Staunton didn't come until 3.00. He said my tonsils are badly swollen – he didn't even look at my arm. Some doctor! Mum has been in an awful naggy mood all day. Sandra + could do no right. We wonder if it's money or something to do with dad or just 'cos she's still in pain. Now I'm feeling bad 'cos mum told us this evening Mr Robinson, a specialist, said she has got a slipped disc which is serious. Oh dear.

18 Tue: Still off school. I am up + dressed but I can't go out. My throat is awfully sore, it really hurts when I swallow, especially at night. Very boring at home until Nannie Salter turned up. Even though I'm not well and mummy is still in bed with her bad back, she started a row. She's a silly woman. She told us off for not being nice to daddy while he's in prison! She said he needs to know he can come home when he's out. She does more harm than good sticking up for him. She's no idea what he's really like. She just does not believe us. She's no sense. I hope she doesn't come again ever. After she went, mummy told me and Sandra that he would have to come back here. NO NO NO

19 Wed: Wendy came to see me after school. She told me how she'd been to a party on Fri and a boy had kissed her a lot. Good heavens! Wendy being passionate! Ha! Ha! Ha! Even worse, she told me that on Saturday night Billy was at the chippy after YC. Oh, I am so unlucky, I could cry. The one week I didn't go to YC. God keeps giving me opportunities to see Billy and I keep missing them!! I've vowed to get a date with him before I'm 15! I didn't go to Confirmation Class cos of my sore throat. I don't care. Just cannot stop thinking about Billy. Awful. Cannot believe even Wendy has a boy and I still don't. So unfair. If all that wasn't bad enough, now dad is coming back soon. HELL.

20 Thu: Back at school. I am glad to be back again, but I feel very jealous + envious inside, cos now Susan has got a boyfriend as well as Wendy. I never chase boys but neither am I chased. I <u>need</u> a boy. I <u>want</u> Billy. I'm getting rather fed-up with Youth Club. The boys are so silly, small and young.

21 Fri: Billy's bus didn't pass ours. I feel that if I don't get a boy soon I'll go mad. I used to think I was pretty, but I can't be. I know I've got a good figure, so what's wrong? Oh I do so want Billy, no one knows how I feel or what it's like to have this overwhelming desire for 'love' + not be satisfied.

22 Sat: I went to Youth Club but I didn't want to. Left at 8.00, just said I was 'bored'. As if to torment me, saw a girl + boy of my age, arm in arm, + a 2nd former with a boy. I'm a 3rd year and NO boyfriend! Dam! Dam! Dam! This is such torment. I'm better off just watching T.V. with mum like we used to but she says it's "good" for me to "mix" so I should go.

23 Sun: Had a bath this morning. Not the treat it used to be when I was first on Bed O. I think my body is ok to look at. Definitely have breasts now, even when I lie down, and lady hair. Did Homework ALL afternoon. Went to church. Told Wendy I'm not coming to Y. C. anymore. I won't enjoy staying in now but I find Y.C. so very boring.

24 Mon: Today Janet said she is giving a mixed party for Minny's birthday. I'm going!!! Goody! I'm going to invite Billy! I hope oh how I hope that he'll take me. I'm sure if I could go out with him once he'd come back for more. Ummm! Bliss! Another boring day at school. I can't even tell Susan how unhappy I am about dad. I know the gang know about him but if I don't say anything, maybe they'll forget. I feel so deeply deeply ashamed still.

25 Tue: All day I've been that excited worried + scared as I'm going to ring Billy to ask him to come to Janet's party. Rang him. He said "Oh yes I'd love to. Thank you very much for inviting me." He's great! He never enquired about the party except the date, so he must be just content to be with me! I like him tons + I think he likes me. God answered my prayers.

26 Wed: Oh I am so happy! Happy! Happy! I didn't think Billy would come but to say he'd love to without even hesitating! No one at school seriously thought he would either I think. At 4.00 he was outside his bus as I went past. Hope he's there tomorrow! I must try to say hello at least. Went to Confirmation Class. After, we (me, Wendy, Janet) went for a walk and met the usual Runcorn Balfour Road boys. NO interest to me.

27 Thu: Saw Billy on the field at dinner time. He waved! Oh, he is nice. I do so like him! He wasn't by his bus tonight, but he waved to me from inside! Oh! Nearly 8 whole days before the party! Oh! Wish it was tomorrow! Hope he goes to the school play on Fri. I think he's super. He seems to like me!

28 Fri: In the evening, I went back to school to meet Susan & co to see Sandra's best friend Carolyn Lister[89] in "Blythe Spirit". It was great -

[89] *Carolyn Lister went on to the Birmingham School of Speech*

very very funny. All the actors were very good but Carolyn was the best. That's two actresses I know! Will it be Carolyn or Helen who succeeds? Maybe I'll know TWO famous people one day! Barry went to the play but not Billy – boo hooooooo!

29 Sat: Got some new shoes – size 7, beige, heels. They are lovely! Went to Y.C. Better than last week. Met Billy after!! Talked to him, alone, for quarter of an hour! Then Janet came across. I could have killed her. He's so gorgeous, polite and wonderful!

30 Sun: Learnt (or at least tried to learn) Geog for a test, but Rita + Teddy came early afternoon so I had to amuse the kids. Didn't mind really but oh! all that unlearnt Geog, to be learnt for Tue! After church at night Janet, Wendy, Minny + I + some boys went for a walk. Met more of Y.C. lot at the Park. They're ok but all I could think about was Billy   Billy   Billy

Training and Dramatic Art and became an actress on TV and stage. In the 1970s, I saw her in a play in London with Michael Crawford. She married the actor William Gaunt.

MAY 1961

1 Mon: School. Goody only 5 more days till the weekend! Wish it was Friday! I'm terrified in case Billy goes off me before Friday – if he's on me now that is! Saw him, he waved. He's great. I like him more each day. In last lesson I was in the library talking to Christine. She said Billy does like me. Oh! It's too marvellous!

2 Tues: I think I love Billy, because I care so much about what he thinks of me, that it hurts. If he doesn't like me + ask me for a date after the party I'll feel most awfully upset. In Physics I felt all nervous and couldn't concentrate. I kept thinking "He doesn't like me I bet he thinks I'm a fool + horrid to look at." I think I am too. I am afraid he's been told to "be nice" to "poor Barbara" 'cos her dad is in prison and she's had T.B. I bet even if he does still come to the party, that'll be it, he won't want to be "nice" to me more than he has to.

3 Wed: In the evening I went to Confirmation Class. Afterwards Wendy, Janet + I went for a walk and met "the boys". Wendy won't go out with Keith (the one with red hair who goes to Balfour Rd Sec Mod) because she wants to be "equally friendly with them all". I think Keith is awfully nice. If Billy (but I hope he does) doesn't ask me out, I'll try for Keith unless Minny does.

4 Thu: All day all we have talked about is the party. I'm terribly excited – and nervous. I do hope Billy likes me. Chris told me he does as he's always talking about me! Also, whenever I see him he waves and gives a lovely, very friendly smile! I do so hope he will ask me for date after!!!

5 Fri: JANET'S PARTY. Billy came at 7.15 + we walked up the road to Janet's house. He wore a black suit + a blue tie (to match his blue eyes). He's fabulous. We 'necked' for 2hrs 20mins. He is awfully passionate. He kissed me long + hard – great! He kissed my neck + cheeks + when he caressed the back of my neck, I felt a shiver down my spine. Billy is marvellous. He is 100x nicer than I thought.

6 Sat: Today I have felt very depressed. "The Party's Over" and so, alas, is my affair with Billy. He didn't ask me for a date. He hinted but he said he wouldn't be able to go out at all now as he has G.C.E in a month. I hope he asks me afterward. He must like me or he couldn't have kissed me so passionately? I returned them so he knows how I feel. I feel empty now without him.

7 Sun: Went to Y.C. last night but kept thinking "Last night I …" Gosh! It's hard to believe I spent 2hrs necking with Billy! I didn't think I was like 'that' but I am + boy do I love it. I ache with longing for Billy. I do so love him, I do, I do. After Church tonight, a boy I hardly know (Terry) who was at Janet's party said "Would you + Billy like to come to my party on Saturday?" It's the answer to my prayers! Hope he'll come!

8 Mon: <u>School</u> Talked about the party. Oh! I do hope Billy will go to Terry's party! Wendy got a bit ratty 'cos everyone has been teasing her about

Friday. She was a bit silly, starting to let a boy kiss her then giggling and getting off his knee. I'm glad I didn't have to kiss anyone else, only Billy. Went to a talk "The Evolution of Jazz" at dinnertime. Alone. The gang wouldn't go. Didn't see Billy there but he may have been 'cos he likes jazz too. His bus passed ours but I was so engrossed in Minny's copy of Lady C.[90] that I missed him. Mmmm … I now know what passionate love is really like but some bits in it I can't ever imagine doing. I'd be embarrassed and giggle.

9 Tue: Christine was supposed to tactfully find out if Billy wanted to go to Terry's party. She just asked him! Fortunately he did! She said he wanted me to ring him up after school, so I did. After school, I rang him. He asked what time etc. He seemed pleased to go but he's still worried about his exams, poor boy. I do hope we have as nice a time as last time! Christine told me in the library that she wrote my name on Billy's jotter + he didn't object! With other girls names he's scribbled them off!

10 Wed: Went to Confirmation Class but I didn't go for a walk after as it was a bit cold (I only had

---

[90] *Lady C:* Following a Court Case, the first unexpurgated copy of D.H. Lawrence's Lady Chatterley's Lover was published in the UK in 1960. Penguin Books quickly sold three million copies and it was said to have been read by ten times that many people. Our copy was read by more than ten of us. It had been written in the late 1920s and so was already a bit dated by the 1960s. We found it hilarious rather than erotic but were keen to learn from the sex scenes.

my cardigan over my dress) and I wouldn't want Billy to think that I flirt with any of those boys. I love being in bed, thinking about Billy and Saturday. Can't wait!

11 Thu: A Latin test today for 3A. Poor things! I'm glad I don't have to do Latin + anyway I enjoy my free periods (talking to Christine about Billy!) I have to face the fact that no matter how well I do in the Summer exams I won't be allowed to stay in the A form without Latin. I just pray I will at least be allowed to go into the 4th year. I could not bear being with girls so much younger than me. I even feel older than my friends of the same age because of Crossley. Yah! Yah! Yah! Soon be Sa- Sa-Saturday. Yipee! Party time! Hope all goes well. Hope a spot on my chin goes. Friction from Billy's chin!!

12 Fri: DEANERY COMPETITIONS PAROCHIAL HALL at 7.00 Minny, Wendy + I went early to help set out. We were told last week at YC we all had to enter something so I did flower arranging. Only three entries so I should at least have got 3rd prize but the judges only awarded 1st and 2nd! Not fair. The quiz team (two boys I don't really know + Minny + I) drew with Norley Y.C. Then after an unfair tie question we lost. Irritating night. Anything I do now that isn't to do with Billy is a waste of time.

13 Sat: TERRY'S PARTY 7.00-10.30 Billy came at 10 to 7. We walked up there. It's quite a way but I didn't mind 'cos I was alone with Billy for longer. When the boys had to go out in the beginning of

Shop, Billy wouldn't go 'cos he said he only wanted to be with me so there was no point! He's great. I do like him. He put his arm round me as we walked home + kissed me goodnight twice. He asked me for a DATE!!!

14 Sun: In the afternoon Rita + Teddy + the kids came (again). I played with them in the garden until 4.30 and then we went to Bluebell Wood. I didn't get back in time for church so I stayed at home + watched T.V. I have felt in a daze all day thinking about Billy. I can't believe how gorgeous he is. He really does like me!

15 Mon: Everyone was talking about the party – how badly Janet behaved (she sulked + wouldn't be kissed) + how gorgeous Billy was + that he's asked me out on Saturday! I wonder where we'll go? Unfortunately there's an X (Camp on Blood Island) on at the Empress. Oh well, so long as I'm with him!

16 Tue: Today in Physics I was daydreaming, fell off my stool, scratched my leg, + hurt my bottom back bone so now I have a 'sprained tail'!! I just keep thinking about Billy. Can't wait until I'm with him again. (P.S. Next day it was only a little bit sore, then my tail was O.K. by Thurs!)

17 Wed: Today I have had a funny feeling that I am GOING OFF BILLY. I hope I'm not. I don't want to but it came over me, all of a sudden. This happened before in Crossley with John then Kenny but they weren't real and Billy is. I think I'm afraid it won't last and I'll be so hurt if it doesn't. Went to

Confirmation Class. Afterwards went for a walk, and when I saw and heard that lot of lousy boys, I went right back on Billy – pronto!

18 Thu: Took Scamp for a walk after school so I could use a telephone box for privacy. I phoned Billy as he asked me to. We were on the 'phone for over ½ an hour! In the end, a man who was waiting got me out of the phone box or we'd have been there til 8.00 I'm sure. Oh he's wonderful! I do so like him! The Fair is here from today until Mon. I hope I go with Billy on Sunday after our date on Saturday.

19 Fri: Went to the Dentist after school as I have a bad tooth-ache which moves round the right side of my mouth. He thought it was a loose filling so he's replaced it. I bet it was Billy's kisses that dislodged it! At 7.15 I went to a 'Tramps Supper' at St. John's Y.C. with Minny. Liz and others from school were there 'cos it's their church. We were funny Tramps! It was good fun. Mummy has finished my new dress. Its super. Sleeveless, round neck, gathered skirt. I'll wear it on Saturday. Hope Billy likes me in it!

20 Sat: At night I went to Warrington on the bus with Billy to see "Suzie Wong". It was a good film + Billy is great. I loved being with him in the cinema. Every bit as good as I'd dreamed it would be! I do like him a lot. I love being held by him. He asked me for ANOTHER DATE! We missed the last bus so Barry came for us and ran me home at 11.30!   The film made me think of Wong in Crossley but I didn't mention that to Billy. I thought of telling him about Mave but decided not to. Suzie Wong was a different sort of prostitute I think. Anyway, I want to forget all that. I can't believe he wants to see me again after 2 parties and 1 date! I was with him for at least 5 hours and it was ALL grrrreat!

21 Sun: WHIT SUNDAY I have a guilty conscience because I have not been to Church. I should go because I have so much to be thankful for. God answered my prayers about a date with Billy and that's where I was instead! I got the 7.20 bus to the village where their farm is. Billy met me + we went for a walk all round - about 7 miles! I did enjoy myself. I do so like him. We talked and kissed and walked and kissed – bliss!! My lips feel bruised!

22 Mon: WHIT MONDAY If I was still at Bethesda, I'd have walked. Last year, I wished I could. This year, I'd rather walk with Billy! He came on the 6.30 bus + we went for a walk. We got home at 8.30 + sat in the sitting room till 9.10, then he went for his bus. It was nice again but not as long and he seemed shy. He hardly kissed me. I hope that was 'cos there were people around on our walk and 'cos we were then in my house. I have an awful feeling that's it. He said he can't go out now 'cos its G.C.E. exams soon, but he said "There's always afterwards" I hope there is. Last time he said he couldn't see me til after his exams, he changed his mind. I don't think he will again. I don't really think he will want to see me after either. This was my FIRST LOVE AFFAIR. Is it already over?

23 Tue: When I woke up today I had a throbbing in my (right) front tooth. It has gone out of the others (I had that pain off + on for a few weeks) + now only this tooth hurts + is very painful. It makes me jump if I touch it so it's a good job I've not got a date with Billy or wow! would I scream after one of <u>his</u> kisses!

24 Wed: Woke up today to find my upper lip, nose + cheeks badly swollen. My tooth isn't too bad now, but I feel horrid with this lip. The inside of my lip is outside its so swollen. I went to see the young dentist, Mr Powell, + he said a nerve has blown up in my front tooth + he'll have to "de-sensitise" it. I've got to suck penicillin lozengers till Friday. I am glad Billy isn't seeing me like this.

25 Thu: Felt much better today. My face has gradually gone down, until at night only my upper lip under my nose + my right cheek is up + not as much as before. Oh! I wonder what Mr Powell will do? Wendy came over. I wanted to talk about Billy but she's not interested. I know I love him. I can't bear the thought that this is it. I am trying to be glad I had 2 parties and 3 dates with him but now that is not enough. If that's it, maybe it would have been better never to have known how wonderful he is and what bliss it is to be kissed by him.

26 Fri: Went to the Dentists after school. Although my face is much, much, better he said he couldn't do anything to it yet, so I'll have to come back on Tues p.m. Wendy came for tea. After, we took Scamp for a walk up Runcorn Hill. We saw the YC boys and girls playing football! Fools! I had to talk about Billy. Wendy said Janet likes him a lot. I like the thought of her being jealous! But what if Billy finds out and asks her for a date? I could not bear that. It's bad enough not knowing til after the exams if he will ask me out again but if he asks anyone else, I will go mad.

27 Sat: At 1.15 I went to Sandbach with the Y.C. where a Youth Rally was being held. Our Y.C. didn't do very well, but in the quiz (me, Minny, + same two boys as last time) we won! It was boring for me. I don't like any of these horrid boys + the silly way everyone acts around them. If Billy had been there it would have been great. Janet can't be that keen on Billy – she was necking with one of the YC boys all the way home on the coach! I wish I could see or speak to Billy. I do so miss him + I think about him a lot. If he really liked me, he'd want us to at least talk on the phone, surely?

28 Sun: All day I have felt very very depressed. I long for Billy and I think about him constantly. When I look in the mirror I wonder how a boy as marvellous as Billy could want me. I feel that, after the exams, he'll forget, or not want us to go out. Rita + co came in the afternoon so, yet again, I got no hmk done. Went to Church. Wendy + I didn't go for a walk. She wanted to but I couldn't be bothered.

29 Mon: Billy Billy Billy What a problem. I like him so much it hurts half the time and yet the other half I think blow! he does annoy me. If he really likes me, why doesn't he talk to me at school? That would not be interfering with his revision. I don't think he really likes me. I really like him, I think. Revised Chem. Took ages to learn 4 pages. I feel as if I only get to be happy in little bits before it all goes wrong. I was happy to leave Crossley, then the dad stuff. I was happy to go out with Billy but that didn't last long. I am happy to be back at school with my friends but unless I do well in the exams, I'll be here but not with them.

30 Tue: Today Billy was down the boys field but he never looked at me, not even when they went in for dinners. He must have seen me near the dividing cinder track. That put me in a "don't-like-him-much-anyway" mood. When I saw him by the bus after school he beamed + said hello. I just said hello back and gave him a little smile but didn't stop. Oh dear, now he'll be thinking I don't like him. Went to the Dentist and had my front tooth de-sensitised by having the nerve out. It didn't hurt at all + I didn't have an injection. Learnt R.K. Not bad.

31 Wed: Life seems to be full of so many problems that I can hardly bear it. Perhaps I shouldn't but I think + worry + wonder + question religion + politics + crime + the H-bomb.[91] Less important

---

[91] _The H bomb:_ _In the late 1950s and early 1960s, fear of nuclear war was a frequent topic in the news. Teenagers were as consumed with worry about that then as many today are about climate change. Then, as now, there was huge frustration that the older generation, having made the mess and created the threat, did not seem to be in any hurry to tackle the issue._

problems to many, but big to me, are Daddy, boyfriends, my nose + my T.B. After Confirmation class tonight I talked to Vicar Barlow for 50 mins about how Church is unreal to me, why God lets so many bad things happen etc but he could not help. I feel as if I'm just not meant to be happy for long. It will be even worse when dad is released.

JUNE 1961

1 Thu: Mummy had a letter from Daddy. He comes out on Tuesday[92] + is coming straight here for a talk. I told mummy that I will do whatever she wants me to, be nice to him or forget him. After Sandra's exams he's coming back to stay. I wish he wasn't. It'll be a hard job, but for mummy's sake I hope it's worth it + life is happier for her. Sandra said she's still not going to speak to him. It does not seem like 6 months since we last saw him. I am very unhappy. I have got a complex about (a) people letting me down. I don't really trust anyone completely, except mum. (b) boys. I think they all dislike me + I'll never be in love + I'll be lonely. (c) my looks. I'm ugly, especially my nose and my hair and now my skin. (d) school. I have tried to work hard enough to catch up so I can stay with my friends but I don't think I have and it's too late now.

2 Fri: In art I did free design. Art, for me, is frustrating because I have lots of idea but not the ability to carry them out! Watched Hancock on B.B.C. As always, very funny! He's great, my favourite. I want us to enjoy our peaceful last days without daddy but bit of an atmosphere 'cos of Sandra's attitude. I agree with her – I hate him and

---

[92] *Date of release:* *The diary says my father was sentenced to six months in prison on 10 February, but as his release date was Tue 6 June, either I recorded that incorrectly or he only served four months of his sentence, perhaps being released with a third remission for good behaviour?*

his drinking and I don't want him to ever come back[93] – but I have to do what mummy wants.

3 Sat: Went to the Dentist – last visit I'm glad to say – then went shopping with mummy. She is smoking a lot and a bit snappy. I wonder if she really wants dad back? Is she just doing her "duty"? In the afternoon I tried to swot Biol, couldn't, so read "Scarlet Pimpernel". It's set in France and is quite exciting. I don't know how I'd manage without books to escape into. I didn't go to Y.C. It is so boring. I think even T.V. is better than Y.C. Mum + Sandra think I'm soft + if I stopped "acting grown-up" I'd enjoy Y.C.

4 Sun: To church in the evening without Wendy. Home (no walk) watched T.V. Talked to Barry while he was waiting for Sandra. Really hard not to ask him about Billy. I'm glad to say I managed it. Dreamt I slept with Billy, not sex, just necking etc. Funny - not really thrilling or exciting. In the morning, I took bunches of roses from our garden to Nannie + Aunty Laura. They were very pleased. I am thinking a lot about Crossley at the moment. Not sure why. Maybe it's because I feel so unhappy most of the time, just like I was there.

---

[93] *Years later, as an adult, I had more understanding. After his awful experiences in Burma and India in WW2, my father might well have been depressed and self-medicating with alcohol. PTSD was, in those days, unheard of, and men returning from the war had no support or counselling.*

5 Mon: I feel very depressed. I am writing down the reasons. 1) I can't learn + exams start in <u>18</u> days. If I don't do well, I won't move up to the 4th year with my friends. 2) I hate the thought of Dad coming back. Our peace will be shattered. I have promised mummy I'll be nice to him but I'm not sure I'll be able to. 3) Billy doesn't even wave to me anymore from his bus. He isn't going to ask me out when his exams are over. He went to a dance at the British Legion in Runcorn on Friday. He'd have asked me if he liked me. So much for not being able to go out because of his exams. I'll cross his name off my ruler now + say I don't like him, but I think I still do. 4) I am ugly and I am getting spots and no one will ever want me. LIFE IS VERY COMPLICATED AND I WISH I WASN'T ALIVE

6 Tue: Today I have been so awfully depressed that I wished life had never been invented. I worry about things like I listed yesterday. I was thinking about Daddy especially. He came for a visit while we were at school. Mum says he's changed. She always believes he has. I don't want our peace disturbed but he ought to come back. Sandra is being very difficult. I want to be as well but I have promised mummy. Learnt Biol (heart) and French tenses. It is very hard to revise when I am so unhappy. I cannot bear the thought of dad living here again.

7 Wed: Didn't feel too depressed today. At least I hid it better I think. When I pretend I'm ok, sometimes I then start to feel ok. Went to Confirmation Class. I listened rather half-heartedly as Vicar Barlow was talking about the same old thing, cracked the same corny jokes! Learnt my French pronouns while he was going on so some good came of it! Cos I wouldn't go for a walk after, Janet said "You are a weird girl". I just do not have the heart to be a jolly teenager at the moment but I can't tell anyone why. If Billy loved me, dad coming back might not seem so awfully bad.

8 Thu: From today until 14th I found my diary a blank and so is my memory concerning the details of this time. Roughly I remember that I revised, felt very miserable, went nowhere + longed + longed + longed for Billy. I know I felt very sad because I knew that despite his promises he would never get in touch with me after the exams yet I loved him as much as a girl of my age can. I feel as if there is nothing to look forward to. It is an eternity since he held me in his arms + kissed me so tenderly + so passionately. As I write this, so many days after our last date, I can still remember every detail of the times I had with him.

15 Thu: When I was going out with Billy I'm sure I was a nicer person. I wasn't so irritable and lazy but happy to show God how grateful I was for granting my prayers. I wanted to be really good. Perhaps it is just the physical side of love that I long for. NOT sex, but kisses and affection. I feel terribly depressed, convinced that no one nice will ever desire me + I'll never meet a boy as nice as Billy. I want love so much that it hurts. I plan desperately how I could get Billy back so that once more I could feel secure + loved by someone else, as well as my mummy. I wonder if my friends go through such agonies? I don't think they do. Anyway, most of them have boys and their fathers aren't alcoholic thieves who've been to prison.

16 Fri: School. In art I started to do a picture poster for "PAVLOV'S PUPPETS". I won't be able to finish it before the exams though. Learnt Geog. If I could go to a dance, I might meet a boy I like who will fall for me + do something about it. If I saw Billy there, holding another girl, how would I bear it? If we could go on holiday this Summer, I might have a holiday romance, but 'cos of dad, we've no money. I do not think I can manage to be pleasant to him when he comes back. I still really hate him. I will never trust him again.

17 Sat: Revised Biol all afternoon. How very, very boring! I seem to have done a lot of work but learnt nothing! This is getting serious. At night I watched another episode of the "Valiant Years" (about Churchill and the war) with mummy. It showed Belsen and mass hangings + graves. It was horrid. How can we say we are civilised when war and things like that still happen?[94] The war must have

---

[94] *"The Valiant Years"* was a documentary based on the memoirs of Winston Churchill. It was televised between Feb and Aug 1961 and was narrated by Richard Burton. I watched almost all the episodes with my mother. I liked that it led her to talk about how she and her family had lived during the war. The episodes about the holocaust disturbed me particularly. Later, I came to appreciate more about other aspects (such as the bombing of Dresden) but, then, I was totally and uncritically patriotic about what 'we' did in the war.

been horrible, even for people not fighting. Mummy seems to have enjoyed herself though, working, and living with her parents so nannie could look after Sandra. Dad was in Burma and India with the RAF but he never talks about it and he doesn't like watching anything to do with the war on T.V. All I know is he lost his faith there (and his hair) and he hates anything to do with Japan.[95]

18 Sun: Wendy and I went to church in the morning. In the afternoon Rita and Teddy and the kids came at 20 to 3 + stayed until 6.15!!!! I got no work done through them. Mummy should let me go upstairs when I've work to do but I'm expected to play with the children so they'll be good. At night I learnt some chemistry but it was a great struggle. I'm dreading that exam. I am really afraid I have not worked hard enough to catch up. If I don't do well in the exams, that's it. Mummy knows that but

---

[95] *A TV documentary I had seen about Hiroshima and Nagasaki had left a deep impression on me. When, later, I joined CND (the Campaign for Nuclear Disarmament) I had many arguments with my father about the American bombing of Japan. He was in favour. In his view, it had ended the war and saved more lives than had been lost, and, based on his first-hand experience of the Japanese forces in Burma and India, he thought it was the only way to persuade Japan to accept defeat. Although he told me not to continue to go to CND, I took no notice. In 2009, I stayed with a Japanese friend in Tokyo and visited Hiroshima. I found in the museum there a much more complex account of the thinking and events that led up to the decision to use the H-bomb than either my father or I had then been aware of then.*

she's not helping. I think dad should stay away until after my exams like he is for Sandra.

19 Mon: Had another bash at Chemistry. I've learnt it all once but by Thurs I bet I will have forgotten it! Watched "Coronation Street" as usual even if it is exam week! Since it started in December – on my last night in Crossley! - we don't miss an episode. Must have some relaxation! Mummy said HE is coming home on Thurs. Sandra's exams are over. I promised to be nice for her sake but I wish he wasn't. That is so unfair. Why can't he stay away until MY exams are over too.

20 Tue: Spent a lot of time on French (Irregular Verbs) at night. They just won't go in. I also learnt some Biol (Hydra) + some Geog that I had somehow missed when I was copying up earlier. I tried to tell mummy how worried I am about the exams. She must know how much it means to me to stay with my friends next year. She said he is still coming home on Thu. She should think of me. I think she is being selfish. Sandra is so lucky. If she does ok in her exams, she'll be going to Teacher Training College or even University in September. I'll be stuck here with him. I HATE him.

21 Wed: Didn't go to jolly old Confirmation Class as I was swotting. I learnt some French irregular verbs + of course Chemistry + Eng Lang. I just can't learn the Chemistry equations or formulae! Ah well, ne'er mind, eh? What will be will be. I say that but I am in HELL at the thought of failing the exams, staying down a year – I'd be repeating work

I've already done with younger girls I don't know – AND all the while living with dad again. HELL.

22 Thu: EXAMS START   The ENG.LANG was very hard. I'm sure I've lost at least 32 marks and as I always lose more than I expect, I'll be lucky to get 50% and I was banking on Eng for a good mark to pull up my average. General opinion is it was hard + so was Chemistry. I've made piles of "boobs" but I didn't think that was as bad as I had expected. Dad came home. He was here when I got back from school. Sandra was all right. We were both polite. He gave me a tobacco tin he'd scratched a picture on for me. I do not want it but I said thank you. I could not bring myself to kiss him goodnight. Mummy looks ill but she's the one who wanted him back. I could not concentrate on revision after tea but I was glad not to have to sit downstairs with him there. Sandra, of course, went out with Barry. If only I had Billy to love and comfort me.

23 Fri: Today we had Religious Knowledge in the afternoon. It wasn't too bad but there was an awful lot to write in 1 ½ hrs + mine was a bit hurried I think. I know a lot from Sunday School as well as from school. I know he is trying but I can't bear dad. I just don't believe he's changed. I don't trust him. I don't like speaking to him or anything. Wish he'd go. I feel sick just being in the same room. He couldn't drink while he was in prison but it won't be long before he starts again. Why does mummy always think this time he means it?

24 Sat: At night I went to a Midsummer hop at the Parochial Hall with Minny. I didn't want to go but I can't bear being in now dad is back. I wish it was just me and mummy. I don't want him in but if he goes out, he'll start drinking again. HELL. Amazingly, I really enjoyed the dance. There was a good group "Bruce + the Cavaliers" really diggy! 3 guitars + drums.

25 Sun: I didn't go to church today. I was too busy trying to learn Physics. I had Sat night off, that's all I dare. It's been fabulously hot so I tried working in the garden but I haven't been able to concentrate at all. I still don't know any physics, but I have tried to learn it. I'm dreading the exam. Mummy made her usual delicious Sunday roast but I didn't enjoy it one bit 'cos HE was there. He is being so "nice" he makes me feel ill.

26 Mon: What a shock! I was told today that Susan had been rushed to hospital with acute appendicitis + operated on immediately. Poor Susan, I hope she's OK now. I wrote to her when 3A did Latin. Physics was horrible. I just couldn't do it. I'll guess at 43% for my mark!

27 Tue: This morning we had Revision and games. In the afternoon we had Eng. Lit. I thought it was a nice paper + I feel that I did it O.K. However when I feel like this it usually means I get bad marks.

28 Wed: Geography this morning. Boy were we rushed! I could have written much, much, more. I thought it was an easy paper but I made a mess of it, no doubt. Maths in the a.m. Ha! Ha! What a laugh! I missed 3 out + made up answers for the rest.

29 Thu: Biology in the morning. What a paper! I knew my Hydra well, but on Vegetative Reproduction I made it up more or less. Art in the p.m. I did a Pictorial Composition called "The Rescue". It was a picture of 3 potholers, one on a stretcher, one coming out of the hole, the other at the side.

30 Fri: French in the p.m. Dam! Dam! Dam! It's not fair, all the time I spent on my Irregular verbs + I got them all wrong I think. Everyone else said it was easy. We revised + had games in the afternoon. I bet I did awfully in French. It's been a tough week with exams but at least it kept my mind off home (dad) and how much I miss Billy. I am dreading the weekend. I don't like being at home anymore.

JULY 1961

1 Sat: Went down town with Sandra in the afternoon, shopping. Watched the T.V. at night with mummy. It was rotten. Corny Charlie Chester visiting military bases and doing shows. She liked it, I didn't. Not much we do both enjoy now. Nearly as bad as Y.C. Surprise surprise – dad was "out". We all know what that means. He hasn't got a job yet.

2 Sun: Learnt my History today. I feel that I know it as well as I am capable of learning any work for an exam. Went to Church. Sexy sermon – "a child is the material sign of physical love between man + wife" etc. Saw Hawaian Eye – since Billy, I'm back to preferring dark haired boys but I'd consider a blond - then back to revising. Life is dull and boring.

3 Mon: Second Maths exam in the morning. It was as bad as the other. I bet I get less than 20% for Maths. History was O.K. I put down all I knew + answered the questions well I think, but who knows what mistakes I made? Awful to think my whole future depends on these exams. The more I think about what failing means the more I find it hard to learn.

4 Tue: Exam results are starting to come in. I am starting to hope I might be doing well enough to convince Miss Bird to let me stay with my friends and go up into the 4th year! I got Chemistry 61% . Geography 74% and English language 70% Very pleased with all three.

5 Wed: Today: French <u>49%</u> and our English Lit <u>67%.</u> I was disappointed in both these marks. In French 'cos I only got 8/20 for verbs and in Eng. Lit 'cos I thought I'd done so well in it. I'd put lots of quotes. Top mark was only 71 though so I know I should be quite pleased.

6 Thu: Biology – what a shock 76! I was 5th! I am pleased cos I thought I'd messed the paper up. Goody! Goody! Maths – 24%, bottom, natch. As I expected, but no help to my total, alas! History a very big disappointment – 59%. I think she marked meanly cos I had all the points I should have had. 63 for Art. I was very pleased + surprised!

7 Fri: DR HUGHES 9.30. I'm getting on very well he said. I told him about my stomach ache when I take cachets and he's going to give me some medicine for it. Mummy came with me but I went back to school on the bus by myself. I've been wondering which is best (a) To go out with no boy as I can't have Billy, though I long for his kisses and love, OR (b) Go out with a boy I'm not really keen on so at least I have A boyfriend. I will wait until there's no chance at all of getting Billy but if I don't ever go out with him again, I hope I meet someone as nice, if such a person exists.

8 Sat: I went to see Susan at her home today. She isn't as ill as I had expected after her appendix op. Linda from school was there. We stayed for tea. After, we went to see "G.I. Blues" at Frodsham. Mmm ... Elvis!! Reminds me of Billy. We chatted to two boys Linda knows. One was quite funny. I enjoyed the evening but after I found chewing gum in my hair – ugh! Someone must have put it there. Sandra had to cut it out for me.

9 Sun: On Friday afternoon Miss Addyman, our form and Geog teacher, took 3A up Helsby Hill[96] so today I was writing it up in my field book. It was lovely being out in the sun with my friends and the exams over! I had that sudden thought – I am happy! At night I went to Church. I sat by Wendy. I want to keep the happy feeling I had on Friday afternoon but today and most days I feel fed-up and miserable. I just don't like being here now dad is back.

10 Mon: Sports Day heats. Even me!! Some of the girls were talking about going on holiday with their parents – two are actually going abroad (Italy and France). I'll be lucky to get as far as Widnes! I don't want a family holiday anymore anyway because he'd have to come. We can't afford one. He's still not got a job. Who'd want to employ him after what he's done?

[96] *Helsby Hill, opposite Helsby Grammar School, is a sandstone ridge, with great views of the Mersey Estuary from the top. Nearby is the similar but higher Frodsham Hill which, in that period, had a helter-skelter and a ballroom at the top (where I saw the Beatles a couple of years later). Later, the Australian film "Picnic at Hanging Rock", made me think of that day because I remember it as hot and having a sense of release after the exams and being happy with my friends but fortunately that is where the similarity to the film ends.*

11 Tue: Today: R.K. marks: 76% - 9th!! Also Physics 67% - 11th (Cor!!!) She then gave us our final average + total: 62.3%   26th (out of 32)! I'm very, very pleased! This MUST be enough to let me go into the 4th Year in September. I did better than I had hoped.

12 Wed: Another day of horrible, cold, wet, windy weather. It was so bad at night that mummy wouldn't let me go to Confirmation class because of the walk there and back. I was glad really as I think it is boring.

13 Thu: I should be happy I've done so well in the exams but I'm not. I know that is important, and I couldn't bear it if I'd had to repeat the year, stuck with younger girls I don't know, but I am so very unhappy about life now. These are the thoughts I constantly have. I wish a boy that I could love would love me. I long for kisses + to be wanted + needed. I don't want sex, just love + kissing like Billy gave me. I pretend to everyone that I do not like him but I do, it's just that I supress my emotions. I wish home was just me and mummy and Sandra. I wish we weren't so hard up. I wish I could stop going for check-ups and forget I ever had T.B. I cannot imagine how my life is ever going to get better.

14 Fri: Miss Lewis wants me to write an article on reading for the School Mag. about all the books I read while in Crossley. I'm not sure I want to draw everyone's attention to that.

15 Sat: Rain! Rain! Rain! I hope St. Swithin's legend doesn't come true, 'cos if it does it will rain till 24 August. Dad is trying to be nice. Mummy wants us to try harder but Sandra won't. He's not drinking at the moment (as far as I can tell) but he will again, he always does. I will never forgive him for what he did. He broke his promise to God and shamed us. I'll never trust him again. I wish he wasn't here.

16 Sun: Couldn't be bothered to go to church or do anything. Just messed about and read. I know now that Billy is not going to ask me out again. His exams finished ages ago. I have been told he was at a dance and behaved commonly with noted low girls. That makes me very miserable. I am determined to forget him. He quite obviously never liked me the way I did him.

17 Mon: Today in Maths Miss Wilkey read out which division we would go into next term. I am going into Div III. There are two others who will but they are going to appeal. I'm not. I am glad I'm going to be in Div III 'cos it's Commercial Maths and Statistics. I don't care if I end up being the only girl out of this form there, I'd rather have a chance to understand and get my GCE.

18 Tue: I gave in my "Reading" article on Mon + today Miss Lewis sent for me. It's very good she said. I've got to copy it out again with the mechanical errors corrected. I didn't really want to write it but I'm pleased she likes it. I am still thinking about Billy. I can't stop. I don't tell anyone I am. I feel massive affection and gratitude that he was my first (and so far only) boy and he was so nice to me. I will always remember those 2 parties and 3 dates.

19 Wed: We aren't doing many lessons at the moment at school. My Geography field book was on display in the Domestic Science room! So now, with all the other merit marks and subject signatures I've had, I'll be able to get Miss Birds signature for "outstanding work" in a number of subjects. More evidence that I have done enough to stay with my friends!

20 Thu: I gave back my article on reading to Miss Lewis. I don't like it, because even if it is well written (+ she praised it highly!) it isn't an interesting subject. Who cares what I read! Anyway it is definitely in the mag. + I'm glad about that. She couldn't believe that I had done it with no help at all! Or that I'd read so much and so widely!

21 Fri: Hurrah! Hurrah! Hurrah! Barbara's in 4A!!! I am very, very, pleased! I thought I'd done well enough to go into 4th year but I did not expect 4A as I don't do Latin. Miss Addyman said 4A is the hardest worked form in the school! They must think I can do it! We take all the subjects for the next year then we can drop two the final GCE year. Our form room is the Physics Lab. with Mrs Bradley! Must try harder not to fall off a stool!! Billy isn't coming back to school in September but I think his blond friend, Mick is, so maybe I'll try for him. I am feeling lucky!!

POSTSCRIPT

In July 1963, in 5A, I passed 8 GCEs (English Language, English Literature, Maths, History, Geography, Biology, French, Art). However, I did not join my friends in the 6th Form because in August that year, my father's drinking – he had remained sober for only a very short time after he came out of prison – had become so much worse and, for the first time, he was becoming aggressive when drunk, not just with my mum, but with me. (Sandra had by then left home, having been to university (for one year only) and married Barry.) Mum and I fled our home and went to live with Nannie and Grandad Wakefield in Bridgewater Street, Runcorn.

Because of my TB and the domestic violence, and the fact that my grandparents' terraced house was only two up two down with no bathroom and an outside toilet, we were given a Council flat a few months later. My mother had to take out an injunction to stop my father coming and threatening us. He, meanwhile, continued to live in our old house. He sold or disposed of most of my childhood and many of my mother's possessions and, eventually, sold the house. We were able to keep very little. Although much of the money to pay for the house and its contents had come from my mother's grocery business – which he had helped bankrupt years before because of his drinking – the house was in his name, as was the way then, and the law regarded it as his, not half my mum's. She came out of the Legal Separation very badly. They never divorced but I did not see him again. He died when

I was 32. Having become a mother by then, I had started to think about my own childhood and his part in it and why he drank.

Knowing that things were becoming bad at home and that it would be difficult for just my mum to support me if I stayed on at school, during my final GCE year I had applied and been accepted for a place on a full-time secretarial course at the local Further Education College, paid for by ICI, who would also pay me a small wage and give me a job at the end. Once we had left home, I was glad to have that option available. We were desperately in need of the money to live, with only my mum's shop wages to support us.

I completed the secretarial course (winning the Course Prize) and started at ICI, Runcorn, in July 1964. I was soon promoted out of the typing pool into a job working for a group of men, then became the Assistant to the Secretary for the Head of Graduate Recruitment, Mr Caird. One day, he told me I was "wasted as a secretary" and that it wasn't too late to try for university.

Mum knew I wasn't finding the work very satisfying so, when I told her that, she contacted my old English teacher, Miss Lewis, to find out if what I'd been told was realistic. Miss Lewis said my best bet was to apply for Teacher Training College but I'd need at least one A level. So, in late October 1964, I began studying, by myself, for English Literature A level, using books (and records) supplied by Miss Lewis, while continuing to work full-time (and enjoy myself as anyone of that age wants to do but especially someone who felt she had a lost year to make up for). Closer to the exam, Miss Lewis gave me some one-to-one tuition for a few Saturday afternoons. I took the exam at my old school. To my astonishment, I achieved Grade A!

I was accepted at Alsager Teacher Training College, Cheshire, but when I arrived there in Sept 1965, I found that they had just begun to offer the new B.Ed degree through Keele University. I therefore enrolled for that (in English Literature and Drama) alongside the Teaching Certificate. I completed the Teaching Certificate in July 1968 and the B.Ed Hons in June 1969. While a student, I had a short story published in a national magazine and poetry in student magazines. I then completed my Probationary Year as a teacher (in a comprehensive school in Manchester) but knew that was not the work I wanted to do long-term.

Through a flat-mate who was a student at Manchester University, I heard of a scholarship available for postgraduate work. I applied and was awarded a one year scholarship (fees plus living expenses) to do an M.A on the English Novel at Manchester University, starting in September 1970. It was a two year degree, including exams and a dissertation, but, as I only had enough money for one year, I asked if I could complete it by the end of the Summer 1971 so I could take up a teaching post. They agreed, so I took the exams in June, completed my dissertation (on Robert Tressell's *The Ragged-Trousered Philanthropists*) by late August and graduated in November 1971.

After that term teaching English and Drama in a comprehensive school near Sheffield, then working for a publisher (on a school edition of *The Ragged Trousered Philanthropists*) and in a variety of secretarial jobs, I joined the Fast Stream of the Civil Service in London in September 1972. That became my main career, although I had 10 years out while I had my three children.

During that period, I did a range of different part-time jobs, including copy-writing, teaching English in a private school in Oxford, and the basic Writing 101 in a university in Indiana, America, where my husband was Visiting Professor. We lived there twice and visited my old penpal Barby in South Dakota and met my father's relations in Indiana and Minnesota.

I returned to the Civil Service (Cabinet Office) in October 1987. I had a variety of job-sharing and part-time jobs before becoming full-time. I worked in a number of different Departments and Government organisations and wrote extensively in my professional capacity. One post involved international negotiation so I travelled to even more of the world than I had dreamed of when doing those jigsaws and reading in Crossley. I retired as a Senior Civil Servant in 2004, having been awarded a CBE.

Not bad for someone who only had four years of secondary education and missed an entire school year!

"As sometimes happens to children whose childhood is blighted by illness, isolation and suffering, a few of those sufferers also later achieved fame, fortune and perhaps happiness in the arts, literature and public life." p.263

The White Death: A History of Tuberculosis by Thomas Dormandy, The Hambledon Press, 1999

NOTE ON TUBERCULOSIS AND SANATORIA

Fri 13 November 1959

<u>Mantoux test and B.C.G</u>: In that period, we were all tested by having a mantoux test (or Tuberculin Skin Test) before we were given the BCG (Bacille Calmette-Guerin) vaccination against TB. It had been known since early in the 20th century that the presence of the tubercle bacillus in the body was not the same as tuberculosis the disease, although they were causally related. According to the current NHS website, the mantoux test is used to test whether a person has latent TB i.e. where TB is present but is not making the person ill. It involves injecting a small amount of a substance called PPD tuberculin into the skin of the forearm. If you have a latent TB infection, your skin will be sensitive to PPD tuberculin and a small, hard red bump will develop at the site of the injection, usually within 48 to 72 hours of having the test. If you have a very strong reaction, you will need a chest x-ray to confirm if you have active TB.

This test (sometimes called the Pirquet test) is no longer routinely given, nor is the BCG offered to children in secondary schools in the UK. It was replaced in 2005 with a targeted programme for babies, children and young adults at a higher risk of TB. This is because TB rates in this country are low in the general population and because TB is difficult to catch as it requires close contact with an infected person, usually over a long period of time.

While TB was not as common a killer then as it had been when my mother was young, in the 1950s, pulmonary TB was reckoned to be fatal within 5-15 years in 80% of cases. It could be acute or galloping but was usually chronic and intermittent. In children, it often attacked the bones and could cause deformity in adolescents who were still growing.

Mon 16 November 1959

Symptoms of TB According to the NIIS, the symptoms of TB include a lack of appetite and weight loss, a high temperature, night sweats and extreme tiredness or fatigue. Most TB is in the lungs (as mine was) and is called pulmonary TB When that moves from the latent to the active stage, it can result in a persistent cough which leads to phlegm being brought up, some of it possibly bloody, and increasing breathlessness. I never had a cough or breathing difficulties.

Sat 28 November 1959

Diagnosis: A chest x-ray, then and now, is usually the first step to diagnosing TB because the infection changes the appearance of the lungs, causing what we called 'shadows' (mild) and 'cavities' (serious). The infection causes a small lesion on the lungs. If it heals, as it may do in an otherwise healthy person or with treatment, it calcifies and shows up as a shadow. If the infection builds up and is not treated, some would be coughed up, and what would be left would be a space lined with tuberculous tissue, forming what is known as a cavity. A specialist would then examine the patient with a stethoscope and by tapping and listening (known as percussion and auscultation).

Sat 29 November 1959

Infectious or contagious – how easy is it to catch TB? My grandparents in particular were worried about my passing TB on to others. I don't know what advice my parents were given but I was allowed to go out shopping etc. although there were some restrictions.

According to the current NHS guidance, TB is spread from one person to another through tiny droplets released into the air when a person with TB coughs or sneezes and somebody else breathes in those droplets. However, TB is not easy to catch because you need to spend a long time in close contact with an infected person to do so. TB cannot be spread through touch or sharing cutlery, bedding or clothes. Not everyone with TB is infectious. Children do not generally spread the infection. People with latent TB are not infectious and not everyone with active TB is.

Mon 30 November 1959

Stigma: TB has, historically, been associated with poverty, poor housing and diet, and, because of that, has a stigma attached to it, hence my Nannie Salter's apparent shock and shame, having thought the poverty of Ireland was behind her family. I lived in a pleasant 1930s semi-detached house with three bedrooms and a large garden, in a residential area. Our family income fluctuated a lot during my childhood as my father gained, then lost, many jobs, so sometimes we were poor and at other times well-off but we always had good, home-cooked food and the house was clean and as well heated as any were in that period.

Nowadays, TB is still often seen as relating to poverty, or as a Third World illness, or is associated with HIV/AIDS so some stigma remains.

Mon 7 December 1959

The history of sanatoria: Sanatoria became established in the middle of the 19th century as the main way of treating tuberculosis and, for about 100 years, they flourished but their decline, once effective drugs were found, was rapid. While the harsh 'fresh air' regimes of the early ones probably did little to help, the bed-rest and graduated exercise of the later ones might have done. The long stays continued for a while, even when the new drugs were being used, but the Madras Experiment (1959) brought that to an end as it showed that patients treated at home did as well (or better) than those given the same drugs in a sanatorium. Perhaps those patients who were then considered unwise to 'sign themselves out' of Crossley actually did better than some who stayed? In 1962, the Medical Research Council said that those three drugs I had been given, taken over two years, was the optimal treatment. However, research soon after showed that they, and other, newer, drugs, could complete the healing in a much shorter time – months, not years. When I first found out that I had been in hospital much longer than was medically necessary, I was angry, but I now think that, awful as it was, at least the approach which combined the old method with the latest medicine meant I was well and truly cured and have remained very healthy ever since.

Tue 8 December 1959

Crossley Hospital/Sanatorium: From postcards of that time, Crossley Sanatorium looks like a red-brick stately home. It was set in 66 acres, about 3.5m away from Frodsham, the nearest town, and near Delamere Forest, Cheshire, a wooded area with lakes, such as Hatchmere. Crossley (East) Hospital (or the Manchester Sanatorium as it was originally known because it was intended initially for TB patients from there) opened in 1905, and was able to take 90 to 100 patients. The buildings included a main block with three storeys. There were 6-bed, 5-bed, 4-bed wards and singles, with men on one side (on the middle floor – it was different on ground floor surgical I think) and women on the other. In addition, there was a basement (housing Occupational Therapy), two large recreation or day rooms, attached kitchens, dining room (known as the canteen and also used for entertainments) and a chapel, nurses' home, mortuary, and out-buildings. In the grounds were wooden huts, open to the elements, for patients to be out in for 'fresh air' but which had fallen into disuse by the 1960s. Instead, we just had the floor to ceiling bay windows open all day and in all weathers.

In 1948, it was taken over by the NHS. By the time I was there, it took any adults with TB, many of whom were from Liverpool. By the early 1960s, there were not enough TB patients, so it started taking in cancer cases, then, later, did small general operations. Later still, it became a geriatric hospital and then an old people's care home. My Nannie Wakefield died there aged 81 (in 1979), in the 6-bedder middle-floor ward where I had been a patient. It was a very odd feeling visiting her there with my husband and young children. According to Wikipedia, it later became a mental hospital. After it closed (1988), it briefly became a boarding school (until 1991) and then lay derelict until 2006 when it was bought for re-development as a residential site.

Wed 9 December 1959

The source of my TB: I was never told what (or who) the source of my TB was. I have always assumed there must have been a carrier as so many of us had positive mantoux tests (or so I was told), meaning we had been exposed to TB. Then, I believed I was "unlucky" as my TB happened to be "active" at the B.C.G time and so was picked up. Now, I think I was lucky it was picked up when I had it so relatively mildly. As I was already a sickly child, I might have gone on to develop TB very seriously had it not been discovered by chance that way. I was also given to understand that a teacher was identified as the 'carrier' but I have no way of knowing if that was true or just told to me to make me feel better that it wasn't my fault that others had positive mantoux tests.

Tues 22 December 1959

Deva: Deva Hospital was originally an old-style mental asylum, dating back to 1829. In 1948, it was taken over by the NHS. From 1965, it was known as the West Cheshire Hospital. Later, it fell into disuse as a mental hospital and, in the 1980s, with new buildings, it became a general hospital. It was further away than I then realised and it appears from the diary that I may have thought Deva and the Liverpool San (mentioned later) were the same place.

Sat 26 December 1959

Galloping consumption: This was the term used by patients and staff at that time to describe a sort of TB that took hold very quickly and against which drugs were ineffective but the patient was too weak for an operation to remove part or all of the diseased lung.

Mon 4 January 1960

Treatments for TB in 1960: As the diary shows, I was being treated at a time of transition. While the life-saving drugs of streptomycin, PAS and INH, usually combined in what was known as Triple Therapy, had recently been licensed for use in the NHS, the older doctors, who ran the sanatorium where I was, still believed that what was needed as well was complete bed rest, followed by gradual increases in activity, and fresh air. It was a 'belt and braces' approach which meant I was in hospital for much longer than was probably actually necessary. I might well have been as fully cured much sooner had I been allowed to have the drugs at home, as long as I rested there in the first few months.

Streptomycin, discovered in 1943 and first tested for TB in 1946, was one of the first really successful treatments for TB. It was given in the form of a daily intramuscular injection. Because of some side effects, and the cost, it is not routinely given now.

PAS (para-aminosalycilic acid) was first discovered in 1936 but was not used for the treatment of TB until 1952. It was usually in liquid form and taken with INH tablets, or the two were combined in a fairly large rice-paper cachet (dipped in water for ease of swallowing).

INH or isoniazid (isonicotinic acid hydrazide) was first described in 1912 but was not registered as an effective drug against TB until 1952.

I am glad that, at the time, neither I nor my family – or perhaps even the doctors – knew of the many adverse side effects listed nowadays for these drugs. Thankfully, I am not aware that I suffered from any of the serious ones. In some 10% of those given streptomycin, there can be problems with the inner ear, affecting 'the organs of equilibrium' (balance), which is perhaps why I've never been a confident bike rider and, despite years of yoga, still find balancing on one leg tricky – or it could be that I've seized upon that as a handy excuse!

Although on 14 July there is a reference to my having been changed to streptoducin, I have not been able to find any modern reference to that so I might have misheard or misspelt it then.

In the back of the diary, I say that on 8 December 1960, I began pycamisan cachets (3+4+3) throughout the day after meals). PAS was then available in a combination formula with isoniazid called Pycamisan or Pasinah.

Wed 6 January 1960

Operations: When the drugs were not effective, people were operated on. The history of TB is full of horrendous accounts of many of these somewhat experimental but not usually successful procedures. In some cases, an operation was done to 'rest' the lung, which was then later re-inflated. In others, a diseased part was cut out or the whole lung removed. Because these were major operations –

and ribs had to be moved apart or removed to allow access – recovery times were slow. Some patients had more than one operation, sometimes years apart, which, combined with months of drug treatment, and rest before and after, ate up large chunks of their lives without necessarily prolonging them by that much. As far as I am aware, such operations are no longer done.

Sun 24 January 1960

Broadgreen Hospital, Liverpool: This was where patients from Crossley went for their operations in that period, even though both Crossley and the Liverpool San had operating theatres. It was established in 1903 and specialised in TB from 1922, becoming a Sanatorium in 1929 and, in 1946, under the NHS, it became Broadgreen Hospital.

Thu 23 June 1960

Barrowmore Hospital, near Chester, was founded in 1920, specialised in TB and was taken over by the NHS in 1948. Patients were sent there occasionally for tests such as a bronchoscopy (a procedure that allows a doctor to look at the airways in lungs). It was closed in 1983.

Sat 23 July 1960

Liverpool Sanatorium (also known as Crossley (West) Hospital) was founded in 1901. Set in about 40 acres, it had about 50 beds, primarily for TB patients, initially only from Liverpool. From the NHS taking it over in 1948, it was run with Crossley as a single entity. It has since been demolished. It was a short, pleasant walk through the woods from Crossley to the Liverpool San.

Fri 29 July 1960

TB and sex: At that time, it was believed that having TB increased a patient's sex-drive. This was repeated in one of the talks the doctor gave us later (as noted in the diary) and can be found in most old histories of tuberculosis. What foundation, if any, it is considered to have nowadays, I do not know. It may be that, because of the long stays young people had to have in hospitals, there was a lot of 'fraternising' (as it was euphemistically called by the staff at Crossley) but simply because they were young and wanted normal life to carry on.

24 November 1960

Other forms of TB: This was the first time I had known TB was not just a disease of the lungs. The thought terrified me. The NHS website says that TB infections are much less common outside the lungs but can occur in the lymph glands, the bones and joints, the digestive system, the bladder and reproductive system, and the brain and nerves. These are now very rare. Fortunately, neither did I know then that having TB when still growing may result in deformity of the spine – although I had suspected it because of Reenie Henson's (not her real name) humped back (see Jan 17 1960) - or that it may lead to infertility in later life, neither of which, I am very glad to say, happened in my case, and I have never had a weak chest (or covid).

SOURCES FOR THE ABOVE

Most of the information on TB is from the NHS website and that on sanatoria from Wikipedia. My understanding of the history of TB has been informed by the highly informative and very readable *The White Death: A History of Tuberculosis* by Thomas Dormandy, The Hambledon Press, 1999. As that publisher has ceased to exist, and Thomas Dormandy is now dead, I have been unable to obtain permission to quote from the book. I recommend it to anyone interested to know more about the history of TB.

BOOKS MENTIONED

Sun 15 Nov 1959   Thomas Hardy *Under the Greenwood Tree* and *Jude the Obscure*

Sun 15 Nov 1959   *Metaphysical Lyrics & Poems of the Seventeenth Century, Donne to Butler,* selected and edited by Herbert J.C. Grierson

Tue 1 Dec 1959   *Paddy-the-Next-Best-Thing* (1912) by Gertrude Page. By the time I came out, I had lost interest, or lost the book, so I never did read it.

Thu 3 Dec 1959   *Jane Eyre* by Charolotte Bronte

Mon 18 Dec 1959   *The Isotope Man* (1957) by Charles Eric Maine

Fri 5 Feb 1960   Elinor Brent Dyer (1894-1969) was a prolific and popular writer of children's fiction (including the Chalet School stories)

Fri 5 Feb 1960   *Pam's First Term* by R. Chatwyn [Not traced]

Thu 18 Feb 1960   *Great Expectations* by Charles Dickens

Tue 8 March 1960	*A Daughter of the Land* (1918) by Gene Stratton Porter (1863-1924)
	Anya Seton books I read included: *The Winthrop Woman* (1958) and *The Mistletoe and the Sword* (1955)
Tue 29 March 1960	*Eight Cousins* (1875) by Louisa May Alcott
Thu 7 April 1960	*The Colditz Story* (1952) by Pat Reid Had already been made into a film (1955).
Thu 7 April 1960	*The Saplings* (1945) by Noel Streatfeild, more famous for the Ballet Shoes books. It was an adult novel, about a middle-class family facing war from 1939. There is a later reference (22 April) to *The Painted Garden*, a 1949 children's novel, by the same author.
Mon 25 April 1960	*Daddy-Long-Legs* (1912) is an adult novel by American writer Jean Webster, told in letter form. It was made into a film in 1955.

Fri 15 July 1960   *Germans Under My Bed*
[Not traced]

Mon 3 Oct 1960   *The Whiteoak Saga* (also
known as the *Jalna Series* or
the *Whiteoak Chronicle*) was
a series of 16 books by a
Canadian writer, Mazo de la
Roche, published between
1927 and 1957. I became
obsessed with the characters
and their exciting, passionate
lives. Throughout the diary,
there are references to them
as I steadily read my way
through them.

Mon 10 Oct 1960   *The Feast of July* by H.E.
Bates (1954)

Fri 14 Oct 1960   *Sherlock Holmes* (published
1887-1915) by Sir Arthur
Cona.n Doyle. No title given
so do not know which book
or whether short stories
(1891-1927)

Thu 20 Oct 1960   *Pavilion of Women* (1946)
by Pearl S Buck

Tue 25 Oct 1960   *1066 and All That: A
Memorable History of
England, Comprising All the
Parts You Can Remember,
Including 103 Good Things,*

	5 Bad Kings and 2 Genuine Dates (1930) by W.C. Sellar and R.J. Yeatman A tongue-in-cheek reworking of English history I found very funny.
Fri 18 Nov 1960	*A Town Like Alice* (1950) by Nevil Shute
Mon 1 Dec 1960	*The Loving Spirit* (1931) by Daphne du Maurier
Thu 22 Dec 1960	*Just William* books by <u>Richmal Crompton</u>. 39 were published between 1922 and 1970. My children listened to Martin Jarvis reading them.
Sun 1 Jan 1961	*Pride and Prejudice* by Jane Austen This began a life-long pleasure in Austen.
Sat 28 Jan 1961	*The Golden Treasury of Modern Lyrics (1911)*
Fri 31 March 1961	*Sea Wyf and Biscuit* by James Maurice Scott (1955) I wanted to read it because I'd heard it as a radio play a few years earlier and something about the story had stayed with me.

Mon 8 May 1961   *Lady Chatterley's Lover* by D.H. Lawrence (1960 Penguin edition)

Sat 3 June 1961   *The Scarlet Pimpernel* by Baroness Orczy (first published 1905)

OTHER BOOKS MENTIONED IN THE SCHOOL MAGAZINE ARTICLE of JULY 1961

A Picnic in the Shade by Rosemary Edisford 1958

Daughters of Divinity by Verily Anderson 1960

The Life of Winston Churchill as a boy [no details]

Gilbert Harding's Book of Manners 1956

Haworth Parsonage by Isabel C. Clarke 1930

Wuthering Heights by Emily Bronte

Under Milkwood by Dylan Thomas

Cold Comfort Farm by Stella Gibbons 1932

A Phoenix too Frequent by Christopher Fry 1951

Room at the Top by John Braine 1957

Look Back in Anger by John Osborne 1956

The Snow Goose by Paul Gallico 1940

Love of Seven Dolls by Paul Gallico 1954

FILMS/PLAYS MENTIONED

Fri 28 Nov 1959   *High Society* (1956) with
                   Bing Crosby, Grace Kelly,
                   Frank Sinatra

Sat 24 Sept 1960   *She Couldn't Say No* (1954)
                   with Jean Simmons + Robert
                   Mitchum

Thu 6 Oct 1960   *Who Was That Lady*? (1960)
                   with Tony Curtis, Dean
                   Martin, Janet Leigh

Mon 10 Oct 1960   *The Baby and the Battleship
                   (1956)* with John Mills,
                   Richard Attenborough

Tue 11 Oct 1960   *The Pets* by Robert Shaw (A
                   play on ITV) He was also an
                   actor.

Wed 12 Oct 1960   *The Spanish Gardener (1956)*
                   with Dirk Bogarde, Michael
                   Hordern

Mon 17 Oct 1960   *The Black Tent* (1956) with
                   Anthony Steele, Donald
                   Sinden

Wed 19 Oct 1960   *A Man Without a Star* (1955)
                   with Kirk Douglas

Mon 24 Oct 1960   *The Kidnappers* (1953) with
                   Duncan Macrae

Mon 31 Oct 1960   *Brothers-in-law* (1957) with Ian Carmichael, Terry-Thomas, Richard Attenborough

Wed 2 Nov 1960   *It's a Wonderful World* (1939) with James Stewart, Claudette Colbert

Mon 7 Nov 1960   *Blind Date* (1959) with Hardy Kruger, Stanley Baker

Wed 9 Nov 1960   *The Long Arm* (1956) with Jack Hawkins

Wed 16 Nov 1960   *The Rainbow Jacket* (1954) with Robert Morley

Mon 21 Nov 1960   *I'm All Right Jack* (1959) with Peter Sellers, Ian Carmichael, Richard Attenborough, Terry-Thomas, Dennis Price

Mon 28 Nov 1960   *Blue Peter* (1955) with Kieron Moore

Wed 30 Nov 1960   *Quartet* (1948) four plays by W. Somerset Maugham (*The Alien Corn*, a man disappointed by his musical talents, had a great impact on me.)

Mon 6 Dec 1960	*Aunt Clara* (1954) with Margaret Rutherford, based on a novel by Noel Streatfeild
Wed 7 Dec 1960	*The Card* (1952) with Alec Guinness, Petula Clark, Glynis Johns
Sat 24 Dec 1960	*Gunga Din* (1939) with Carey Grant, Douglas Fairbanks Jr
Sat 24 Dec 1960	*The Bells of St Mary's* (1945) with Bing Crosby, Ingrid Bergman
Fri 20 Jan 1961	*Let's Make Love* (1960) with Yves Montand, Marilyn Monroe, Frankie Vaughan
Fri 27 Jan 1961	*The Lost World (1960)* with Claude Rains
Fri 27 Jan 1961	*The Man Who Never Was* (1956) with Clifton Webb
Fri 3 Feb 1961	*Solomon and Sheba* (1959) with Yul Brynner, Gina Lollobrigida
Fri 24 March 1961	*No Kidding* (1960) with Leslie Phillips, Geraldine McEwan, Irene Handl

Mon 3 April 1961   *Pollyanna* (1960) with
Hayley Mills, Jane Wyman,
Karl Malden

Fri 28 April 1961   *Blithe Spirit* by Noel Coward
(1941 play; 1945 film)

Sat 20 May 1961   *The World of Suzie Wong*
(1960) with William Holden,
Nancy Kwan

Sat 8 July 1961   *G.I. Blues* (1961) with Elvis
Presley

NEWSPAPER ARTICLES   transcribed from
British Newspaper Archives

THE LIVERPOOL ECHO AND EVENING EXPRESS   Thursday, January 5, 1961

FORMER ASSURANCE MAN IS ACCUSED

CHARGES AT RUNCORN

FOR TRIAL

After a hearing of over five hours, Edward Salter, of 58 Victoria Road, Runcorn, a former local agent for the Prudential Assurance Company Limited, was committed for trial at the next Chester Assizes at a private Committal Court at Runcorn yesterday.

He appeared on 16 charges, four of fraudulent conversion, and 12 of intent to defraud by forgery.

Salter was alleged by Mr. Phillips Owen, (prosecuting) to have been concerned with industrial insurance in Runcorn.

The 16 charges could be split into four groups he said. The first group related to the family of Mr. Kurt Kriesal, of Okar, Chester Road, Sutton Weaver, the second to Mrs Barbara Joan Hewitt, of Delph Lane, Daresbury, the third to Mrs Marie Urey, of Lawton Terrace, Moore, and the fourth related to Mr. John Male, of Runcorn Road, HIgher Walton, near Warrington.

The people concerned had all made claims on their insurance policies and handed them over to Salter, said Mr. Owen.

The witnesses all stated in court that signatures on documents produced by the prosecution had not been made by them.

RESERVES DEFENCE

Mr. Ronald Haughton, the clerk in charge of the district office of the Prudential Assurance Company, Sankey Street, Warrington, gave evidence of having received documents from Salter, all of which appeared in order. He had drawn cheques, which had been forwarded to the Runcorn agent. When the receipts for the sums had been received back at Warrington, they, too, had appeared to be in order.

Two bank clerks, Mr. Kenneth Hebden, or 45 Devonshire Road, Birkenhead, and Mr. John David Halme, of 20 Avonmore Avenue, Liverpool, gave evidence of having cashed cheques for Salter at the Runcorn branch of the Midland Bank.

Salter, who pleaded not guilty, reserved his defence and was allowed bail in his own surety of £25. He was represented by Mr. J.A. Reston.

RUNCORN WEEKLY NEWS   Thursday 16 February 1961

FORMER ASSURANCE AGENT JAILED

While Edward Salter, of 58 Victoria Road, Runcorn, was a Prudential Assurance Company area agent at Runcorn, he obtained £81 by a series of frauds, said Mr Philip Owen, prosecuting, at Chester Assizes on Friday.

Salter pleaded guilty to four charges of fraudulent conversion, six of forgery and six of uttering forged documents.

He was sentenced to six months' imprisonment.

Salter asked for other similar offences to be considered, the amount involved being £56 6s. 2d.

Detective-Constable Ernest Robertson said that Salter at one time had a grocery business in Runcorn. He was now a timber checker with the National Dock Labour Board. He had averaged £16 9s. 9d. with the insurance company. His area was between 32 and 40 square miles and he would cover 300 t0 400 miles weekly in his car.

OFFERED RESTITUTION

Replying to Mr. Justin Price, defending, the detective said that, when he saw Salter, "he was showing signs of considerable strain". Before the offences came to light, he admitted what happened quite voluntarily and wrote a letter offering restitution. There was about £160 of his superannuation in the company's possession.

Chairman of Runcorn Urban District Council last year, Mr Charles Joseph Helsby, said he had formed a high opinion of Salter's character and was surprised when he knew what had happened.

Mr Price said that, in a few years, Salter had brought in £40,000 of new business. His car expenses were £7 10s. 0d. a week and he received £1 6s 0d weekly, later rising to £1 14s. 0d. expenses weekly.

His superintendent had said "Yours is not an easy wicket to bat on." Difficulties had beset him on all sides.

Mr. Justice McNair said that Salter was a trusted agent, and when humble policy holders tried to surrender their policies, he put some of the money in his own pocket. It was not a single lapse from honesty.

Printed in Great Britain
by Amazon